Writing Opinion for Impact

Writing Opinion
for Impact

Conrad C. Fink

Iowa State University Press • AMES

CONRAD C. FINK is William S. Morris Professor of Newspaper Strategy and Management and Director of the James M. Cox Jr. Institute for Newspaper Management Studies at the University of Georgia, Athens. He is the author of five other books, one of which, *Media Ethics,* is also published in Korean.

© 1999 Iowa State University Press

Designed by Dennis Anderson

Iowa State University Press
2121 South State Avenue, Ames, Iowa 50014

Orders: 1-800-862-6657
Office: 1-515-292-0140
Fax: 1-515-292-3348
Web site: www.isupress.edu

♾ Printed on acid-free paper in the United States of America

First edition, 1999

International Standard Book Number: 0-8138-2606-3

Library of Congress Cataloging-in-Publication Data

Fink, Conrad C.
    Writing opinion for impact / Conrad C. Fink.
        p.   cm.
    Includes index.
    ISBN 0-8138-2606-3
    1. Journalism—Authorship.   2. Newspapers—Sections, columns, etc.
    3. Periodicals—Sections, columns, etc.   I. Title.
    PN4784.C65F56   1999
    808′.06607—dc21   98-23368

The last digit is the print number: 9 8 7 6 5 4 3 2 1

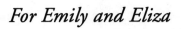

For Emily and Eliza

Contents

Introduction

Do you want to learn to write editorials and columns that will *blister* your targets, really tear their hides off?

Want to rampage across the pages of a newspaper or magazine, writing opinions and commentaries that stab, slash and wound?

If so, you're reading the wrong book.

However, you have the *right* book if you want to study opinion writing that's reasoned yet forceful, balanced yet pointed, thoughtful but also colorful, engaging and readable.

You have the right book if—above all—you are deeply, even solemnly aware of the enormous responsibilities carried by opinion writers who help set the agenda for this country's public dialogue on the compellingly important issues of our day.

Be aware of this reality: With skills you'll begin to learn in this book (I promise only a beginning), then sharpen later in your writing career, you can do more good than a battalion of Red Cross volunteers. You also can do more harm than a bomb-throwing terrorist on a crowded street corner.

So, let us—you and I—move forward to study the art (yes, *art*) of opinion writing that is graced with creative beauty whenever possible and that hits hard frequently—but *always* is written with knowledge that serious business is afoot when we journalists enter the realm of ideas and opinions and, thus, people's minds.

Don't get too self-important, however, about the role of opinion writers in America. It's difficult to prove their impact.

Do editorial writers and columnists truly shape public opinion or merely shadow it? Even after more than 40 years practicing journalism and teaching it, I'm not certain.

Do editorial writers win the wars of ideas? Or do they merely stir up trouble, then watch from the hilltops until the battle is over before descending to shoot the wounded?

Of this I am certain: Your duty as an opinion writer is on the battlefield, not overlooking it, and you must engage fully and early enough to lead readers toward solutions best for them, their communities, their nation.

Newspapers take all this very seriously. They regard their *editorial* mission—commenting, criticizing, applauding—as an essential complement to their *news* mission of providing the factual information that any informed democratic society must have to function properly.

Readers clearly are attracted to editorial pages and their "op-ed" cousins, the pages of analysis and columns of commentary opposite editorial pages. Research shows that adults frequently read opinion pages.

For magazines, which lack the spot-news timeliness of daily newspapers, writers increasingly are moving into analytical and interpretative writing that not only probes deeply beneath the surface of news but also comments on it.

Editorial comment is also carried by some television stations. New electronic media—"online newspapers"—provide some editorials and commentary.

So, move ahead in this book confident that meaningful career opportunities await *if* you can identify and understand the complex problems and opportunities facing our society, and *if* you then can write opinion about them with persuasive clarity, a sense of social responsibility and intellectual leadership.

Of course it's unlikely you'll get that opportunity immediately upon graduation. You first will need seasoning—call it "journalistic street smarts"—as a reporter and newswriter.

But, *somebody* will write editorials and columns in the future for, say, *The Wall Street Journal,* for *The New York Times,* for *Forbes* magazine, for *Time.* Why not *you?*

In the next generation of journalistic stars, nationally syndicated columnists will be writing about politics, international affairs, business, sports, the arts. Why can't *you* be one of them?

Closer to home, you may have opportunities in community journalism to write opinion for local newspapers, magazines or other media so essential to the public dialogue in thousands of cities and towns across America.

To help your first steps toward such a goal, I've organized this book to let you move gently through the process of discovery central to learning how to write *opinion with impact.*

Organization of This Book

PART ONE: SETTING THE SCENE

is composed of three chapters on subjects you should consider *before* launching forth as a writer of opinion and commentary.

Chapter One, The Responsibilities of Opinion Writers, discusses societal values and journalistic principles generally accepted as important influences on ethical, responsible opinion writing. Your *power* in opinion writing is awesome. So are your *responsibilities.*

Chapter Two, Identifying Issues for Comment, looks at how to identify your audience and its needs and desires, then focus your opinion writing to achieve maximum impact. Misjudge your audience, blur your writing focus—and your effort is wasted.

In Chapter Three, Reporting and Researching Your Opinions, we turn to the absolutely crucial question of how you can ensure your editorials and commentaries give readers "added value." Your opinion alone won't do; strong reporting, and basing your opinion on fact and logic are essential.

PART TWO: WRITING TO WIN READERS

addresses this reality: Identify the crucial issue, report it strongly, but you'll not score if your writing is dull and wooden.

Chapter Four, Writing Newspaper Editorials, distinguishes the subjective and at times passionate writing of opinion from the objective and dispassionate writing of news. Structures, forms and styles of writing are presented from leading newspapers.

We turn to Writing Magazine Editorials in Chapter Five, discussing the differences in audience, content and publication frequency that distinguish this form of writing from newspaper editorial writing. There *is* a difference, and we examine how leading magazine writers handle it.

PART THREE: WRITING PERSONAL COLUMNS

turns (in three chapters) to one of the most coveted jobs in all of journalism—writing personal columns.

Chapter Six, Commentary That Hits Hard, focuses primarily on columns dealing in hard news, especially politics and public policy. You'll study the writing styles of some of journalism's biggest stars.

We turn to humor in Chapter Seven, Amusing, Entertaining or Making 'em Cry. Writers who can stroke the keyboard with a light, entertaining touch are sought by editors and readers alike.

Sports is a major dimension of newspaper, magazine and electronic coverage, and we turn to it in Chapter Eight, The Fun and Business of Sports. We'll discuss how leading sports commentators structure and write their columns.

PART FOUR: ARTS REVIEWS AND CRITICISM

is a single Chapter Nine dealing with a journalistic specialty that's hugely popular with writers and readers, You and Arts Commentary. All newspapers and magazines review and critique the arts—if only books—and many of the country's top publications make arts commentary one of their principal attractions for readers.

PART FIVE: EXTRA DIMENSIONS IN COMMENTARY AND OPINION

is in two chapters.

Chapter Ten, Specialty Columns and Comment, is designed to give you ideas on how to get started, right now, in column writing. It illustrates how your hobby, special personal interest or, even, your fantasy may be the subject of a column. We'll also look at writing for broadcast and cyberspace.

Chapter Eleven, On Campus Today: How It's Done, reports on my study of 45 campus newspapers at colleges and universities nationwide. I've found strengths—and weaknesses—in them, which may help you improve your own writing.

PART SIX: YOU AND THE LAW: WRITE DEFENSIVELY!

concludes the book—but its subject, libel and how to avoid it, should be high among your priorities as you begin writing. As Chapter Twelve, Avoiding Legal Traps for Opinion Writers, explains, the legal traps out there are threatening.

Acknowledgments

I've seen before the willingness of newspaper and magazine professionals to pass on some of what they know to journalism students. But I am amazed—and gratified—at the number who agreed to contribute to this book. To them, my deep gratitude.

In order of appearance, I thank those of you who wrote special contributions for this book:

Richard Oppel, editor of the *Austin* (Tex.) *American Statesman;* Susan Laccetti, editorial writer for the *Atlanta Journal;* Burl Osborne, publisher of the *Dallas Morning News* and president of the publishing division of A.H. Belo Corp.; George Melloan, deputy editor (international) of *The Wall Street Journal;* Tom Teepen, national correspondent for Cox Newspapers; Karen Woods, former dancer with the Merce Cunningham Company and now a teacher of dance at Ohio State University; Jackie Crosby, news editor of Star Tribune Online in Minneapolis.

Throughout the book I've reproduced examples of newspaper and magazine writers too numerous to list here. But for each I've extended the best salute one writer can give another: a byline credit is attached to each writing example.

Special thanks to:

Maria Henson, associate editor and editorial writer for the *Charlotte Observer,* who consented to be interviewed for the "Case Study: The Murder of Jeannie Purcell," in Chapter Three.

Christopher Callahan, assistant dean of journalism at the University of

Maryland, who graciously shared, for Chapter Three, his insights into using the Internet as a reporting tool.

Scripps Howard Newspapers for permission to use the piece by Fredric Koeppel of the *Memphis Commercial Appeal* on his life as a restaurant reviewer. That's in Chapter Ten.

Dr. Kent Middleton of the Grady College of Journalism at the University of Georgia for his counsel in my writing of Chapter Twelve, "You and The Law: Write Defensively!" Dr. Middleton is an expert in media law, and his guidance was most valuable.

Dean Tom Russell of the Grady College has my continuing appreciation for his support of my teaching and writing efforts.

To Sophie Barnes goes my admiration for her efficiency in deciphering my editing hieroglyphics and somehow producing a cleanly typed manuscript.

PART ONE

Setting the Scene

THE FIRST thing to learn in opinion writing is that you must *un*learn one thing probably central to your idea of what a journalist is all about.

You've picked it up in journalism courses: a journalist must stay out of the story, stay objective, stay dispassionate. Right?

Well, that was then—in reporting or newswriting courses—not now, when you must move from objective into *subjective* writing, when you must insert *your* ideas and *your* emotions into your writing, not eliminate them.

A second lesson upfront is that if you think newswriters have impact on how the world turns, think of yourself as an opinion writer, bursting into the marketplace of ideas backed by the institutional prestige and power of a newspaper or magazine. And, no matter what the size of your publication, it likely will be one of the most influential institutions in your community.

It follows, then, that you'll carry enormous journalistic and societal responsibilities as an opinion writer—responsibilities quite beyond those of *news*writers (and theirs is no easy burden, either). Understanding and preparing for those responsibilities is covered in the three chapters of Part One.

In Chapter One, I discuss how to approach—carefully and

methodically—the influence you'll have over reader-thinking and public policy. You'll look at values and principles, some embodied in professional codes, which should help you sort out question of ethics and social responsibility that arise frequently in opinion writing.

Chapter Two addresses your responsibility for commenting primarily on those issues of compelling, not secondary, importance. Occasional light pieces—your opinion of last night's sunset, your musings on the stray cat problem—are okay. But wander too far from subjects the public wants to read about and, often, desperately needs to read about and you'll waste your opportunity *to change things that count.*

In Chapter Three, I'll pass along hints on backing your opinions with facts. It's not enough to shout, "I believe, I believe" and rush to the keyboard. Measured against the flow of history, what you (or I) believe will wear thin quickly as the sole rationale for opinion writing.

1 The Responsibilities of Opinion Writers

IN THE 1700s, America's first opinion writers unleashed their quill pens—and helped start a revolution.

In 1831, the *American Rail-Road Journal* (later, *Railway Age*) began commenting on how railroads were run—and thus were born the "trade" publications that have commented on, and forced change on, American business and industry ever since.

In 1925, *New Yorker* magazine was launched with dazzling new and sophisticated commentary and social analysis—and changed how Americans walked, talked, dressed, ate and drank.

From our earliest days, it's been clear that you can change things in virtually every sector of American life with what you write in editorials, commentaries and columns. And, you can change them for ***better or worse.***

In this chapter, we'll look at your responsibilities and at societal values and journalistic principles you might consider when deciding what to write about and how to write it.

Goals to Guide Your Writing

When editorial writers talk about their responsibilities, many mention four goals as most important in opinion writing:

1. Serve your public.
2. Provide a forum—a marketplace of ideas—for readers, community, nation.
3. Be society's watchdog.
4. Inform and guide your readers to cause change.

Note that pursuing those four goals not only will lead you from ***objec-***

tive newswriting into *subjective* advocacy writing but also force you to presume you can lead your readers through fact and fiction to the truth; to presume you know some paths are wrong, others right; that you know some solutions are better than others.

A huge responsibility?

You bet, and to understand why many editorial writers are sobered by it, let's look more closely at those four goals:

Serve Your Public

Editorial writers regard this as so important that it is the very first thought expressed in the Basic Statement of Principles adopted by the National Conference of Editorial Writers (NCEW), the leading professional organization of print and broadcast opinion writers.

"Editorial writing," says the statement, "is more than another way of making money. It is a profession *devoted to the public welfare and to public service*" (emphasis added).

In its code of ethics, The Associated Press Managing Editors Association, a nationwide group of newspaper members of the AP, counsels newspapers to use their advocacy powers "in the public interest."[1]

Lesson: Take a position—a strong one—in your editorials and opinion columns. Back one candidate, not another; support one side of an issue, attack the other; but *always* do so in the public interest, not your interests, not those of your newspaper or magazine employer, certainly not those of any special interest group whose goals run counter to those of the wider public.

Great power devolves to you as an opinion writer; wield it for the greater good.

Provide a Public Forum

Creating a marketplace of ideas for public dialogue is considered profoundly important by leading news organizations.

The Washington Post's Code of Standards and Ethics states one of that paper's "special responsibilities" is "to listen to the voiceless."[2]

The nation's leading professional organization of editors, The American Society of Newspaper Editors, emphasizes in its Statement of Principles that, "The *primary purpose* [emphasis added] of gathering and distributing news and opinion is to serve the general welfare by informing the people and enabling them to make judgments on the issues of the time."

The editorial writers' group, NCEW, states that "voice should be given to diverse opinions, edited faithfully to reflect stated views."

Lesson: Making *your* views known is important in opinion writing; creating a marketplace of ideas for others—letting *all* be heard—is crucial.

Serve as Society's Watchdog

This mission—stand guard in the night while others sleep—is embodied in all codes of ethics and principles published by leading news organizations.

This, of course, is the "Fourth Estate" concept—the idea that the media, on behalf of the public, are independent counterbalances to three other "estates," the executive, legislative and judicial branches of government.

The American Society of Newspaper Editors' Statement of Principles is blunt on this point:

> The American press was made free not just to inform or just to serve as a forum for debate but also to bring an *independent scrutiny* [emphasis added] to bear on the forces of power in society, including the conduct of official power at all levels of government.[3]

But, you may ask, does that mean that, as an opinion writer, you may end up confronting, disagreeing with, arguing against powerful societal institutions, ranging from the local city council to the White House and U.S. State Department?

Yes. When he wrote *The Washington Post*'s code, Ben Bradlee, then executive editor, put it this way:

> *The Washington Post* is vitally concerned with the national interest and with the community interest. We believe these interests are best served by the widest possible dissemination of information. The claim of national interest by a federal official does not automatically equate with national interest. The claim of community interest by a local official does not automatically equate with the community interest.

Lesson: As an opinion writer you will be expected—*required*— to monitor the powerful, to comment on and, if necessary, criticize their use of power. *And,* you must remain independent and serve the public's interest while doing so. That can mean bucking the folks you live with, maybe attacking the most respected people in town; indeed, it can mean taking on the President of the United States and Leader of the Free Western World!

If you find there is too much heat in that, you should stay out of the editorial-writing kitchen.

Inform and Guide Your Readers

This is an editorial writer's responsibility that's at least half understood by even beginning reporters. After all, most of us entered journalism to report for our readers, to *inform* them.

But *guide* them? *Stir them to action?*

Yes, it is not only informing readers but guiding them—recommending, persuading, advocating, cajoling—that distinguishes opinion writing from newswriting.

The National Conference of Editorial Writers says the "chief duty" of editorial writers "is to provide the information *and guidance toward sound judgments* [emphasis added] that are essential to the healthy functioning of a democracy."

Lesson: In opinion writing, do your reporting and research; immerse yourself in facts and conflicting views; think through the issue at hand, then step forward with courage to write, in effect, "Follow me ... this is the way."

That equation, by the way, explains why you're unlikely to land a job writing editorials or opinion columns fresh out of college. You'll first need plenty of experience. This is recognized by the Radio/Television News Directors Association, which declares in its Code of Broadcast News Ethics that analysis, comment and editorial opinion must be written "by individuals whose competence, experience and judgment qualify them for it."[4]

Other Goals in Opinion Writing

In sorting out your personal approach to the responsibilities of opinion writing, you can gain much from the editorial writers' Basic Statement of Principles (see Box 1-1). Guidance also is in codes published by other professional organizations (see Box 1-2).

| Box 1-1 | National Conference of Editorial Writers Basic Statement of Principles |

Editorial writing is more than another way of making money. It is a profession devoted to the public welfare and to public service. The chief duty of its practitioners is to provide the information and guidance toward sound judgments that are essential to the healthy functioning of a democracy. Therefore, editorial writers owe it to their integrity and that of their profession to observe the following injunctions:

1. The editorial writer should present facts honestly and fully. It is dishonest to base an editorial on half-truth. The writer should never knowingly mislead the reader, misrepresent a situation, or place any person in a false light. No consequential errors should go uncorrected.
2. The editorial writer should draw fair conclusions from the stated facts, basing them upon the weight of evidence and upon the writer's considered concept of the public good.
3. The editorial writer should never use his or her influence to seek personal favors of any kind. Gifts of value, free travel and other favors that can compromise integrity, or appear to do so, should not be accepted.

The writer should be constantly alert to conflicts of interest, real or apparent, including those that may arise from financial holdings, secondary employment, holding public office or involvement in political, civic or other organizations. Timely public disclosure can minimize suspicion.

Editors should seek to hold syndicates to these standards.

The writer, further to enhance editorial page credibility, also should encourage the institution he or she represents to avoid conflicts of interest, real or apparent.

4. The editorial writer should realize that the public will appreciate more the value of the First Amendment if others are accorded an opportunity for expression. Therefore, voice should be given to diverse opinions, edited faithfully to reflect state views. Targets of criticism—whether in a letter, editorial, cartoon or signed column—especially deserve an opportunity to respond; editors should insist that syndicates adhere to this standard.

5. The editorial writer should regularly review his or her conclusions. The writer should not hesitate to consider new information and to revise conclusions. When changes of viewpoint are substantial, readers should be informed.

6. The editorial writer should have the courage of well-founded convictions and should never write anything that goes against his or her conscience. Many editorial pages are products of more than one mind, and sound collective judgment can be achieved only through sound individual judgments. Thoughtful individual opinions should be respected.

7. The editorial writer always should honor pledges of confidentiality. Such pledges should be made only to serve the public's need for information.

8. The editorial writer should discourage publication of editorials prepared by an outside writing service and presented as the newspaper's own. Failure to disclose the source of such editorials is unethical, and particularly reprehensible when the service is in the employ of a special interest.

9. The editorial writer should encourage thoughtful criticism of the press, especially within the profession, and promote adherence to the standards set forth in this statement of principles. (Adopted Oct. 10, 1975)

| Box 1-2 | What Other Codes Say |

Codes of ethics or statements of principles are drawn up by many journalism groups and news organizations. Here's a sampling of guidance they offer editorial writers, analysts and commentators:

The primary purpose of gathering and distributing news and opinion is to serve the general welfare by informing the people and enabling them to make judgments on the issues of the time. Newspaper men and women who abuse the power of their professional role for selfish motives or unworthy purposes are faithless to that public trust.

The American press was made free not just to inform or just to serve as a forum for debate but also to bring an independent scrutiny to bear on the forces of power in the society, including the conduct of official power at all levels of government. ...

Every effort must be made to assure that the news content is accurate, free from bias and in context, and that all sides are presented fairly. Editorials, analytical articles and commentary should be held to the same standards of accuracy with respect to facts as news reports. ...

To be impartial does not require the press to be unquestioning or to refrain from editorial expression. Sound practice, however, demands a clear distinction for the reader between news reports and opinion. Articles that contain opinion or personal interpretation should be clearly defined.

AMERICAN SOCIETY OF NEWSPAPER EDITORS' STATEMENT OF PRINCIPLES

The public's right to know of events of public importance and interest is the overriding mission of the mass media.

Broadcast journalists recognize the responsibility borne by broadcasting for informed analysis, comment and editorial opinion on public events and issues. They accept the obligation of broadcasters for the presentation of such matters by individuals whose competence, experience and judgment qualify them for it.

RADIO/TELEVISION NEWS DIRECTORS ASSOCIATION'S
CODE OF BROADCAST NEWS ETHICS

The newspaper should strive for impartial treatment of issues and dispassionate handling of controversial subjects. It should provide a forum for the exchange of comment and criticism, especially when such comment is opposed to its editorial positions. Editorials and other expressions of opinion by reporters and editors should be clearly labeled.

ASSOCIATED PRESS MANAGING EDITORS' CODE OF ETHICS

[P]ublic enlightenment is the forerunner of justice and the foundation of democracy. The duty of the journalist is to further those ends by seeking truth and providing a fair and comprehensive account of events and issues. ...

[Journalists should] support the open exchange of views, even views they find repugnant ... give voice to the voiceless.

SOCIETY OF PROFESSIONAL JOURNALISTS' CODE OF ETHICS

We fully recognize the power we have inherited as the dominant morning newspaper in the capital of the free world carries with it special responsibilities:

—to listen to the voiceless.
—to avoid any and all acts of arrogance.
—to face the public politely and candidly.

We avoid active involvement in any partisan causes—politics, community affairs, social action, demonstration—that could compromise or seem to compromise our ability to report and edit fairly. ...

On this newspaper, the separation of news columns from editorials and opposite-editorial pages is solemn and complete. This separation is intended to serve the reader, who is entitled to the facts in the news columns and to opinions on the editorial and "op-ed" pages. But nothing in this separation of functions is intended to eliminate from the news columns honest, in-depth reporting, or analysis or commentary when plainly labeled.

THE WASHINGTON POST'S CODE OF STANDARDS AND ETHICS

However, codes drawn by professional groups or media companies suffer two major failings.

First, they are consensus documents, written after often laborious discussion by journalists with differing, sometimes conflicting, goals. Such codes give you general guidance only ("serve the public" falls short of the specific guidance many young writers desire).

Second, newspapers or other media companies write codes primarily to protect their institutional competitive and marketplace positions, not to give you personal guidance. (*The Wall Street Journal*'s "conflict of interest policy" warns against causing "embarrassment and damage" to the company—not much help to young journalists struggling to create their own standard of right and wrong to guide their professional life.)[5]

So, intense introspection is required if you're serious about creating a meaningful personal code of ethics. Some things to think about:

Avoid Conflict of Interest

As writer of an institutional editorial (one representing your newspaper's or magazine's corporate position) or a personal column, you can:

• Build voter support for a new public sports complex in your city's downtown.
• Divulge good and bad news about companies, causing their stock prices to rise or fall.

- Say nice things about a new movie, sending viewers flocking to the box office.

All three scenarios listed above happened. Nothing wrong with that, you ask? Well, in all three cases, the writers were, shall we say, *not fully forthcoming.*

That is, one writer didn't tell readers his newspaper's owners had nearby property holdings that would soar in value if the sports complex were built; the stock market commentator didn't reveal he and friends were secretly investing—and harvesting huge gains—*before* informing readers of the price-moving news; the movie reviewer didn't reveal he had flown to Hollywood and dined and wined at a studio's expense for his screening of the new movie.

News of these obvious conflicts of interest seeped out (it always does) and many were the rationalizations:

- No matter who owns land downtown, the city and all of us would benefit from a new sports complex.
- What if I did make a buck or two by trading on inside information? Fat cat investors do it all the time.
- Hey, I would have reviewed the movie favorably even if I hadn't gobbled up thousands of dollars in freebies laid out by the studio.

Whatever the rationalizations in our three cases, the writers simply were unethical. Period. They were wrong to use their powers of persuasion in behalf of causes from which they (or, their employer) stood to benefit. And, they were wrong to conceal from the public their conflicts of interest.

When all was revealed, the newspapers and writers suffered enormous loss of credibility, and credibility is all that newspapers—or writers—have to offer.

Report and Write With Honesty

Let's say your newspaper supports local business expansion, and you're assigned to write an editorial arguing that Acme Industries—and its 600 jobs—should be induced to build a new plant in town.

You write that Acme's huge payroll would boost the local economy. The company's tax contributions would help finance new schools, new roads.

But, your editorial doesn't mention that you know Acme produces dangerous chemicals and twice was fined in another state for polluting skies and streams.

You've just committed a journalistic felony—reporting with prejudicial selection of facts and writing with special "spin" to make a point dishonestly.

Reporting fully and honestly for your opinion pieces is so important that it gets its own chapter later in this book. Suffice to say here that your *writing* can be ethical only if your *reporting* presents the facts fully and impartially.

Then, you must reach *fair conclusions* drawn logically and clearly from those facts. It's dishonest to do otherwise. Besides, your readers cannot be fooled by unfair, illogical, biased writing. They have too many other sources of fact and opinion and will not rely solely on your judgment—not about Afghanistan, not about Princess Diana, not about any other subject, near or far.

Open Yourself to Diverse Views

Mix strong personal opinions you formed years ago on hot topics—abortions, public education, drug addiction, crime in the streets.

Stir in a writing style you've developed to strike hard, focusing intently to make your personal point.

Add a measure of refusal to listen to the views of others.

You've just read a recipe for submerging yourself, anonymously and probably ineffectually, among hundreds (perhaps *thousands*) of writers who labor diligently day after day on those subjects, concocting mixtures of the same old tired words in support of personal positions adopted long ago and not re-thought since.

But, ah, how you will stand out *if* you display intellectual honesty by listening to the opinion of others. And, what impact you will have *if* you hold open the possibility (however slim) that your path to the truth may not be the only path!

A real ego kick, a feeling of power, can develop for opinion writers who find themselves at the center of the marketplace of ideas. For some, that feeling yields to arrogance that inevitably shines through their writing.

The result: A lost opportunity to persuade the uncommitted or convert the opposing side. The writer is dismissed by discerning readers and is left with only the applause of co-believers—left preaching to the choir.

It takes courage to change course publicly, to admit error, to bow before superior wisdom or new facts. But the great ones do it.

Tom Wicker, a highly respected *New York Times* columnist, devoted one column annually to acknowledging error, misinterpretation and other ills that afflicted his writing during the year.

Box 1-3	A Professional's Viewpoint

There isn't any one way. There isn't any one truth. There isn't any one wisdom.

—Geneva Overholser, then editor of the *Des Moines* (Iowa) *Register,* "The Great American Tragedy: Few Say Much About Anything," *The Masthead,* Fall 1992, p. 15.

Keep the Institutional Record Straight

It's profoundly important that editorial pages readily and fully acknowledge error and that newspapers, as institutions, keep the public record straight.

First, it's simply the right thing to do. Absent any probing, regular scrutiny by other institutions in society, the media institution—society's watchdog—has to bark at itself at times.

Second, readers will sense quickly any effort to cover up past error or blur editorial wrongdoing. Fast, full admission of error helps protect a newspaper's credibility.

Truly great newspapers are open in such matters. Examples:

- *The New York Times* endorsed President Clinton for a second term, then just a week after the election, outraged by new information on his fund-raising activities, strongly criticized Clinton, their own pick.
- *The Atlanta Constitution* endorsed former U.S. Sen. Paul Tsongas in his presidential campaign, then strongly criticized him for withholding from voters news that he had suffered a recurrence of cancer. The *Constitution,* in effect, said it had been misled—and thus had misled readers of its endorsement editorial.
- *The Columbus* (Ga.) *Ledger-Enquirer,* in a long editorial, noted that newspapers are quick to criticize other businesses for race prejudice in hiring. The newspaper added that "it is only fair to turn the tables on ourselves" and reported minority hiring was slowing in the newspaper industry. The newspaper then detailed its own minority staff—22 percent of total staff.

Newspapers are fond of publishing their own editorial standards—the principles that guide their editorial pages (see Box 1-4 for the *Milwaukee Journal Sentinel's*). It's important that editorial pages reflect those principles, day in, day out.

| Box 1-4 | Tenets of an Editorial Policy |

Milwaukee Journal Sentinel writers structure editorials against a backdrop of what the newspaper stands for. These tenets of editorial policy were published on the newspaper's editorial page:

- We are independent, beholden to no special interest or political party.
- We have an overriding concern for the best interests of the city and state.
- We believe in the American free enterprise system and minimal governmental interference with business and finance.
- We are conservative on fiscal issues.
- We believe that a just society must have compassion for the unfortunate, that a responsible society must erase any inequities that impede access to

employment, and that a wise society must be skeptical of policies that diminish initiative.

- We will be defensive of the rights of individuals as guaranteed by the Declaration of Independence and the U.S. Constitution.
- We believe that diversity unites us all for our ultimate role as shareholders of the planet.
- We support a strong national defense.
- We will be a tenacious enemy of violence, crime and fraud.
- We will try to lead our readers to the truth.
- We will strive to be accurate and fair.
- We will be a relentless change agent, determined to fix what is broken, right what is wrong, affirm what is wise and build a better future.

Used with permission

Beware the "Bad News Syndrome"

Starving children in Africa ... AIDS in America's streets ... corruption in Washington. The drum roll of horror is continuous—and addictive. If you're not careful, you'll write exclusively to its rhythm.

It's easy to succumb to the bad news syndrome, to write always with a woe-is-me tone about bad news, not good news; about darkness, not light, about conflict not conciliation.

Syndicated columnist William Raspberry puts it this way:

> We are at our most comfortable with bad news. Whatever our attitudes as men and women—as citizens—as reporters, we love conflict. It's what we understand best, and it is what we cover best.
>
> Let the basketball coach at your local college come under fire from the NCAA, and you'll be all over the story like a cheap suit.
>
> But I defy any of your readers to tell you, on the basis of anything they find in your newspaper, the name of even one outstanding professor at the university, or to describe the nature of anything important going on there.[6]

Believe it: Some parts of Africa are doing better, medical researchers may be closing in on AIDS, some honest politicians work in Washington and there even are outstanding professors (and coaches) doing good work.

Don't relent in your attacks on evil and darkness, but take time to applaud good and cheer the light.

Write to Engage

Here's a writing formula to *avoid:*

Thorough + Lousy   = Failed
Reporting   Writing   Editorial

Obvious, you say? Yes, but pick up a newspaper—*any* newspaper—and odds are you'll find that formula followed to its dismal end.

Fact is, much editorial writing is disabled by two misapprehensions by writers:

First, editorials mostly are about serious subjects, therefore the writing must be *serious* (read that, stuffy, pompous, dull).

Second, serious editorials attract only serious readers, so the writing must be "pitched" to an educated elite in *appropriately upscale language* (read that, long words, convoluted sentences, dense paragraphs).

Jack Hart, senior editor for writing at the *Portland* (Ore.) *Oregonian* and a distinguished writing coach, says standard readability tests show writing in American newspapers is "beyond the comfortable reading reach of all but audience members with advanced college degrees."

Yet, Hart says, "The average American adult on the other hand, has completed about a year of college. Forty percent hold only a high school diploma."[7]

Remember: The responsibilities of an opinion writer include developing a writing style that engages readers and *communicates effectively.* More—much more—on that later in this book.

| Box 1-5 | A Professional's Viewpoint |

Write it well, and they will come.
Make it eye-appealing, and they will read.
Make it fair, and they will respect your opinion.

—Rena Pederson, *Dallas Morning News*, "The President's Letter," *The Masthead*, Fall 1996, p. 1.

To Thyself Be True

Your opinion writer's checklist of responsibilities must include consulting your own conscience—your own sense of whether your writing is right or wrong.

Listen to *instinct?* Yes, it can be your first early warning of an ethical problem. Or, of course, you can get an "all clear"—your conscience murmurs that your subject matter, your reporting, your writing angle *seem* right.

But flying merely on instinct is dangerous in these days of heated controversy swirling around the enormously complicated subjects we write about. Can't we be more methodical in discerning right from wrong? Read on.

The Final Checklist

Call it conscience, call it instinct, but that little voice whispering to you is the sum total of your life experience—what your mother told you, what you heard in church, what you learned in school and on the playing fields.

Those sources (especially mom) can help guide you through many ethical complexities you'll face in opinion writing. However, I suggest you also use a checklist drawn more broadly from societal values and journalistic principles.

Societal Values

These are standards most citizens accept as characteristics of a civilized society. When confronting your responsibilities in opinion writing, run your finger down this list:[8]

✓ *Truth-telling.* It's a value held dear and to trash it is to fail utterly as a journalist.

✓ *Humaneness.* Will your piece harm people unnecessarily? If so, rethink it.

✓ *Stewardship.* You must respect and guard the rights of others. If you benefit from a system, you must protect it and pass its benefits to others.

✓ *Justice.* This promises reward or punishment as deserved, not on basis of race, color, creed or social or economic status. Is your writing just? Do you monitor whether society applies justice even-handedly?

✓ *Freedom.* Our society stands for independence and liberty. Are you protecting the freedom of others? Are you enmeshed by special interests and conflicts that restrict your freedom in writing?

✓ *Golden mean.* Since Aristotle (384-322 B.C.), humankind has striven for a middle ground, somewhere between dangerous extremes. Can you offer a middle ground—an editorial that, for example, urges the city council to lure Acme Industries to town but only with safeguards against polluting skies and streams?

Journalistic Principles

Generations of journalists have adapted societal values to job-related journalistic principles. Check them, too:

✓ *Serve your public.* Basic to what we do.

✓ *Monitor the powerful.* Yes! Bark in the night.

✓ *Be balanced and fair.* Without this, an editorial or column is just personalized ranting.

✓ *Be compassionate.* Can you write about the corrupt politician without harpooning his innocent wife? Try.

✓ *Guard the First Amendment.* Rush to its defense. Without it, we're silenced, the watchdog is mute, democracy is threatened.

✓ *Be courageous and independent.* Some journalists who came before us died in pursuit of truth; others will follow. Risking unpopularity at City Hall over an editorial on Acme Industries and polluted skies seems a relatively small price to pay.

It's Not Painless, You Know

Get used to the idea: You'll not get far into opinion writing without causing—or taking—pain.

That's because, inevitably, some of the societal values and journalistic principles we've studied often are in conflict.

For example, *serving the public* may conflict with **compassion** if, say, your readers must be told about the scandalous behavior of a politician, but by revealing it you inflict unspeakable agony on his wife, a sideline innocent.

Or, let's say you must do a piece on an *alleged* rapist (in your role of monitoring the justice system), yet you know your writing might impair his chance of a fair trial.

Such conflicts of principles are resolved by many editorial writers in accordance with the concept of *utilitarianism*—in sum, serving the interests of the larger number of persons, even if that causes pain to an individual.

At times, you will take the pain. You can suffer deep agony, for example, in a conflict of your loyalties—loyalty to yourself (and your conscience), loyalty to society and to the hand that feeds you (your employer).

What if you are ordered to write an editorial that's contrary to your personal beliefs? Let's say your boss wants an editorial welcoming Acme Industries to town and *not* mentioning its record of polluting skies and streams?

Think about this scenario:

- The hand that feeds you hired you to help get the newspaper on the street. It's the owner's newspaper, not yours.
- Your loyalty to society (your community, your neighbors, their children) demands you insert a warning about Acme's polluting past.
- Your loyalty to self is divided: (a) Your need to keep your job (you have rent to pay, car payments to meet), but (b) you're revolted at the prospect of writing something you don't believe.

What to do?

Well, much of this book is devoted to helping you establish your own decision-making process for use when your time comes to make such tough decisions. And, your time *will* come.

Summary

In opinion writing, you must *un*learn the basic rule of newswriting—stay objective, dispassionate and neutral; in subjective advocacy writing, *your opinions belong in your writing.*

- Editorial writers serve their public, provide a forum for discussion of public issues, serve as society's watchdog and inform and guide readers to cause change.
- Many ethics codes are consensus documents providing only general guidance to young writers; some are written primarily to protect the marketplace position of a newspaper or magazine.
- Opinion writers must avoid conflicts of interest and should serve the public's interests, not their personal interests, not the interests of any special group.
- Honest reporting and writing must go into opinion pieces, and you must reach fair conclusions based on facts presented.
- Beware holding so intently to your personal opinions that you neglect the views of others; when the facts change, so should your position.
- Don't become obsessed with bad news; take time to applaud good.
- Superb reporting plus lousy writing yields failed editorials. Write to engage readers and communicate effectively.
- Listen to your conscience, respond to your instincts but also ensure your writing is in accordance with societal values and journalistic principles such as truth-telling, humaneness and fairness, stewardship, the Golden Mean, justice.
- Be courageous in your writing but expect to cause—and take—pain before you're far into opinion writing.
- Many writers adhere to utilitarianism, or serving the greater number of persons even if that means causing pain for an individual.

Recommended Reading

The Masthead, published quarterly by the National Conference of Editorial Writers, is must reading for any aspiring opinion writer. The full range of opinion writing—institutional editorials, personal columns, commentaries—is covered in this publication.

Excellent guidance is available in *The American Editor,* published by the American Society of Newspaper Editors; *The Quill,* the magazine of the Society of Professional Journalists; *presstime,* a Newspaper Association of America periodical, and *Editor & Publisher* magazine.

Of course, the very best guidance for students of opinion writing comes from reading editorials and columns published by leading newspapers and magazines. Learn from the professionals!

I discuss the ethics of writing and reporting more fully in *Media Ethics*, 2d ed. (Boston: Allyn & Bacon, 1995) and in two books on writing: *Introduction to Professional Newswriting*, 2d ed. (New York: Addison Wesley Longman, 1998) and *Introduction to Magazine Writing* (New York: Macmillan, 1993).

Notes

1. Texts of APME's code and codes drawn by APME and other media organizations are published in Conrad Fink, *Media Ethics* (Boston: Allyn & Bacon, 1995).
2. Ibid.
3. Ibid.
4. Ibid.
5. Ibid.
6. William Raspberry, "Look for the What-Works Angle," *The Masthead*, Winter 1994, p. 18.
7. Jack Hart, "Why Worry About Words?", *Editor & Publisher*, Feb. 1, 1997, p. 13.
8. I present a five-step process for ethical decision-making in *Media Ethics*, op cit.

Exercises

1. Study the lead institutional editorial in today's *New York Times* (or another newspaper your instructor designates) and write, in about 250 words, *your opinions* on these questions:

   (a) What societal values and journalistic principles do you think motivated the writer? Is the editorial designed to *serve the public, monitor the powerful, exercise stewardship?*
   (b) Is the editorial well-rounded and does it meet the standards of *truth-telling, balance* and *fairness?*

   In completing this exercise, write persuasively and engagingly about the editorial. Write to *communicate* clearly your views of it.

2. Interview an editorial writer for your student newspaper (or a community newspaper designated by your instructor).

   In about 300 words, describe that writer's personal approach to ethics in opinion writing. Does the writer follow a written code of ethics? If so, is that code drawn by the employing newspaper or a professional organization such as American Society of Newspaper Editors?

   Does the writer seem sensitive to issues of societal values and journalistic principles that arise in opinion writing?

   In your opinion, does the writer follow the ethical guidelines outlined in Chapter 1?

3. Think deeply about this: Editorial writers and opinion columnists frequently endorse political candidates, recommend readers take certain actions, or

otherwise attempt to lead their audience toward solutions to important public issues.

In about 250 words, describe your *personal* feelings about the responsibilities inherent in this.

Are you confident you possess background, experience and education that fit you to provide such intellectual leadership?

If so, which subjects or issues can you write about with confidence?

If not, how do you intend to prepare for the day when you would feel confident to enter a career in opinion writing? Which news specialities—politics, say, or economics, community affairs—interest you most?

4. Look again at the Basic Statement of Principles drawn by the National Conference of Editorial Writers and reproduced earlier in Chapter 1.

In 250 *persuasive* words describe:

- What do you think is the single most important principle raised in that statement?
- If you were to *re*write the statement, which value or principle would you strengthen or emphasize?

5. Study institutional editorials published in five consecutive issues of your college newspaper (or another paper designated by your instructor) and, in about 250 words, state whether the writers fulfilled these journalistic principles:

Serving the public.
Monitoring the powerful.
Being balanced and fair.
Being compassionate.
Guarding the First Amendment.
Being courageous and independent.

2 Identifying Issues for Comment

H OW'S THIS as an issue for your first editorial or column: Looking ahead, scientists say the earth may cool in a couple billion years or so and all life may vanish. You can warn your readers they better start thinking about that.

Or, perhaps this issue: Looking back, not enough voters turned out for the mayoral election 12 months ago, and you can tsk, tsk about that.

Ridiculous? Yes, but those absurdities illustrate how very wrong you can be if your opinion writing deals with issues too far *ahead* of the news curve ("The earth is cooling!") or too far *behind* it (belatedly moaning about low voter turnout a year ago).

In neither scenario could you fulfill a basic responsibility in opinion writing: Identifying issues of compelling importance to your readers and writing about them in *timely fashion*. It's not easy.

Mike Royko, the late syndicated *Chicago Tribune* columnist, described the challenge: "Eighty percent of the job is deciding what to write about."[1]

In this chapter, we'll look at ways you can identify important issues to ensure you are timely, relevant—and helpful—to readers struggling to get through another day, struggling to build better lives for themselves, their community, their nation.

First Priority: Know Your Audience

Your selection of issues to write about must flow, of course, principally from your readers' needs and desires.

Determining reader desires is relatively simple. Opinion polls, focus groups, on-the-street reporting and other journalistic devices give us good insight into what readers *want.*

Determining what they *need* to read about is tougher. This requires you, as a trained journalist, to sift through the hundreds of issues, problems and opportunities confronting your readers and identify those that are crucial, even if readers don't recognize their importance.

Then, you must write alluringly and avoid "castor oil journalism" (the imperative, "Read this! It's good for you!"). Write pointedly, even sharply, but always engagingly so your message can be digested easily.

Whichever you're writing about—reader wants or needs—you must have detailed and precise understanding of your audience.

How the Media Define Audiences

Long gone are the days when editors merely surveyed the world of news and issues, then wrote about those that interested them before throwing the "product"—the newspaper, the magazine—before a faceless, anonymous audience of strangers.

Box 2-1	A Professional's Viewpoint

An editorial writer has only one excuse for existence: that he has a positive opinion about a subject on which he is well informed, on which he knows more than the average man.

—H. L. Mencken

Mencken, the "Sage of Baltimore," made this comment in 1947 to an American Press Institute Writing seminar that led to formation the following year of the National Conference of Editorial Writers. The text of his remarks is in "Still Wise Advice: Get Out of the Office," *The Masthead,* Fall 1996, p. 36.

Today, editors use extensive research to determine who their readers (and nonreaders) are, where they live, what their annual household incomes are, how much schooling they have, even what they buy at supermarkets.

This research aids media strategists in identifying and analyzing a "market" to be served. All newspapers and magazines try to fashion news and editorial content that attracts a certain type of reader who, in turn, is attractive to advertisers (who provide about 50 percent of revenue for magazines, 80 percent for newspapers).

Your selection of issues for comment must be in general accord with the marketing strategy that results.

All media generally identify three types of markets:

Geographic Market

For community newspapers and magazines, this might be the city of publication plus two or three surrounding counties. For large publications, the targeted geographic market might be the entire nation.

Broadcast stations serve geographic markets, called the "designated market," covered by their signal patterns.

In both print and broadcasting, marketing strategy requires serving advertisers who want to reach prospective customers within the geographic market.

Obviously, news and editorial content must focus principally on issues that break within the geographic confines of the market *or, if they develop elsewhere, are of interest locally.*

However, avoid the parochialism that afflicts many editorial pages—a journalistic myopia that sees only Main Street and what happens on it as worthy of comment. Today, a "local" issue can break in Afghanistan or outer space and have impact on your Main Street. You must alert your readers when you see such an issue develop afar.

| Box 2-2 | A Professional's Viewpoint |

If a story is exceptionally boring, it may result in an editorial. Editorials are written by people who have agreed to have several strong opinions a day and write them down, provided they do not have to sign their names. It is very much like writing on the walls of public restrooms, except that people read the walls of public restrooms.

Most editorial writers run out of strong opinions after a couple of weeks, so what they do is just seize some issue at random and demand that the nation develop a cohesive policy about it. Or it can be a coherent policy. Either one is okay.

Humorist Dave Barry in a 1984 syndicated column that's as funny today as it was then.

Demographic Market

Within their geographic markets, all media target audiences by age, income, education and other *demographic characteristics* extremely important to advertisers.

Advertisers increasingly use media that reach desirable audiences precisely defined demographically. Cadillac car dealers want their ads to ride into affluent homes on upscale newspapers; fancy department stores and real estate brokers selling $500,000 homes love glossy elitist magazines.

News strategists build content likely to attract such niche audiences—stories about ballet, the stock market and Caribbean vacations for Cadillac owners; photo layouts of beautiful homes, beauty care stories and society gossip for the wealthy.[2]

Opinion writers must address issues of concern to their medium's niche audience. *But*—as watchdogs, as keepers of the social conscience—opinion writers must expand their view beyond limited horizons, to include all sectors of society. (See Box 2-3 for one editor's suggestion that you comment on issues that "make good things happen" in your community.)

| Box 2-3 | A Professional's Viewpoint |

Richard Oppel is a veteran journalist who has reported and edited for The Associated Press and Knight Ridder. He currently is editor of the *Austin* (Tex.) *American Statesman*. He advises opinion writers to select an agenda of issues that will "make good things happen" in their communities.

BY RICHARD OPPEL

An editorial page should be a powerful instrument for community good, but many newspapers today fail to take advantage of their privileged position in a democracy.

Years ago, the failure may have been one of abuse, with a publisher or editor favoring friends and punishing enemies.

Today, the failure is often one of timidity. I see pages of local newspapers filled with long, boring editorials about the United Nations or Congress; tedious letters from organizational representatives; and op-ed columns by a handful of syndicated writers.

I think a good editorial page should have an agenda. The editors should publish that agenda at the first of each year. It should say, "Here's what we believe. These are the issues that we think should be resolved. We will be pushing these points through the year." And then the paper should do so.

Our readers think that a newspaper has an agenda. They take it to be a hidden agenda. Well, most good editors do have editorial agendas. We believe in working to make good things happen in a community. So, why not publish that agenda?

Similarly, we need to recruit good letter-writers by encouraging comment in editorials and editors' notes. We should nurture those writers, polishing their prose through good editing. We should develop local columnists, too, placing special emphasis on thoughtful, articulate people *who disagree with the paper's point of view* [emphasis added].

Our editorial writers should be encouraged and supported in taking controversial positions on local and regional matters. In local matters, we can hope to have some influence. Editorializing forcefully and locally is riskier than commenting on the United Nations, but those editorials will bring response and reaction.

Given an agenda, local columnists and emphasis on local editorials, how much further should we go in terms of community leadership? In some instances, we can be a "convener of the community"—calling together disparate groups to talk about solutions to lingering, hard-to-solve problems. Consider, for example, a river running through the newspaper's hometown. Because of increased industrial, recreational and other uses, the river is becoming more and more polluted. Yet, it runs through several other cities and counties, and no one political unit seems capable of addressing the problem. Yet a newspaper—perhaps working with an area college— could invite elected officials, business executives, environmentalists, boating enthusiasts, academics developers and others together to discuss how to address the problem.

Should we go beyond that? Nothing wrong with the newspaper "setting up" the discussion by publishing conventional, in-depth reporting of the river's condition, and the causes of the pollution, prior to the meeting. And all's right with publishing news of the proceedings, presenting the major alternatives that emerged in discussion, taking editorial stands, and finally encouraging readers to come to their own conclusions.

We need to remember as journalists that our principal roles are to report and comment. We arrogate a bit too much to declare "This is the solution," and set ourselves up as the ultimate arbiter. We should respect the right of citizens to elect their representatives, and the responsibilities of those officials to make decisions. We are not the decision-maker on policy; we are not the instrument of implementation.

Psychographic Market

This involves targeting, also on behalf of advertisers, *audiences defined by attitudes and beliefs.*

That is, news and editorial content is aimed at persons with common psychographic characteristics, such as conservative (or liberal) political beliefs or interests in, say, wildlife conservation or lifestyle activities.

Obviously, opinion writers for media serving psychographic niches must be expert in the subject matter—liberal politics, wildlife conservation or whatever—and write primarily on issues dealing with attitudes and beliefs of the niche audience.

Here are examples of media that target audiences with precise geographic, demographic and psychographic profiles:

The Wall Street Journal, with 1.8 million circulation the largest newspaper in America, offers high-quality news and editorial content that's conservative politically and fiscally. Result: Readers in business, finance and industry throughout the United States who average more than $1 million net worth and, of course, are prime targets for upscale advertisers. *Journal* opinion writers aim directly at issues of compelling importance to their elitist audience.

The *Journal* "delivers" even more attractive readers internationally with editions published in Europe and Asia, and opinion writers for those editions adjust their sights accordingly.

Forbes magazine, heavy in financial and corporate news, attracts readers at the top of America's socio-economic scale.

Rolling Stone, once targeted at youthful swingers, now aims upscale at demographically more attractive readers and thus courts different advertisers than in the old days.

Opinion writers for both magazines select issues and pitch their writing appropriately for their audience.

Many community newspapers and magazines are less aggressive in moving upscale. Their advertisers need deeper "household penetration" into all demographic sectors of their markets to sell groceries, furniture, discount store goods. Nevertheless, the higher their income and education, the more people read, so even community publications are becoming somewhat elitist. Opinion writers on 50,000-circulation newspapers, for example, might be writing for readers who average, say, $40,000 annual income and a couple years of college.

Television, counting its viewers in the millions, offers a more diverse and somewhat downscale audience. (Persons of low income and education generally are heavy watchers of TV, not readers.) But some TV programming attracts upscale viewers, so opinion writers for community television stations must take that into account.

Radio stations target specific audiences through their music or talk programming. Youthful listeners seek stations playing the hottest, newest tunes; older listeners head for stations offering classical music or Glen Miller's "Golden Oldies." News programming and editorials are scarce on many stations. But radio does offer commentary via all-talk formats, and content is selected with the same attention to audience demographics that motivate other media.

CASE STUDY: *ATLANTA JOURNAL* AND *CONSTITUTION*

Envisage yourself writing opinion for the *Atlanta Journal* or *Constitution,* sister papers with combined circulation of about 450,000 weekdays, 720,000 on Sundays.[3]

Your *geographic market* is the city of Atlanta and four surrounding counties, called the "city zone," plus 55 other counties, termed the "retail trading zone," in northeast Georgia.[4]

Your *demographic market,* defined in *Journal* and *Constitution* research, looks like this:

- Most of your weekday readers (73.3 percent) have annual household income over $35,000 (for 19.3 percent, it's $75,000 or more).

- Of all readers, 51.8 percent are aged 25-44; 36.8 percent are 45 or older. Only 10.5 percent are 24 or younger.
- In education, your audience is "upscale": A whopping 74.4 percent have some college or technical school background (32 percent are college graduates, 17.2 percent have postgraduate education).
- In occupations, readers are upscale, too: 33.8 percent are professionals or managers; 12.4 percent are employed in technical or sales jobs; 9.9 percent are in administrative or clerical jobs; 16.6 percent have blue-collar or service jobs, and 15.6 percent are retired.[5]

Psychographically, your audience is terribly complex. Some readers have attitudes and beliefs born of family ties dating back generations in the "Old South." However, thousands are newcomers who migrated to Atlanta searching for jobs and better weather. Their attitudes and beliefs tie back to Toledo, Los Angeles, Miami, not to the Old South, not to Georgia.

In merely a decade or two, Atlanta has exploded with growth, evolving into an international city with major banking and commercial firms, one of the world's busiest airports and urban sprawl extending miles from downtown.[6]

How can you sort through all of that and identify issues of timely, compelling interest to your readers?

Role of the Editorial Board

The *Constitution* and *Journal* have separate editorial boards that select topics for comment in institutional editorials.

Each board operates with a high degree of autonomy, although each broadly represents its newspaper's overall strategy. The *Constitution,* for example, has one of the most liberal editorial views among major daily newspapers; the *Journal* takes a moderate-to-conservative stance.

Susan Laccetti, a *Journal* editorial writer, explains how her paper's editorial board selects issues for comment:

> There are five members of the *Journal*'s editorial board: Jim Wooten, a veteran newsman who is editor of the editorial page; Jeff Dickerson, a former editorial writer at the *Detroit News* who is one of the few black conservative columnists in the country; Richard Matthews, an expert in Asian affairs and a 25-year veteran at the Atlanta newspapers; Martha Ezzard, a former legislator and attorney from Colorado and the only liberal on the board; and I, a reporter who spent 12 years covering government, politics, growth and education.
>
> The board meets daily at 9 a.m. after all members have read the morning newspaper and *The New York Times* or sometimes *The Wall Street Journal.* Wooten convenes the meeting around the board's conference table and gener-

ally steers the board toward topics he believes the newspaper should comment on.

The board members divide up topics *based on what's going on in the news* [emphasis added] and their personal interests. For example, Dickerson often writes about minority affairs, welfare reform, affirmative action. Ezzard is the legal and environmental expert. Matthews is the foreign affairs guy who also is well-versed in city of Atlanta matters. I write about metro Atlanta governments and schools, education and some state government matters. Wooten rarely writes editorials, instead commenting on topics such as health care, state government and pension abuses in his thrice-weekly columns.

At each meeting, board members bring up topics they would like to write about. Then there is discussion about each topic. Some topics generate little discussion. Others can generate a firestorm.

At recent board meetings, Ezzard pursued every chapter and verse of Atlanta's water and sewage woes. The board generally agreed with her position to come down hard on the Atlanta mayor for continued illegal dumping of raw sewage into the Chattahoochee River, water source for most of Georgia's population.

On topics such as welfare reform, the board has been more divided. Dickerson, Matthews and I have been the more conservative members wanting strict reform and short time limits for recipients to get off welfare and get a job. Ezzard has been the sole crusader for giving identical welfare benefits to immigrants.

Perhaps the most controversial topic recently broached by the board has been partial-birth abortion. The board has not taken a position on abortion in a decade or more. I pushed for the board to urge the Legislature and governor to adopt a ban on partial-birth abortion. The most fractious debate in recent months occurred the days the board voted on that issue.

Again, only Ezzard fought to keep the board from commenting on the ban. After two days of debate, a vote was taken because the issue was so emotional. The vote was 4-1 for the board to take a stand urging a ban on the controversial abortion procedure. The resulting editorial tried to move the abortion debate to middle ground, arguing that banning a particular procedure was not the same as eliminating abortion. The Legislature later adopted the ban with the governor using the editorial page's language to support his decision to sign it.

Editorial topics also are broached by the writers in other ways. Each week, the board meets three times with visitors who want the board's support on topics of interest to them.

Gov. Zell Miller visited with the board to discuss welfare reform prior to the 1997 legislative session. Lewis Jordan, president of ValuJet, visited the board to try to ease criticism leveled at his airline since the 1996 crash of a plane near Miami. Metro Atlanta school superintendents, promoting referendums to hike the local option sales tax a penny to build schools, visited several times to promote their plans, which eventually were endorsed by the board. Corporate executives, ambassadors, congressmen and others frequently visit the editorial board.

The board also takes on projects to write about that may not be stories in the news. For example, I have been doing investigative reporting on wasteful spending practices at Grady Memorial Hospital, the city's only public hospital that serves indigents in north Georgia. I have written a series of editorials about the hospital's resistance to efficiency studies; the hospital's refusal to return federal reimbursements to its support counties (Fulton and Dekalb); and the hospital's bid to move into an HMO market. Ezzard's series of editorials on Atlanta's water and sewer woes is another example of the project-like direction Wooten likes to send board members.

At no time in the editorial page process does the publisher, Roger Kintzel, ever try to influence what is said on the *Journal* editorial page.[7]

Clearly, *Journal* editorial writers comment principally on timely local issues—many of them "pocketbook" issues—having direct impact on their readers' money and lives. However, the *Journal's* total offering of opinion, interpretation and analysis goes beyond two-a-day institutional editorials. Op-ed columns feature syndicated writers, as well as local commentators.

Over a four-day period in 1997, at the time of Laccetti's writing, these topics were covered in institutional editorials and op-ed commentary:

Table 2.1.   Editorial and op-ed topics appearing in the *Atlanta Journal,* March 18–21, 1997

EDITORIALS	OP-ED COLUMNS
March 18	
Welfare reform (local angle)	Welfare reform
Clinton/cost of living	U.S. conservative leadership failing
	Teenager values
	Fire ants (light, humorous)
March 19	
Government red tape (local)	Welfare reform
Lottery scandal (local)	Quality of education
	AIDS/needle exchange
	Gardening (light)
March 20	
Sales tax increase (local)	Car air bag dangers
Regulation of Internet	Equal Rights Amendment debate
content (national)	Multiculturalism vs. assimilation
	Labor union contributions
	to Democrats
March 21	
Welfare reform (local)	Legal regulation of small business
Medicaid (local/national)	U.S. at peace, world in turmoil
	National Endowment for Arts
	Polygraph evidence in trials

Box 2-4	A Professional's Viewpoint

One good idea is enough for a lifetime if you're the inventor of the Frisbee or the Hula-Hoop. If you're the editorial writer at a small daily, however, one good idea will barely get you through lunch.

You need 13 good ideas. A week.

—Tom Dennis, editorial writer, *Wilkes-Barre* (Pa.) *Times Leader*, "Small Shop Generates 13 Good Ideas a Week," *The Masthead*, Fall 1993, p. 9.

Meanwhile, at the *Constitution* ...

For strategic purposes, *Constitution* opinion writers take a different approach to selecting issues for comment.

First, the *Constitution*'s institutional editorials and many of its staff-written columns take a liberal stance, compared to the *Journal*'s generally conservative position. This is planned by the newspapers' owners, Cox Newspapers, to ensure readers have a choice in political and societal comment.

Second, the *Constitution* is a morning paper and is distributed over empty predawn highways to a much larger geographic market across Georgia and beyond. The *Journal*, like most metropolitan afternoon papers, generally is aimed at readers in or tightly around the core city. Circulation trucks for afternoon papers, which are printed in mid-morning, simply cannot get through daytime traffic to reach the outer fringes of a large geographic market. *Constitution* editorials and columns, therefore, often take a geographically wider view, serving needs and interests of readers distant from Atlanta.

Third, the *Constitution* is much larger than the *Journal* (310,000 circulation vs. 140,000) and much more influential. The *Constitution*'s audience is upscale; its influence nationwide.

Out of those factors come *Constitution* selections such as those in Table 2.2.

Table 2.2.   Editorial and op-ed topics appearing in the *Atlanta Constitution*, March 18–21, 1997

EDITORIALS	OP-ED COLUMNS
March 23	
Welfare reform (national)	Welfare reform
Tobacco company suits (national)	CIA failures
	Give working families breaks
	Japan's technology
	Campaign financing
	Oklahoma City bombing trial

Table 2.2.   *(Continued)*

EDITORIALS	OP-ED COLUMNS
March 24	
Tornado survival tips (regional)	Save city's green spaces
	Save old baseball stadium
	Spring brings bugs (light)
	Southern barbecue (light)
March 25	
State legislation on business takeovers (statewide)	Restore civil discourse
	Mexico/drug smuggling
Nature conservance (statewide)	U.S. House leadership
Middle East unrest (international)	
March 26	
Baseball stadium (local)	China money in U.S. politics
Fed Reserve Board/interest rates (national)	Public transportation in large cities
Annual black student gathering (local)	Incest

CASE STUDY ENDS HERE

Fine Tuning Issues for Comment

Newspaper space— "newshole"—is limited and precious. Magazine pages are "tight," and editors can't afford to misjudge reader desires with *any* irrelevant copy. For television and radio, time—broadcast's equivalent of space—is extremely limited.

How, then, can you focus on just those essential issues that will give you maximum impact in the space or time available?

Many newspapers seek reader assistance by establishing structured two-way communications with community groups and citizens.

Advisory boards are created from selected community leaders or, more broadly, from representative readers drawn from throughout the newspaper's market.

The *Fort Worth* (Tex.) *Star-Telegram* has three community advisory boards which, in the words of senior editorial writer Tommy Denton, serve as "critics/counselors and sources of feedback as to our numerous journalistic shortcomings and our rare complicity in random acts of modest competence."[8]

One *Star-Telegram* advisory board is for 20 black leaders assembled following strong criticism from blacks about the paper's news coverage and editorials.

Lynnell Burkett, associate editorial director of the *San Antonio* (Tex.) *Express-News,* reports her newspaper's community advisory board serves these purposes:[9]

- Establishing relationships with citizens traditionally without access to the newspaper.
- Assuring that editorial writers hear from women and minorities (particularly important, she says, if the writing staff itself lacks diversity).
- Introducing community leaders to the newspaper's key people and how the newspaper works.
- Developing varied sources and viewpoints for editorial (and news) writers.

The *Express-News* selects about eight advisors to meet monthly for one year, then rotates in new members. Effort is made to ensure board diversity in gender, ethnicity, geography, interests and professions.

Express-News advisors meet informally at the newspaper or over lunch at local restaurants. Some papers favor relaxed coffee-and-doughnut chats with editors in the newsroom or editorial board room.

However, formal *focus groups* are preferred by some newspapers because trained discussion leaders often are capable of eliciting truly effective guidance.

Research selects group members broadly representative of the newspaper's geographic and demographic markets, or who represent specific niche audiences. Some newspapers with large black or Hispanic audiences use such precision research to ensure editorial (and news) policies meet the needs of all readers, not just the educated, affluent elite who are both highly visible in most communities and naturally attracted to newspaper reading.

Under a facilitator's guidance, focus groups can deliver probing, in-depth critiques that often don't emerge in more informal settings. Group members, for example, can be assigned to study editorials in advance of meetings and arrive ready to discuss how they cover local issues.

But, some editors see dangers in advisory boards.

First, advisory boards, like letters columns, tend to attract activists or, even, cranks. (Watch who signs letters to the editor of your college or local community newspaper and you'll likely see the same names time and again.) Although activists may represent a wider reader constituency and, thus, should get a hearing, they often bring narrow personal or special interests to advisory boards and can skew discussions.

Second, many editors fear relying too heavily on advisory boards could lead editorial writers to abrogate their responsibilities, as trained journalists, to nonjournalists. Sample diverse opinions, listen to outsiders, take seriously any criticisms advisory boards deliver, but *always* reserve to yourself the ultimate decision on what to write about and how. And, editors warn, don't turn editorial pages into mere reflections of community extremists, into print versions of talk radio, where screamers and extremists can dominate. (However, does the popularity of talk radio and television signal newspapers aren't creating community forums in their editorial pages? David Awbrey, editorial page editor of the *Wichita* (Kan.) *Eagle,* says broadcast's popularity indicates alienation of many Americans from mainstream media.)

It's not only in identifying issues that editors strive to preserve their prerogatives (and responsibilities). They value the individuality of their *writing*—the structure of their arguments, the shape and form of their language—and take firm steps to protect that from community advisory boards or their own newspaper's editorial board.

Dan Radmacher, editorial page editor of the *Charleston* (W. Va.) *Gazette,* warns: "We shouldn't write by committee—I have never seen anything good result from that. But we can *think* by committee."[10]

<table>
<tr><td>Box 2-5</td><td>Viewpoints of Two Professionals</td></tr>
</table>

Every person has only so much attention to give and politics and government takes up only a fraction of what it did 25 years ago. Look at the declining television coverage. Look at the declining voting rate. Economics and economic news is what moves the country now, not politics.

—Robert Teeter, long-time Republican campaign consultant, quoted in R.W. Apple Jr., "Why a Capital Uproar Is a Hinterland Beep," *The New York Times,* national edition, March 13, 1997, p. A12.

The *Hartford Courant's* editorial page is never reluctant to comment on major topics like the war in the Middle East, the unification of Germany and a new Connecticut governor. ... But now we also dare to tackle the really controversial stuff, such as traffic lights in rural towns.

—George Graves, *The Hartford* (Conn.) *Courant,* "Zones Feed Hunger for Local News," *The Masthead,* Summer 1991, p. 20.

Focus on Core Issues

As always in journalism, it's up to *you,* the writer, to decide ultimately which issues are crucial to your readers.

Michael Goodwin, editorial page editor of the *New York Daily News,* counsels that every editorial "must not only present an opinion, but also have a reason for being."[11]

To accomplish that, Goodwin says, "Focus on the core issues that affect the daily lives of readers: crime, education, jobs, health, transportation."

Those core issues, Goodwin says, take up about two-thirds of *Daily*

News editorial space. He says, "To expect busy readers in Podunk or Brooklyn to wade through a tome that analyzes, say, the strike of French workers, is not only a waste of time and space; it's downright foolish. What, pray tell, is the point?"

Goodwin's identification of core issues is supported by a national survey by the Roper Center. Findings: Most Americans (95 percent) want to know about crime, 94 percent are interested in local news, 92 percent in the environment, 88 percent in the national government, 87 percent in global news, 67 percent in the arts, 63 percent in sports.[12]

And, how do you stay current in so many subjects? Well, reading your own newspaper is a good start.

Dr. Ernest C. Hynds, a University of Georgia researcher, finds virtually all editorial writers list their own newspapers as a source of ideas and *66 percent* report it is the source used most often.

Second as a source of ideas are regional dailies published near the writers' cities. Nearly half the writers surveyed found ideas in nearby competing papers that could be refined and localized for their own readers. Other sources: *Newsweek* (a source for 18 percent of respondents), *The New York Times* (14 percent), *Time* (11 percent), *The Wall Street Journal* (10 percent), *U.S. News & World Report* (8 percent), *The New Republic* (5 percent), *USA Today* and *The Economist* (both 3 percent).[13]

But precisely where in the hundreds of newspaper pages you'll see every week do you search for what interests readers? Follow your readers. They'll show you. Newspaper Association of America research gives you guidance:

Table 2.3.   Adult Reading (weekdays)

	(*percent*)
Read every page	57
General news	94
Editorials	78
Entertainment	77
Sports	76
Food/Cooking	74
Business/Finance	72

Source: "Facts About Newspapers 1995," Newspaper Association of America, p.6.

Lessons for editorial writers in Table 2.3:

• Many (57 percent) readers report reading (more likely, scanning) every page. First cast your net wide when searching for ideas. Your readers buy newspapers for their wide view of the world. Note 94 percent of readers look at general news.

- However, quickly identify niche issues and isolate precisely what in the wider world is on your readers' minds. Note, for example, the high percentage (72 percent) of readers attracted to news of business and finance. Those readers obviously are looking for news on investments and the pocketbook issues they confront daily. Reader pocketbooks are fertile ground for opinion writing and editorial leadership.
- Be cautious with research showing high readership of editorials. Some surveys show low interest among readers, although Newspaper Association of America studies found 78 percent of all adults read editorial pages. Incidentally, readership was found strong across gender and ethnic lines: Editorial reading was reported by men (76 percent), women (79 percent), whites (78 percent), blacks (71 percent), and Spanish/Hispanics (70 percent).

Finally …

In search of issues demanding editorial comment, nothing beats reading, talking, walking, thinking.

Read as the pros do—your own newspaper, competitors' papers, regional and national magazines. *The Wall Street Journal* does a national *news* story on college tuition? Localize that for your college newspaper. A debate erupts in a neighboring town over a school bond issue? For your newspaper, localize the question of quality of education in your town's schools.

Talk to everyone you meet. Have an idle moment in the supermarket checkout line? Talk to the person next to you. Talk to the cashier. *Listen* to what they say about food prices, jobs, traffic, taxes. What they *say* is what many of your readers *think*.

Nothing beats walking through your community, be that a university, village or city. How are downtown businesses doing? Busy, vibrant? Or, boarded up? Either way, you have an issue. Are all stop lights working? Are all the street signs up and visible? Are streets clean? There, in such subjects, is where your readers live. Comment is needed.

Don't rush to the keyboard with a half-formed idea. *Think it through. Research it.* We turn to this in Chapter 3, Reporting and Researching Your Opinions.

Summary

- Your selection of issues for comment must flow principally from your readers' needs and desires.
- The media define their audience "markets" *geographically* (a city and sev-

eral surrounding counties, for example), *demographically* (age, education, income) and *psychographically* (beliefs, attitudes). Write to those markets.

- Richard Oppel, editor of the *Austin* (Tex.) *American-Statesman,* says opinion writers should select an agenda of issues that will "make good things happen" in their communities.
- Many newspapers establish editorial boards that define issues and set institutional policy.
- Advisory boards often are formed of local officials or representative citizens to give opinion writers insight into issues crucial to readers.
- Focus groups are favored by some newspapers because trained discussion leaders often are successful in eliciting truly effective guidance for editorial writers.
- Advisory boards and focus groups tend to attract activists who can skew discussions toward their own special interests; some writers fear outside advisors can lead writers to abrogate their responsibilities, as trained journalists, to select issues crucial to readers.
- Effective editorials focus on *core issues* that affect your readers' daily lives—crime, education, jobs, health, transportation.
- Research shows editorial writers most frequently find ideas for their commentary in their own newspapers or neighboring regional papers, but also in *The New York Times, The Wall Street Journal* and other national newspapers and magazines.
- Most adult readers (94 percent) are attracted to general news but business/finance and other niche subjects are high on their reading lists, too.
- In searching for ideas, nothing beats reading, talking, walking and thinking about your community and the crucial issues in readers' lives.

Recommended Reading

Make it a habit to read newspapers and magazines for ideas that can be localized for comment. A *Wall Street Journal* national roundup on, say, real estate taxes should lead you to think of how you could treat that for a local community newspaper. If you're a campus journalist, a newsweekly article on underage drinking should start you thinking about commenting on student drinking at your college.

Important research on reader attitudes and issues appears regularly in *presstime, Editor & Publisher* magazine, The American Society of Newspaper Editors' *The American Editor, American Journalism Review, Columbia Journalism Review* and *Journalism Quarterly.*

The Masthead regularly publishes research and analysis by editorial and opinion writers who are members of the National Conference of Editorial Writers. This is must reading for aspiring opinion writers.

Notes

1. Clarence Page, also a *Tribune* columnist, reported this quote by Royko. See John Kanelis, "If You Aren't Excited, Neither Are Readers," *The Masthead,* Winter 1996, p. 36.

2. I discuss marketing research by newspapers in Conrad Fink, *Strategic Newspaper Management* (Boston: Allyn & Bacon, 1996).

3. "Audit Report," Audit Bureau of Circulations, for 12 months ended Sept. 30, 1994.

4. Ibid.

5. "How Do AJC Readers Compare With the Atlanta Market?," a research report drawn from Atlanta Consumer Market Study, 1992, and issued by *The Atlanta Journal* and *Constitution.*

6. For a deeper look at evolutionary change in the Atlanta market and its impact on these sister newspapers, see Conrad Fink, *The Atlanta Journal* and *Constitution,* a case study published in 1989 by The Poynter Institute for Media Studies.

7. Susan Laccetti, letter to author, April 10, 1997.

8. Tommy Denton, "Uninitiated Unclear on the Concept," *The Masthead,* Summer 1995, p. 8.

9. Lynnell Burkett, "Three Steps to a Successful Advisory Board," *The Masthead,* Summer 1995, p. 12.

10. Dan Radmacher, "Listen to Your Nagging Voices," *The Masthead,* Fall 1996, p. 12.

11. Michael Goodwin, "Leave Ho-Hum Editorials to 'Foreign Affairs'," *The Masthead,* Spring 1996, p. 12.

12. This survey was published March 2, 1997 by the Roper Center, in conjunction with the Freedom Forum's Newseum, 1101 Wilson Blvd., Dept. P, Arlington, Va., 22209.

13. Ernest C. Hynds, "Editorial Pages Become More Useful," *The Masthead,* Fall 1995, p. 38.

Exercises

1. Interview the lead editorial writer for your campus newspaper (or another newspaper your instructor designates) on his/her understanding of the newspaper's geographic, demographic and psychographic markets. Then analyze five days of editorials and discuss, in about 250 words, whether the issues selected for comment in those editorials show he/she truly understands the newspaper's market.

2. Read again Richard Oppel's advice that editorial writers select agendas of issues that can "make good things happen" in their communities.

Select for your campus newspaper (or another newspaper your instructor designates) an agenda of five issues on which you could comment and perhaps "make good thing happen" at your college. Explain, in about 300 words, why you selected the five issues and what general position you would take on them.

3. Construct a hypothetical editorial board of seven persons for your campus newspaper (or another newspaper your instructor designates).

In about 300 words, explain the diversity, backgrounds and viewpoints you think would best reflect issues crucial to your college's student body. What would be the racial, gender and other components of your board? Which five important issues would you place before this board for discussion?

4. Michael Goodwin, editorial page editor of the New York *Daily News*, is quoted in this chapter as saying *core issues* for his readers are crime, education, jobs, health, transportation.

Discuss, in about 250 words, the core issues you think are crucial to students on your campus (or in another community your instructor designates). Prioritize the issues by importance.

5. Read today's *The Wall Street Journal* (or another newspaper your instructor designates) and select four stories you would localize for editorial comment in your campus newspaper.

Be certain to pick stories that truly have student angles and discuss, in about 250 words, why those stories are important to students. For each idea, present the general approach and tenor of editorials you would write.

3 Reporting and Researching Your Opinions

ATTENTION, YOUNG WRITERS! H.L. Mencken left this advice for you:

> No editorial writer ought to be permitted to sit in an editorial room for month after month and year after year, contemplating his umbilicus. He ought to go out and meet people.[1]

That advice from a great opinion writer of another era—Mencken lived 1880–1956—is as important today for you, the aspiring writer, as it was then for your predecessor writers.

Mencken, one of our most memorable writers in his years at the *Baltimore Sun,* was stressing the importance of *reporting* as the foundation for valid and effective opinions. Investigate your subject, he said. Master it. Act as a reporter. *Then*—only then—write your opinion.

It's to this crucial function—reporting—that we now turn.

CASE STUDY: THE MURDER OF JEANNIE PURCELL

Even today, there is passion in Maria Henson's voice as she describes the dismal end of Jeannie Purcell.[2]

"It made me angry," Henson says.

Out of that anger—and deep-dig, investigative reporting over nearly two years—came a Pulitzer Prize in editorial reporting for Henson and fundamental changes in how the state of Kentucky deals with spouse abuse.

It all started in 1989, when the *Lexington* (Ky.) *Herald-Leader* reported on its front page the tragic story of Jeannie Purcell. Then 33, she fled to Lexington from Virginia to escape her abusive husband. She got a protective court order to restrain him from hurting her. Police said she should call if he showed up.

Jeannie's husband did show up, but she had no time to call for help. He broke into her house and held hostages (including small children) for 17 hours. When the shooting ended two men had been wounded. Jeannie was dead, three bullets in her chest, one in her back. Her husband killed himself.

For Maria Henson, then a *Herald-Leader* editorial writer, the immediate question was, "What now?" Rush to the keyboard? Write a quick editorial to follow closely the spot news coverage?

As a trained journalist, Henson could have been in print the next morning, of course. Writing on deadline is second nature to experienced journalists. But such a quick-reaction editorial would have been written necessarily light on facts, if heavy on outrage. Without substantive reporting, Henson would have been reduced to expressing righteous indignation and calling for action—action by whom and how would have to be left a little unclear at this early stage, naturally.

Henson recalls in fact starting such an editorial. Its focus was on the Lexington community's failure to protect Jeannie.

"I couldn't get it finished," Henson says. "It sat in my computer for two years."

But the following day, David Holwerk, *Herald-Leader* editorial page editor, had more immediate, if simple, guidance: "Find out what's out there."

"That," Henson says, "was my ticket for reporting that you'd normally see on the news side."

Henson "set out just as a reporter would—east to meet beaten women in Appalachia, north to the Kentucky outskirts of Cincinnati, and west to near the Mississippi River ... traveling and interviewing beaten women. Victims' advocates served as my brokers by finding women who would be willing to tell their stories on the record. I was also reading anything I could find about domestic violence."

All the while, Henson was writing editorials on other subjects. But spouse abuse never was far from her mind.

"After seven months of off-and-on research, confrontational interviews, and appeals for court documents and tapes that were not public records, I was ready to write," she says.

Even while starting to write her series, Henson continued reporting.

"What I learned would later fill nearly 30 editorials (published) over 13 months," Henson says.

Her series, "To Have and To Harm," led to profound changes: Domestic-violence records and hearings throughout Kentucky were opened to the public. Judges and prosecutors received special training in handling spouse abuse. The state attorney general reported on domestic violence statewide. A computerized system was established to track abusers throughout the state. Spouse abuse became a political issue in statewide races. New legislation was passed.

CASE STUDY ENDS HERE

Reporting Gives Writing "Added Value"

Henson, now associate editor and an editorial writer for the *Charlotte* (N.C.) *Observer*, says important lessons arose from the Jeannie Purcell case:

- First, through their own research, editorial writers *must add to a newspaper's treatment of an issue.* Don't merely comment on what is in the news pages, she says, do reporting that gives your readers "added value."
- Second, "Reporting gives your editorial writing authority ... the writer brings passion but if you do the reporting, you have a channel for that passion."
- Third, "Translate issues into people," Henson says. "An editorial page can spark change, can crusade, and can strike a chord with its readers. We did it by telling stories of individuals. We did it by including photographs of the women."

Henson had advantages going into her prize-winning series. Her newspaper, the *Herald-Leader*, is owned by Knight Ridder, a company renowned for high-quality journalism. It was natural for her editor to turn her loose to report over a long period on this significant story. And, Henson's fellow editorial writers picked up the slack: They "had to work harder and write more editorials when I was on the project full time."

But, how can you focus research and reporting to corral such a sprawling, ill-defined subject as spouse abuse? Where do you start? You start by reviewing the basics of daily journalism.

Box 3-1	A Professional's Viewpoint

As we all travel around these days, it is easy to read editorials that contain virtually no facts. With very few exceptions, editorial writers seem to have abandoned the idea that they are reporters first.

—Reg Murphy, president of the National Geographic Society and veteran newspaper editor and publisher, quoted in Tom Dennis, "Awash in Hogwash," *The Masthead*, Winter 1996, p. 31.

The First Steps in Editorial Research and Reporting

We're in the *news*paper business, and that creates a very special reporting environment for you, as an editorial writer.

It's not that we still define "news" the old-fashioned, knee-jerk way—get it now, write it now, publish it now. Editorial writers *must* take time to think through the subject, to report and research it, then to write with meaning, analysis and interpretation.[3]

Nevertheless, editorial writers, like news writers, must respond to those characteristics that help define news. As you start reporting for editorials, keep these in mind:

IMPACT

How many people are affected—and how deeply—by an event? Your reporter's judgment here is crucial. Write about taxes and you've touched every American; write about rose growing and you've appealed to relatively few.

PROXIMITY

How close an event is to your readers is important. But remember our Chapter Two discussion of proximity: A distant event can be news *if* it affects local lives. You meet the test of proximity if you find—and comment on—local meaning in a revolution in faraway Afghanistan or a breakthrough in the equally faraway worlds of, say, biology or astronomy.

CONFLICT

The struggle between good and bad, right and wrong, the political left and political right ... conflict helps us define news. Of course, you cannot assume conflict *automatically* is news. Much conflict is meaningless noise. Posturing by politicians comes to mind—such as two old pros loudly slanging each other on the floor of the U.S. Senate, then walking out, arm in arm, for a friendly lunch. That's not conflict or news; it's stagecraft.

PROMINENCE

Much of the time, what important, well-known people do—and what is done to them—is *newsier* than what happens to less important unknowns. That's because readers so readily recognize or even identify with the well-known. (Note how people still talk about Princess Di.) The smart writer uses that recognition factor as a "peg" to carry readers through a complex subject. Thus, an editorial reporting on, say, the drug woes of a well-known baseball player can pull readers through the long, sad story of addiction more effectively than would writing that's pegged to faceless, anonymous, nameless addicts. But, don't let "prominence" mislead you into overlooking the extraordinary effect you can have with writing pegged to an anonymous unknown. Recall, for example, how the *Herald-Leader*'s Maria Henson accomplished that with Jeannie Purcell, whose sole claim to fame, tragically, was her brutal demise. Here's the point: Jeannie Purcell's prominence was not *who* she was but, rather, *what* she was—a particularly graphic example of a nationwide scandal—the battered woman. Jeannie Purcell's *who* was obvious; it was great reporting that uncovered her *what*.

TIMELINESS

There is journalistic merit in being fast with the news. People are listening to radio right now to hear what's happening; they'll watch television tonight to learn what happened today; they'll read newspapers tomorrow morning to find out what happened overnight; they'll buy newsweeklies early next week to catch up on what happened this week. And—here's the rub—from newspapers and newsmagazines alike, readers will expect the first quick analysis by opinion writers on *what the news means.*

So, your reporting for an editorial or column should move initially along the same avenues explored by newswriters—toward what interests readers and, importantly, toward what has impact on all of us. That means exploring three particularly fruitful avenues:

- People. Report on—write about—people, *not vague issues.* Write about the Jeannie Purcells of America, not the vague, distant issue of "spouse abuse." Tell me Jeannie's story and you've told me a story of spouse abuse I can understand.
- Money. Also translate this into impact on people. Comment on, say, the size of the Federal budget deficit and you'll throw around figures in the trillions. *What is a trillion?* Who can comprehend that much money? But, ah, do reporting that translates the deficit into a per-capita figure—what each of us owes—and you have both my attention and understanding.
- Power. It comes in many forms—political, economic, military, psychological. Translate power into people—those who have it, those abused by it. Report for me on the physical and emotional power Jeannie Purcell's husband had over her and you help me understand what spouse abuse is all about.

Well, you rightly may think, it's a tall order to sort through all those characteristics of news, do appropriate research and still meet a *news*paper's responsibility to deliver timely comment on events. Can it be done? Yes.

Adding Value in a Hurry

Maria Henson's series on spouse abuse was unique for more than winning a Pulitzer Prize. It also was unusual for the time, effort and money the *Herald-Leader* let Henson put into her reporting that achieved the "added value" she says an editorial must offer readers.

Fact is, many editorial writers put an hour or two *at most* into researching a piece, not days, weeks, months or, in Henson's case, nearly two years. And that troubles many writers.

Lack of time for research was cited as a major problem by 58 percent of editorial writers responding to a nationwide survey in 1994 by Dr. Ernest C. Hynds of the University of Georgia. Lack of time to *write* editorials was cited as a major problem by 44 percent.

Only 14 percent of editorial writers responding said they spent more than two hours researching an editorial; another 14 percent said they spent *less* than one hour; 50 percent said their reporting normally got one to two hours for each editorial.

As for writing time, 17 percent said they normally spent less than one hour on an editorial; 67 percent said they wrote theirs in one hour or more.[4]

Of course, you must remember that Maria Henson was reporting on *statewide* spouse abuse in Kentucky. Writing a one-shot editorial doesn't take the time Henson put into writing nearly 30 editorials in a series published over 13 months.

Here is an example of how to quickly give your readers added value:

It's April 15—the day income taxes are due—a news peg recognizable to every adult American. *The Atlanta Constitution* uses that peg for the day's leading institutional editorial, under the headline, "Good Day to Review Taxes."[5]

The *Constitution*'s lead paragraph—the "intro"—establishes additional pegs in readers' minds:

> It's April 15, the day that Lincoln died and the Titanic sank. As if to round out the day of tragedy, this is also the annual deadline for filing income tax returns. All over the country, accountants are harried and postal clerks are busy. Up in Washington, politicians are going through a Tax Day ritual of their own, spouting rhetoric designed to milk the taxpayers' resentment for future votes.

The editorial reports—*reports,* mind you—that House Speaker Newt Gingrich proposes elimination of federal estate and capital gains taxes. This would cost the U.S. Treasury $350 billion in five years, the *Constitution* says.

Then, the editorial turns to the estate (or "inheritance") tax. With added value reporting, the *Constitution* reduces this complex subject to understandable terms: "The Gingrich proposal to eliminate the federal estate tax would benefit only the descendants of the wealthiest 1 percent of Americans."

Estate tax complexities almost defy comprehension. But that 1 percent I understand!

Here is some added value reporting that uses a recognizable personality to express the capital gains tax in human terms:

> Then there's the capital gains tax, assessed on profits from the sale of stocks and property. It is predicted to raise $250 billion over the next five years.
> Last year, for example, Coca-Cola Chairman Roberto Goizueta exercised a stock option allowing him to buy 200,000 shares of Coke stock for $928,000. Today that stock is worth more than $11 million. If Goizueta sold

that stock, most of his profit would be taxed at 28 percent as a capital gain.

However, if the capital gains tax is eliminated, much of Goizueta's $10 million profit would be tax free. And while Coke's chairman was paying little or nothing on a huge profit, a lowly secretary at Coke would still be paying 20 percent of her $30,000 salary in federal taxes, even after deductions.

In the example above, the *Constitution* uses a man and a company—the late Roberto Goizueta and Coca-Cola—as recognizable in Atlanta as General Motors is in Detroit, Wall Street in New York City, breakfast cereal in Battle Creek. Reader recognition is instantaneous.

And, by comparing Goizueta's millions to a secretary's paltry $30,000, the *Constitution* drives home its central theme: eliminating the capital gains tax would be unfair to low-income taxpayers. The *Constitution* sums up that point:

> Tax policy is an either-or situation. Either you take from Peter or you take it from Paula. The estate tax recognizes that it's better to take money from the wealthy dead than to take it from Paula, who is struggling day to day to raise a family, pay a mortgage and keep a car on the road.

It's worth emphasizing: The added value reporting in *The Atlanta Constitution* example above—the writer's use of Goizueta and Coca-Cola—took just 131 words. Yet, even that brief factual comparison of millionaire vs. low-paid secretary added an entirely new dimension of understanding to the much-debated federal estate tax.

Much opinion writing, however, deals with subjects so complex that deeper reporting is needed before you touch your keyboard.

Let's look at some suggestions to guide your in-depth reporting.

Hints on In-Depth Reporting

Broadly, your in-depth reporting should follow three guidelines:

First, readers on average spend 26 minutes or so on the *entire content* of a newspaper. (It's more for magazines.) That means lots of competition for your writing. In the fight for readers, factual substance—true added value—is needed if your opinion writing is to catch their attention. Passionate writing devoid of facts won't do. Additionally, you have limited newshole for editorials or columns; editors will limit you to hundreds of words, not thousands. So, your reporting instincts must be very sharp, leading you unerringly toward the factual substance necessary to draw readers to—and through—what you are able to write in limited space. *Don't let your reporting stray into matters of secondary importance.*

Second, your reporting must build a *bridge of confidence* between you and your readers, between your paper and the community it serves. At stake are your personal credibility and your newspaper's institutional credibility. So your reporting should be painstaking, accurate, thorough and *based on authoritative sources.* Interviewing six students on the steps of the main library lends only anecdotal background to an editorial on your college's spending on controversial new buildings; factual substance—added value—must come from interviews with the college's vice president for finance; from comparing this year's capital budget against last year's; from talking to authoritative sources on both sides of the controversy—lawyers, accountants, members of the board of regents and others.

Third, direct your reporting and research toward material that will *identify* the issue precisely and reveal its true importance; material that will *compare* what's happening against the expected norm, and *characterize* for your readers its meaning.

Let's look more closely at reporting that will identify, compare and characterize issues.

Identifying Issues

Precisely what is the issue? Superficially, it may appear to be spending by your college for unneeded buildings while needed structures are ignored.

But, in-depth reporting might peel back layers of bureaucratic mumbo-jumbo (including spin doctoring that's intentionally misleading) to reveal issues of compelling importance to your readers: The spending will force students to pay even higher tuition and will deny faculty needed raises.

And this illustrates the basic difference between fast-reaction reporting for a news story and in-depth reporting for an opinion piece: A reporter, on deadline, might be forced to limit research to a few quick telephone calls in search of "balancing comment."

In opinion writing, you are obliged to dig deeper, to reveal new insights, to sketch for readers the true dimensions of the issue. The first quick look at an issue in the news seldom reveals its true meaning or likely impact on readers.

Box 3-2	A Professional's Viewpoint

There is a lot of spinning and a lot of lying in our times—in politics, government, sports and everywhere. It's got to the point where if you are like me, you no longer believe the first version of anything.

—Ben Bradlee, former editor of *The Washington Post,* quoted by M.L. Stein, "Finding the Truth Is Not Easy," *Editor & Publisher,* Feb. 15, 1997, p. 11.

Compare What's Happening With What's Expected

It's in the reporting of *departures from the expected norm* that you often will find issues demanding your comment.

For example, superficial research reveals students expect tuition increases. After all, the costs of most goods and services are rising.

In-depth reporting, however, reveals tuition increases at your college averaged 2.3 percent over the past five years, that tuition increases will average 2.2 percent next year at comparable colleges elsewhere in your state—and that your college's spending for new buildings will force up your readers' tuition by a whopping 6.6 percent next year.

Bingo! You've scored with in-depth reporting that compares what's happening with what's expected to happen.

That is, *you need to learn the pattern of things.* You need to learn how things have worked, how they should work—and how to compare all that with how things really are working. Many are the ways to determine how things should work:

- A comparison of your college's capital spending budget against actual expenditures will reveal variances.
- A call to your college's governing body (a board of directors or the state's board of regents) will reveal whether your college president has the authority to personally order the new construction.
- Comparing zoning regulations, on file at the city clerk's office, with zoning permits issued will reveal whether the new buildings are being constructed in appropriate neighborhoods (and, if not, you then dig deeper to determine whether a little political hanky-panky is under way).

In just such ways must your deep-dig reporting seek substantive matter. Compare reality with what's expected—and what's expected is reflected in law, ordinances, financial budgets, tables of organization. Opinion writers never should stop learning about how things work—and should work—in local, state and national government.

Ensure Your Reporting Characterizes Meaning

Did you notice above that I described that projected 6.6 percent tuition increase as "whopping"?

A 6.6 percent increase may not sound like much. But against the 2.3 percent average increase annually over the past five years, 6.6 percent is significant—thus "whopping" as an initial characterization to catch your attention.

Now, however, in-depth reporting comes into play as I characterize more fully that 6.6 percent by including, in my editorial, a little arithmetic for my readers:

Note that the 6.6 percent tuition increase required to finance these new and unneeded buildings will add $429 annually to Our College's $6,500 undergraduate tuition and $495 to the $7,500 paid by graduate students.

Those increases (enough for one month's apartment rent or a down payment on a used car) are three times what students will pay at comparable colleges elsewhere in the state.

Your reporting will characterize meaning if you reduce the incomprehensibly huge and complex to small bites of facts your readers can chew on and understand.

Reduce, for example, the many millions of dollars in your college's capital budget to the per-student equivalent of a month's rent or a down payment on a used car.

That controversial new building can be characterized as merely "big" or as "46,000 square feet." Neither characterization means anything to readers. But you can draw a meaningful comparison: "46,000 square feet, almost exactly the size of the Law Building on South Campus Drive."

Let's say you are commenting in your college paper on the football coach's new contract. You can characterize his pay by comparing it to the average salary paid other coaches in your college's conference or by comparing it to the average faculty salary.

Note in both examples above that you would need to use reporting techniques in finding comparisons.

Some Reporting Tools and Techniques

For every fact you seek, you'll encounter thousands.

For every fact you use, you'll discard hundreds.

This is a reality of in-depth reporting: Your problem is not having too few sources but, rather, too many; it's not that too little information is available but, rather, that too much is.

Your challenge is to fashion reporting tools and techniques that will help you cut through the nonessential to find the essential; help you winnow, sift and evaluate until you find what truly is operative for your readers.

First, what *not* to do:

1. Do not assume there are easy shortcuts in good reporting. There aren't any. Good reporting is hard work. It requires passionate curiosity, strong legs and a nose for news.

2. Do not confuse volume of information with quality or, especially, reliability. A few stabs at a computer keyboard and you're awash in information, some that is reliable and useful, a great deal that is not.

3. Do not let exciting delivery technologies—namely, the Internet—so dazzle you that you confuse surfing cyberspace with the value of old-fashioned, one-on-one, face-to-face interviews with authoritative sources. Don't let technical sources force people sources out of your reporting. (Note in Box 3-3 some old-fashioned reporting sources recommended by members of the National Conference of Editorial Writers.)

Box 3-3	Professional Viewpoints

Editorial writers throughout the country were asked by the National Conference of Editorial Writers to list indispensable reference tools they use in reporting and research. Some of their tools of the trade:

Congressional Quarterly
The Wall Street Journal
Editorial Research Reports
Encyclopedia Britannica
Almanac of American Policy
My Rolodex
My dictionary
My wife
Newspaper library
Nexis
The New York Times
Bartlett's Quotations
Richard Morris' *Encyclopedia of American History*
Roget's Thesaurus
The Washington Post
Webster's Dictionary
The morning mail
WordPerfect Thesaurus
World Almanac
Statistical Abstract
The Internet
Rystrom's *Why, Who and How* of the Editorial Page
MacDougal's *Editorial Writing*
The wire (Associated Press and others)
Telephone
The Encyclopedia of American History
State statutes
Congressional and federal staff directories

William Safire's *Safire's Political Dictionary*
Stylebook
Rodale's synonym finder
Webster's synonyms
Legislative guide
Oxford English Dictionary
The State budget
Aristotle's *Rhetoric*
Foreign Affairs
America Online
Columbia Encyclopedia
A good atlas
A college library
Local metro staff
Local interviews
The criminal code
Facts on File
Grolier Yearbooks
The Bible
My own clipping files
Campaign literature
Government budget papers
Magazines
Dictionaries
Infinet to search
My squirrel pile of possibly-useful—the someday stuff
The World Wide Web
The U.S. Constitution
City charter
John Bremner's *Words on Words*
Longest-serving reporter

SOURCE: "Tools of the Trade," *The Masthead,* Spring 1997, p. 39.

4. Do not build your reporting on reporting by others without challenging original sources. Those old front-page stories in your newspaper's morgue (library) may contain errors passed unwittingly from reporter to reporter, through what has been called the "media food chain." And, much Internet data, don't forget, comes straight from originator to you without any hint of the author's motives or, certainly, cross-checking by an intervening editor or dispassionate "gatekeeper." The Internet is a spinmeister's heaven that has launched much fiction as well as fact into mainstream media. But, of course, it also is a splendid source of much authoritative material, see Box 3-4.

| Box 3-4 | A Professional's Viewpoint |

Christopher Callahan, assistant dean of the University of Maryland's College of Journalism, is a recognized expert on using the Internet as a reporting tool.

Callahan—ccallahan@jmail.umd.edu—points out that the Internet gives you electronic mail capability to "talk" to sources worldwide, access huge amounts of data and open the pages (including editorial pages) of electronic newspapers everywhere.

Electronic mail is useful particularly for receiving press releases (eliminating delays inherent in mail or fax delivery). Also, you can reach many sources directly without playing telephone tag, even sources who are ducking you. ("I am writing an editorial on new construction on campus and I know you will want your views reported in this controversy.")

You can gain quick access to much data through listservs, which are electronic mail groups of people interested in the same subject. Group discussions can help you identify trends and ideas for your writing, Callahan says. He lists these as among the most useful:

Computer-Assisted Reporting & Research (CARR-L)
CARR-L@ulkyvm.louisville.edu
Investigative Reporters & Editors (IRE-L)
IRE-L@lists.missouri.edu
Freedom of Information (FOI-L)
L@listserv.syr.edu

New Information Technologies (NIT) (send to nit-request@chron.com and message: subscribe NIT your e-mail address)

Society of Professional Journalists (SPJ-L)
SPJ-L@psuvm.psu.edu
National Institute for Computer-Assisted Reporting (NICAR-L) NICAR-L@lists.missouri.edu
Cops and Courts FOI-Reporters (CRR-L) CRR-L@reporters.net
Online News (ON-LINE NEWS) (send majordomo@marketplace.com and message: Sub Online-News your e-mail address)

Just as you can search your own newspaper for valuable ideas and information, so can you gain instant access to major newspapers elsewhere:

Washington Post
http://www.washingtonpost.
  com

USA Today
http://www.usatoday.com

The Baltimore Sun
http://www.sunspot.net

Mercury Center Home Page
(San Jose, Calif. *Mercury News*)
http://www.sjmercury.com

The Gate
*(San Francisco Examiner and San
  Francisco Chronicle)*

http://www.sfgate.com

New York Times
http://www.nytimes.com

Boston Globe
http://www.boston.com

Nando.Net.
(Raleigh, N.C. *News and Observer*)
http://www.nando.net

Los Angeles Times
http://www.latimes.com

A truly astonishing amount of information is available via sites through World Wide Web:

Federal Government

Census Bureau
http://www.census.gov

Federal Election Commission
http://www.tray.com/fecinfo
http://www.soc.american.
  edu/campfin
http://www.fec.gov/finance

Federal Register
http://www.counterpoint.com

Congress
http://thomas.loc.gov
http://pathfinder.com/CQ

Government Printing Office
http://www.access.gpo.gov/su_docs

General Accounting Office
http://www.gao.gov

Inspector General
http://www.sba.gov/IG/index.html

White House
http://www.whitehouse.gov

Library of Congress
telnet: locis.loc.gov
http://lcweb.loc.gov

National Archives
http://www.nara.gov

Securities & Exchange Commission
http://www.sec.gov

Federal Budget
http://ibert.org
http://www.doc.gov

Federal Reserve
http://home.erols.com/scambos/
  ta24000.htm

Links to various federal agencies
http://www.law.vill.edu/fed-agency
http://www.lib.lsu.edu/local.html
http://www.webvertising.com

State Governments

Many state governments have their own Internet sites. Some, like California and Texas, have full-text access to all state legislation. http://www.globalcomputing.com/states.html

Vital Records
http://www.inlink.com/-nomi/vitalrec/staterec.html

Courts and Legal Documents

U.S. Supreme Court
http://www.law.
cornell.edu

Code of Federal Regulations
http://www.pls.com:8001/his/
cfr./html

U.S. Code (federal laws)
http://www.pls.com:8001/his/
usc.html

House Internet Law Library
http://www.pls.com:8001

U.S. Circuit Court of Appeals
http://www.law.emory.edu

And Don't Overlook These

Political Parties
http://www.democrats.org
http://www.gop.org

Freedom Forum
http://www.freedomforum.org

**Reporters Committee For
Freedom Journalism**
http://www.rcfp.org

**Center for Environmental
Journalism**

http://campuspress.colorado.
edu/cej.html

Associated Press Managing Editors
http://www.apme.com

Gallup (polling data)
http://www.gallup.com

Newspaper Association of America
http://www.infi.net/naa

Used with permission

Now, some things you *should* do in reporting for your opinion writing.

1. Look for facts *through your readers' eyes.* What's important to them? What's truly crucial to how they lead their lives today, tomorrow? Discard what isn't.

You'll eventually write opinion from your personal viewpoint—often a sharp one, at that—but be dispassionate and objective in searching for facts. Understand—and compensate for—your own prejudices. If you don't research with an open mind you'll surely arrive at illogical conclusions, and your readers will sense that.

2. Use *inductive reasoning* to examine objectively examples and arrive at a valid generalization. (Thus, examining examples of wild overspending by your college president lets you conclude and write, with validity, that not all is correct with how money is handled on campus.)

3. Use *deductive reasoning*, which involves moving from generalization to specific illustration (writing, for example, that not all is correct in campus financial affairs, then examining and explaining specific examples to prove that).

4. Whatever your approach, inductive or deductive, *let readers see the structure of your reporting and your reasoning* as you arrived at a conclusion. You add enormous strength to your writing—and to your persuasive powers—if the professionalism of your reporting and the logic of your reasoning are apparent.

Your biggest chore will be assessing many bits of information for their relative veracity and meaning. Retaining authoritative bits and *ruthlessly discarding* the questionable is one step in the process. Other steps:

- Early in the reporting process, ask yourself if the *writing angle* that's emerging is close to your original idea. If so, continue; if not, is new direction required? Must you rethink what you need to write—and where to find data on the new emerging idea?
- Is your reporting revealing merely "old news" (drugs are used on campus, and that's bad) or are you breaking new trails (drug use on campus is way up)? *Follow new, unexpected angles.*
- Is your reporting following avenues of crucial importance to readers or uncovering facts that, even if titillating or amusing, aren't operative in daily life? Barbara Mantz Drake, editorial page editor of the *Peoria* (Ill.) *Journal Star,* applies the "so what standard": It may be true but if it isn't important, "so what?"—why write about it?[6]
- Begin again the same cycle of asking, interviewing, reading, then sitting back for a moment to question your direction and the validity of your idea and avenue of investigation. Continue repeating the same cycle until you're ready to write.

Our Extra Burden in Reporting

Job Description

Liberal writer who unfairly uses
the power of the media to push a
personal left-leaning agenda on
the American people.

Boil down what many Americans say about journalists these days and you're left with roughly that job description.

REALITY #1

Our image is lousy. We are perceived by many Americans as being biased ideologues who report the news unfairly from a liberal perspective.

REALITY #2

Many readers fail to distinguish between objective *news* reporting and subjective *opinion* writing, or to believe both dimensions of journalism can co-exist fairly in the same pages. Many readers, for example, judge an entire newspaper or magazine—news, editorials, op-ed columns, commentaries and all—on, say, one institutional editorial they deem to be "liberal" or, much less frequently, "conservative."

| Box 3-5 | Professional Viewpoints |

Our reliance on polls is growing a lot more quickly than our sophistication about using them.

—Mark Mellman, Democratic pollster

∽

People look at a number and they say, "Aha, the mystery of politics has been quantified." The truth is, I think we have gone absolutely out of our minds about polls.

—Jeff Greenfield, ABC News

In a word, beware pegging editorials solely on polling data. That warning sounds throughout journalism, particularly come election time.

Depending on polling methodology, the motives of pollsters, the way they summarize their results ... depending on those variables—and many more—polls may or may not give you reliable substance for opinion writing.

At minimum, before relying heavily on any poll or survey, determine (and share with your readers) these facts on how the poll was conducted: Who sponsored the survey? How many people were sampled? When was the polling done? What methodology was used in selecting the sample and interviewing or otherwise questioning participants? What is the margin for error in the results?

Quotes are from James Bennet, "Polling Provoking Debate in News Media on Its Use," *The New York Times*, national edition, Oct. 4, 1996, p. A10.

REALITY #3

A majority of journalists indeed describe themselves as liberal in their thinking or leaning toward the Democrat Party in political attitudes. An American Society of Newspaper Editors survey found 36 percent describe their political orientation as Democrat/liberal; 25 percent as leaning to Democrat/liberal views; 24 percent as independent; 8 percent as Republican/conservative; 7 percent as leaning to Republican/conservative attitudes.[7]

REALITY #4

Many Americans, particularly in view of Reality #3, don't believe individual journalists can rise above personal beliefs and be objective in their reporting, or that newspapers or magazines can rise above their institutional endorsements of candidates or issues and present readers with fair, unbiased, balanced content.

In sum, as unfair—and, to our notion, unfounded—as public attitudes may be, journalists deal with *reader perceptions* as much as *journalistic realities,* as we see them. And, if your opinion *writing* is to be effective, your *reporting* must be demonstrably fair, well-rounded and credible.

I don't suggest pulling your punches in opinion writing. Don't subordinate your subjective personal opinions to objective reporting that turns every editorial, every column into, "On the one hand ... and on the other." Nor should newspapers or magazines pull back from forceful institutional positions that take a stand, that show choice and leadership on even the most controversial subjects.

I *do* suggest, however, that your reporting and writing for institutional editorials demonstrate balance and your willingness to look at, consider and *share with readers* the other sides of an argument (there are more than two sides to most, you know). *The Atlanta Constitution* will lose credibility quickly if it bangs away constantly on the theme of Coca-Cola millionaire vs. poor little secretary, without reporting for its readers there is another side—that some tax experts and economists say the economy as a whole, including secretaries, would benefit from killing the capital gains tax.

And, I certainly suggest that in personal opinion writing—in columns and byline commentary—you *demonstrate* fair reporting and balanced writing. That doesn't mean turning every column into news reporting, into a dreary recital of all sides of an issue. Rather, demonstrate over a period of weeks and months that you're open to arguments other than your own. Make your reporting and writing demonstrate, "Reader, dear reader, I've been out looking at all dimensions of this question for you, and here is my opinion, arrived at fairly and logically."

Report with balance and fairness; then take a stand and write with passion.

Summary

- Solid, in-depth reporting will add substance to your passion in writing opinion.
- Maria Henson, Pulitzer Prize winner for editorial writing, says readers demand "added value" —new information in editorials, not only opinion.
- In defining issues and writing opinion, consider the characteristics of news: impact on people, proximity to your readers, conflict, prominence of individuals in the news, and timeliness.
- To communicate effectively with readers, write about people (what they do; what is done to them), money (and its impact on people) and power (political, economic, military, psychological, and how it's used).
- You'll have just an hour or two to research most editorials and even less to write them.
- Readers will give you even less time, so ensure your writing contains factual substance; merely writing passionately won't catch and hold them.
- Reporting from authoritative sources helps build a bridge of confidence to your readers.
- Your reporting should identify the precise issue you'll write about and reveal its true importance.
- Compare what's happening against the expected norm and characterize for your readers its meaning. That requires learning the pattern of how things work.
- Internet and other electronic sources deliver mountains of information, but don't confuse quantity with quality; question and double-check information, whatever its source.
- Many Americans distrust the media, so your reporting must be demonstrably fair, well-rounded, credible.
- Report with balance and fairness; then take a stand and write with passion.

Recommended Reading

For insights into tools and techniques of in-depth reporting, see John Ullmann, *Investigative Reporting* (New York: St. Martin's Press, 1995); Lauren Kessler and Duncan McDonald, *The Search* (Belmont, Calif.: Wadsworth, Inc., 1992); Donald L. Shaw, Maxwell McCombs and Gerry Keir, *Advanced Reporting*, 2nd ed. (Prospect Heights, Ill.: Waveland Press, Inc., 1997); Carl Hausman, *The Decision-Making Process in Journalism* (Chicago: Nelson-Hall, Inc., Publishers, 1991.

I discuss reporting in Conrad Fink, *Introduction to Professional Newswriting*, 2nd ed. (New York: Addison Wesley Longman, 1998), and in *Introduction to Magazine Writing* (New York: Macmillan, 1994). I discuss the ethics and social responsibility of reporting in *Media Ethics* (Boston: Allyn and Bacon, 1995).

Notes

1. Mencken made this remark in a 1947 speech to an American Press Institute gathering of editorial writers, which was followed by organization of the National Conference of Editorial Writers. Full text is in, "Still Wise Advice: Get Out of the Office," *The Masthead*, Fall 1996, p. 36.

2. Material for this case study was developed in an interview with Henson on April 16, 1997, and drawn in part from her written account of the incident, "Writer Dug for Facts Just Like a Reporter," *The Masthead*, Fall 1992, p. 38.

3. I discuss the definition of news and its coverage in *Introduction to Professional Newswriting* 2nd ed. (New York: Addison Wesley Longman, 1998), and the ethics of reporting in *Media Ethics* (Boston: Allyn and Bacon, 1995).

4. Hynds' survey, conducted in 1994, drew a 50 percent response from a random survey of editorialists on daily newspapers of various circulation sizes and regions of the country. He reports results in, "Editorial Pages Become More Useful," *The Masthead*, Fall 1995, p. 38.

5. "Good Day to Review Taxes," *The Atlanta Constitution*, April 15, 1997, p. A16.

6. Barbara Mantz Drake, " 'So What' Says a Lot," *The Masthead*, Fall 1992, p. 5.

7. Everette E. Dennis, "Liberal Reporters, Yes; Liberal Slant No!," *The American Editor*, January/February 1997, p. 4.

Exercises

1. Recall the case study that opens this chapter: Maria Henson of the *Lexington* (Ky.) *Herald-Leader* editorialized on spouse abuse in Kentucky by focusing her reporting initially on one woman slain by an abusive husband.

Select an issue that's meaningful and topical to the student body of your college. Outline, in about 300 words, how you can use a single person as your writing "peg" to make this issue come alive for student readers. How will you locate such an individual? What information will you seek about that individual? How will he or she be the writing "vehicle" for your editorial message?

2. Select a new event being covered in your college paper (or another newspaper your instructor picks) and outline an editorial that would present readers with "added value" on that event.

How will *news* coverage be the starting point for your added value reporting? What significant new dimension will you seek to add to reader understanding of the event? In about 200 words, outline the direction your reporting and research will take.

3. Pick a continuing news story breaking on (or near) your campus and examine it as potential material for an editorial.

Using definitions outlined in Chapter Three, comment on the story's characteristics—impact, proximity, conflict, prominence, timeliness.

In about 250 words, define the news story's merits as the subject of an editorial.

4. Recall the discussion in Chapter Three of people, money and power as being three particularly fruitful avenues of investigation for editorial writers.

In about 300 words, outline an issue on (or near) your campus that combines *all three* and is worthy of editorial comment. Is there, for example, a powerful official who misuses the power of office or position in a way that affects money and people? Outline the paths your reporting would follow.

5. Interview five students (not in journalism) on their views of the media. Discuss, in about 250 words, whether they distinguish between the objectivity of news columns and the subjective writing on editorial and op-ed pages.

Do the students suspect media motives? Do they trust one newspaper, but not another? Is one medium regarded more highly than another?

Summarize how those students' attitudes affect your view of the role of editorial writers. How should writers deal with public attitudes toward the media?

PART TWO

Writing to Win Readers

I T ' S S I M P L E, really: You can do a brilliant job of defining and researching the compellingly important issues of our day *but your effort is wasted if nobody reads what you write.*

And nobody will read your writing if it's dull, wooden, cumbersome, dense.

So, let's turn in Part Two to editorial writing that's colorful and snappy, yet thoughtful and engaging—writing designed to win readers.

In the next two chapters, you'll learn how professional newspaper and magazine writers shape editorials. You'll see many examples of style, structure and content.

As we move ahead, it's important that you think deeply about your own writing style, where it's weak, where it's strong. And, as you do, consider which techniques and styles to accept from professional example and which to reject.

We'll look first, in Chapter Four, at writing newspaper editorials. The rhythm of daily publication and the expectations of daily readers put special pressures on newspaper writers.

In Chapter Five, we'll turn to writing magazine editorials.

The different publishing rhythms of magazines—weekly or monthly, not daily—create their own influences on writers.

Throughout the pages ahead, think of how you can apply lessons learned to getting started—now—as an editorial writer for your campus newspaper or magazine or another publication.

Think strong writing!

4 | Writing Newspaper Editorials

WHETHER WRITING editorials or news stories, you follow the same ethical standards discussed in Chapter One. Right or wrong in journalism are right or wrong, whether on Page One or the editorial page.

In newswriting and editorial writing alike, you respond to the same news values and judgments—the same reader needs and interests—discussed in Chapter Two.

Basic reporting techniques similar to those discussed in Chapter Three are used in researching news stories or editorials. Whether writing news or opinion, you hunt along the same trails for facts and authoritative sources.

So, when do we study fundamental differences separating newswriting and editorial writing? Now, in this chapter. Now we've reached the true point of departure between the two forms of journalism. *The difference is in the writing.* One is objective and dispassionate, the other subjective and at times very passionate.

Think of the differences this way:

In news you write a front-page piece on, say, the mayor's new policy on crime. Your balanced reporting and neutral language yield a straight, objective account of *what* the policy is.

In that news story—or in a separate news-page interpretative piece labeled "analysis"—you explain *why* the mayor formulated the policy.

In editorial writing, you express opinion on whether the mayor *should* implement the policy.

In a news story, you quote sources—he said, she said, they said that the mayor's policy is "scandalous," and that characterization, as always in newswriting, is surrounded by quotation marks. In editorial writing, *you* judge whether the policy is scandalous—and *you* say so, without quote marks.

In just those ways you now venture into the exciting arena of writing opinion, commentary and criticism.

The Basics of Strong Editorial Writing

In newswriting, you learn to lean back after writing a couple paragraphs and tick them off—who, where, what, when, why and how. If those basic elements are there, your news story is off to a good start.

In editorial writing, those five Ws and How also must be somewhere in your piece, but once they are, you ask yourself another question: "Does my writing SEA—Stimulate, Explain, Advocate?"

That is, does your editorial *stimulate* public dialogue on a compellingly important issue of the day? Does it stimulate readers to think in new, different ways? Will they talk—at work, around the dinner table—aided by new information they've read in your editorial?

Keep ticking 'em off. ...

Does your editorial *explain* issues in ways that add entirely new dimensions to your readers' thinking? Does your reporting provide information—added value—beyond what's in news stories on Page One?

And, does your editorial *advocate* a position? Is your reporting logical and persuasive, your writing engaging and convincing? Have you gone beyond "on the one hand, but on the other" and persuaded readers to move toward new ideas, new conclusions?

Of course, on occasions you'll ask not SEA of your writing, not whether it informs or persuades, but rather whether it amuses and entertains. For providing a lighter look at our world and how we live in it is part of editorial writing, too.

Many are the functions of the editorial page, diversified are its goals.

| Box 4-1 | A Professional's Viewpoint |

The editorial page is the heart and the soul of the newspaper. It is the place for passion and outrage, for humor and kindness, for wisdom and caring. It is the place for the pure idea, the intriguing thought, the graceful phrase. It is the place for hot debate and cool analysis. It is the place for truth; it is the place for fun.

—Michael Gartner, Pulitzer Prize-winning editor of the Ames, Iowa, *Daily Tribune*; columnist for *USA Today* and former president of NBC News, "How Sad That Editorials Need Defending," *The Masthead*, Fall 1996, p. 27.

And, despite its spirit of advocacy and opinion, good editorial writing need not take you far from the news of the day or the mission of a reporter. (See Box 4-2 for the views of a news reporter who switched to editorial writing and who says her news experience lends real strength to her opinion writing.)

Box 4-2	A Professional's Viewpoint

Susan Laccetti, editorial writer for *The Atlanta Journal,* describes her transition from news reporting to editorial writing—and how her training as a reporter strengthens her opinion writing.

BY SUSAN LACCETTI

Many reporters believe they are crusaders for the truth. They have the knowledge and power to get to the bottom of issues more than almost anyone in society.

So why would a reporter, especially one who loves investigative reporting, want to switch to editorial writing? I wondered myself after accepting a transfer to *The Atlanta Journal*'s editorial board.

I always perceived editorial writers as middle-aged white guys who smoke pipes and sit around in conference rooms and do "big thinking" about the day's events, foreign policy or long-term economic trends. My perception was that editorial writers had it easy. They just had to have lots of opinions. And they had to be able to turn out an opinion quickly, based on today's news for tomorrow's newspaper.

I found out quickly I was quite wrong.

Some editorial writers write off-the-cuff editorials—quick opinion pieces just to get the newspaper on the record about a particular verdict, proposal or congressional action. Usually those writers have been writing editorials for years, are uninspired and can quickly make judgments.

The best editorial writers, I believe, are ones who are reporters. Not former reporters but reporters. Writing editorials—good editorials—takes careful research and digging to make sure you have an argument that nobody will poke holes in, especially sassy readers who love pouring in letters to the editor.

As an editorial writer, I do many of the same things I did as a reporter. I go to meetings, sometimes to cover them for a breaking editorial. I go and interview public officials or those involved with public policy that the board likes or doesn't like. I attend sessions of the state Legislature. And I do some digging and investigative work, including searching documents to find evidence to support my opinion.

For example, I recently wrote editorials about the poor management of Grady Memorial Hospital, the public hospital in the city of Atlanta. I used correspondence between board members of the hospital and management to show how the hospital wasted money, including $750,000 to lease office space when the hospital had several empty floors. Those kinds of details or an occasional quote add life or meat to an editorial.

Surprisingly, I did not find it difficult to shift from reporting to editorial writing. Each morning, my five-member editorial board meets to hammer out its position on certain issues. If it is an issue I will write about, I have the guidance of the opinions of my colleagues, which generally is a consensus. When I am working on a long-term piece that takes a lot of research, I generally get guidance from the editor of the editorial page, Jim Wooten, on which direction to go. Like a reporter, I research the editorial but write it with advice or criticism, instead of objectively.

A rule of thumb on our board, however, is that Wooten does not make anyone write an editorial he or she doesn't agree with. That made the transition easier from being a veteran reporter to an editorial writer. For example, we recently wrote an editorial about home schools and a legislative proposal to require home school teachers (generally mothers) to have a college degree. I usually write education editorials. But because I loathe the entire home-school concept, I did not have to write the editorial. Another member of the board wrote it instead since a majority of the board favors home schooling.

Like a good story, the easiest editorials to write are those you feel strongly about. I recently wrote editorials supporting a referendum for a sales tax increase that would result in a millage reduction in a metro Atlanta county. Since I am a homeowner and taxpayer in that county, it was easy for me to take sides on the issue. And it was fun to go talk with commissioners about the plan because I had a true interest in the details of the millage reduction. In turn, my editor said my editorials did a better job of explaining—as well as advocating—the proposal than the news stories in the paper.

Sometimes, when it is a slow news week or no one is working on longer-term projects, the board struggles to get editorials to fill the page. Not much different than a slow news day in the newsroom. Those rare days are the least fulfilling. Usually, we then write editorials about less-meaty items in the news, such as a new traffic plan for around the new stadium or something similar to fill the page. Thankfully, those days are rare. And on those days, we can always rely on world or national news to give us pegs or subject matter to write quick editorials.

Stay Close to the News

Must you disengage from spot news in order to take the long view on issues of our time?

Is unhooking from the daily rhythm of newspaper publishing required for a writer who would be contemplative, reasoned, deep?

No—a resounding no—to both questions.

Indeed, it could be argued—I do so argue—that staying close to breaking news can add enormous strength to your editorial writing and add timeliness, topicality, pertinence to your newspaper.

That certainly is the judgment of major newspapers. Let's look at examples.

The Day Before: The Precede

The day before an important move in Congress, a *Los Angeles Times* editorial writer reasons through the likely outcome. The next morning, the editorial is published, carrying a "today" time element:

> The end of the protracted and bitterly partisan federal budget impasse is in sight. After months of a frustrating stalemate, White House and congressional negotiators have reached agreement on an omnibus spending bill that would fund the federal government through the end of the fiscal year, which ends Sept. 30, about a month before the presidential election. Now all that is needed is approval by the House, the Senate and the White House. Agreement is likely today, the players in the final compromise say ... [1]

The editorial then discusses Republican and Democratic positions on the impasse in several hundred words, concluding, "without further ado, this ugly budget battle should be put to rest."

Thus does the *Times,* a morning paper, publish a "precede" to equip its readers to understand an issue they'll hear about all day on radio and television, then read about in evening papers.

The Morning After: The Follow

The morning after a much-discussed news event, *The New York Times* is in print with comment on its deeper meaning:

> After all the hype and exploitation surrounding the actress Ellen DeGeneres and Ellen Morgan, the woman she plays on television, it was easy to lose sight of what actually was taking place on television last night. The "coming out" of the title character on "Ellen" was accomplished with wit and poignancy, which should help defuse the antagonism toward homosexuals still prevalent in society. The show was not simply a provocative sitcom episode that followed months of advance teasing. Rather, it marked the brave decision by a comic actress to go public with her identity as a homosexual, and to weave this highly personal coming-to-terms into the fabric of the fictional character she portrays. As a result, last night's performance was rich and memorable.

Several hundred words later, the *Times* writer comments that the television show promoted tolerance of homosexuality. The editorial concludes:

> Every few years, it seems, television tosses up an episode that provokes public discussion and debate. In this contentious era, when personal identity and sexual choices are so often intertwined with political or public posturing, it is no surprise that television would try to mine the subject for its value as entertainment. In the end, the fate of Ellen and "Ellen" will be decided not by the

Rev. Jerry Falwell or potentially skittish advertisers or by her own off-screen romances, but by the ratings that have always determined success or failure on television. If Ms. DeGeneres can sustain the quality of last night's show, she deserves to succeed.[2]

Note these points about the *Los Angeles Times'* "day-before" and the *New York Times'* "morning-after" editorials:

First, both news events were widely discussed for months before the writers sat down to their keyboards. That is, the writers had time to fully research the budget impasses and TV show before publishing conclusions.

Second, nevertheless, both editorials carry fresh time elements—pegged to "today" in the *Los Angeles Times* example, "last night" in the *New York Times* illustration. Both papers demonstrate they are on top of major news issues being widely discussed by their readers and both offer *timely* comment and opinion.

Third, both writers monitored their respective news events right up to the moment of writing, *as would spot news reporters.* Both writers acted as reporters with opinions.

Looking Backward: The Sum-Up

Some news events are too complex for quick, morning-after analysis. Writers do well to take time to talk to sources and think through possible ramifications.

Note the *Los Angeles Times* approach, on a Thursday, to an event *earlier in the week:*

> In refusing to hear another controversial abortion case, the U.S. Supreme Court this week signaled that a solid majority of the justices are unwilling to permit further restrictions on abortion and want to withdraw from the fray. In so doing, the court reflects the views of most Americans on this enduringly divisive issue. Republican leaders, take note. [3]

Supreme Court decisions are complex enough, without considering their implications for the Republican Party, subject of several hundred words of commentary following the opening paragraph reproduced above. In such cases take a few days to reflect on the meaning of it all! Then, sum up the action.

But, don't wait too long, as did the *Schenectady* (N.Y.) *Daily Gazette:*

> It came as a surprise to New York officials when the federal Department of Housing and Urban Development announced last month that it was going to make $120 million available for developing the state barge canal. While the officials should gratefully accept the money, they should also make sure that it's used as effectively as possible. The best way to do that is to dust off the

original master plan, which the Pataki administration shelved earlier this year.

That document was the result of four years of planning, including discussions with local officials, meetings with regional groups and public hearings.[4]

Note the example above refers to a "surprise" announcement the previous month. Two points:

First, so many news events break daily that the "crest" of most stories—the time most are in the public mind—passes very quickly. Waiting until next month to comment on a news break risks being so far behind the news crest that your comment is irrelevant.

Second, it's not that the *Daily Gazette* didn't have time to prepare for faster analysis and comment. The so-called master plan had been discussed openly *for four years.*

The Combo: Look Backward, Look Ahead

Effective editorials can be written by tying your commentary to a recent event that is widely discussed, then looking ahead with suggestions for improvement.

Here, a *Columbus* (Ga.) *Ledger-Enquirer* writer looks backward and establishes the tie-in:

> As staff writer Ken Edelstein reported this week, Georgians are producing more and more garbage per person, in spite of a statewide mandate to reduce the output. By law, the state is supposed to be reducing the amount of garbage we produce. But we're increasing it instead. That's the bad news.

Now, the *Ledger-Enquirer* editorial looks ahead:

> The good news is that in Columbus, we're reducing our input into the landfill, if not our output of garbage.

Finally, the *Ledger-Enquirer* discusses solutions:

> Our landfill is nearing capacity. Had we started the current programs years ago when that landfill was opened, we probably wouldn't be nearing that capacity. But we didn't, and there is no way to remedy that.
>
> What we can do is approach the new landfill as we now see we should have approached our old one—with careful scrutiny of what goes in, and with solid, effective garbage reduction programs in place.[5]

You may think abortion, homosexuality on television and costly barge canals are controversial, but you haven't touched controversy if you haven't written about garbage! It's a hot issue in local journalism across the country (perhaps because we all create garbage; most of us have a bad conscience as a result, and none of us has a solution to the mounting problem).

In editorial writing, you can't go wrong by digging deeply (figuratively speaking, in the case of garbage) into such hot local issues and proposing solutions.

But be prepared to take criticism, to take lots of heat.

| Box 4-3 | A Professional's Viewpoint |

The editorial page is where the sword of advocacy is sheathed. We brandish it daily, display it proudly on ceremonial occasions. We are far from the days of John Peter Zenger (1697-1746) when commentary was considered libelous, if not treasonous. But in all too many places in the world such advocacy means taking a very real risk. Like a canary in a mine shaft, commentaries remain the vulnerable first defense against the abuses of power and privilege.

—Fred Fiske, *Syracuse* (N.Y.) *Post-Standard,* "Look How Far We've Come," *The Masthead,* Fall 1996, p. 4.

Timeliness and Meeting the SEA Test

Writing with fresh time elements aids you enormously in passing the SEA test—that is, producing commentary that stimulates readers, explains issues, advocates solutions.

Why? Because if you are close to the news your readers likely have more than passing knowledge of the event and, thus, much greater interest in it.

That TV show on homosexuality discussed by *The New York Times* was watched by an estimated 42 million Americans and probably was talked about the next day—the day of the *Times* editorial—by many more millions. What a strong base of reader interest for the writer![6]

And, *everybody* has a personal position on abortion—another huge foundation of reader understanding.

In commenting on those subjects, writers could devote minimum wordage to backgrounding readers on the underlying issues involved. By contrast, get too far behind the "crest" of a news story and you must use precious space to bring readers up to date and explain fully the issues involved. That happened to the *Schenectady Daily Gazette* writer who commented on an announcement made the previous month and a planning process launched four years earlier.

Lesson: The closer you stay to breaking news, the better your chances of entering the marketplace of ideas and serving as what Burl Osborne, publisher of the *Dallas* (Tex.) *Morning News,* calls the "honest broker in the debate of public issues."

Box 4-4	A Professional's Viewpoint

Burl Osborne is publisher of the *Dallas* (Tex.) *Morning News* and president of the publishing division of A.H. Belo Corp., a large and diversified media company that includes the *Providence* (R.I.) *Journal-Bulletin,* the *Owensboro* (Ky.) *Messenger-Inquirer,* and *Bryan-College Station* (Tex.) *Eagle.*

In the following Q and A, Osborne shares his thinking on what editorial writing is all about:

Q. What's the basic mission of editorials?

A. The best opinion pages will provide a forum for the education, discussion and debate that citizens must have in order to fulfill their duties as members of a democratic society. It isn't enough to stand on the sidelines and carp. Just raising hell isn't enough. Just comforting the afflicted and afflicting the comfortable isn't enough. Clever satire isn't enough and "gotcha" isn't enough.

Q. If "raising hell" isn't enough, what more is needed?

A. To be effective, a newspaper must preserve its role as the honest broker in the debate of public issues. Raising hell about what is wrong and shouldn't be allowed is fine, so long as we spell out what is right and ought to be done about it. Even this, though, may not be enough. For example, if a state is contemplating difficult and complex decisions about, say, education, then the newspaper has an obligation to explain the issues in terms that its readers can understand—on the news pages, with differing views on the op-ed pages and finally the institution's own opinion on the best course to take.

Q. But it doesn't end there, with offering institutional opinion?

A. Editors must recognize that someone else may have a better idea. If there are clear-cut moral issues, the newspaper can and should go much further down the road to persuasion. If City Hall is discriminating against would-be employees on the basis of race, then raising hell, explaining, recommending, persuading and insisting are all appropriate courses.

Q. How do you feel about endorsing specific individuals who may have solutions to such issues?

A. One issue we debate from time to time is whether *The Dallas Morning News* ought to be endorsing political candidates. Does it cause readers to think our news coverage is biased? Does it do any good? Does anyone care? Thus far, we always have come down on the side of continuing to endorse, for reasons we believe to be controlling. First, in the case of down-ballot races, ours is likely to be the only non-partisan research done on the issues or candidates for that contest. Most people can decide without much help from us their choice for president or governor. When it comes to judges, or the state school board or the local city council, voters may feel themselves in need of background information they can trust. In these contests, if a newspaper can put itself above party or ideology, it can enhance its role as honest broker, and provide genuine service to readers.

Q. Do you really change voters' minds?

A. It is not uncommon in Dallas to see voters entering the polls in local elections with that day's editorial page summary of endorsements folded in their hand. Whether they use this to decide whom to support or whom to oppose is an open question, of course. Second, leaders of both major parties have told us that the newspaper's endorsement has significant impact on down-ballot races. The newspaper's research can be helpful, and I believe we ought to provide it.

Q. Do you, as *Morning News* publisher, participate in your editorial board's decision making?

A. I do participate in the process, both in advancing ideas and issues and in discussing those emerging from the group's own discussions. In the case of issues where the company has a direct involvement, we may establish the position from the top. As an example, we own 16 television stations, all of which will be investing heavily in high definition television technology. We have an institutional view about HDTV and related matters and that view is the newspaper's view—*always presented with full disclosure about our business interests* [emphasis added]. In the case of a very few endorsements, such as the presidential endorsement, I will discuss this with my two colleagues who are inside directors and members of the corporate management committee. We could overrule the editorial board, but we haven't.

Q. You're president of all Belo papers. Do you call the shots for them?

A. At all of the other newspapers, the publisher has the final say on endorsements, without consultation with me or others. Some of our newspapers endorsed Bill Clinton, some Bob Dole. In routine discussions about editorial recommendations, I don't vote in a literal sense, but we all understand that I have a very heavily weighted vote should it need to be cast. In practice, that almost never happens because we almost always work through issues until we find common ground.

Q. How do you describe all this to outsiders, especially Wall Street analysts. After all, Belo is a publicly owned company that must respond to shareholders.

A. We tell the world, including the analysts, that our business is run in the interest of journalistic excellence and community service. Internally, we believe we should always act with integrity and a sense of purpose, always seeking fairness, inclusiveness and excellence. With each other, we believe we must build common understandings of our goals, apply our values, practice respect and candor and work as a team. Individual (Belo) companies use these guides to formulate their own missions.

Q. Yes, but what do you tell Belo operating companies about shareholder demands for increased profits every quarter? How do those demands affect your view?

A. *The Dallas Morning News* wants to be, and most days is, a newspaper of distinction. This means that the quality of our people, journalism, service and business practices must be very high, that we must exercise leadership in the community and the industry, that we must take a long view and not get caught in quarter-to-quarter earnings madness and that we must earn sufficient profits to please our shareholders and compare favorably with our peers. Once this kind of philosophical underpinning is communicated to operating companies, a lot of the decisions become much less complicated.

Q. Finally, there are many print and electronic competitors out there—so many voices clamoring to be heard. Is editorial writing for newspapers less important because of that?

A. Newspaper opinion pages are among the most important ways that newspapers can be differentiated from competitors. Well-edited and respected pages are places where calm and reasoned debate can occur, where town hall meetings can be held every day with everyone included, and where real interaction with citizens and their leaders is easy to manage. The forums of television are necessarily contrived and managed; those of the Internet are anonymous. Ours can be powerful and rewarding if we invest the time and effort and money to make them so.

—Burl Osborne, letter to author, April 25, 1997.

Writing Forms and Structures

Early in our journalism careers, we all learn a basic news story structure: Jam the Five Ws and How into the first and second paragraphs, then feed readers information in manageable bites. What's most important is on top; everything else is tacked on in order of descending importance.

That's the inverted pyramid, of course. It's the plow horse of daily journalism—it plods steadily ahead and it gets the job done; it's strong and effective. But it's not very pretty.

We also have "plow horse" structure in editorial writing. Picture it this way:

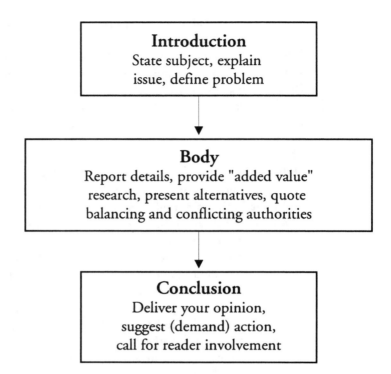

Figure 4.1.   Example of plow horse structure

You'll see lots of plow horse structures in daily journalism because (a) many writers think readers understand them easily, but (b) even more writers are too lazy to stretch for new, exciting ways of writing.

Though functional and easy to write quickly in deadline-crazy journalism, inverted pyramids and intro-body-conclusion editorials have one basic weakness: They are artificial and often dull structures that prevent you from telling a story the way stories should be told, around a campfire or across a kitchen table.

Neck of the Vase: A Writer's Salvation

Tell me a story.

We've all said it; we've all heard it. And, we all know storytelling is a marvelous way of communicating an underlying theme, of teaching a lesson. Think of the lasting lessons learned: perseverance from a little train that could; good-guy cowboys always fight evil; little girls shouldn't trust wolf-like grandmothers with sharp teeth.

So, we come to Tina Rosenberg, assigned by *The New York Times* to comment on new child welfare initiatives. Dullsville, right? Who wants to read once more about *that!*

Well, read on:

When New York's child welfare system took [Bob Brown] from a neglectful mother at age 7, he had no idea that what lay before him was going to be even worse. He and his four brothers and sisters were placed with a foster mother in Queens. [Brown], now 21, says she beat them repeatedly with belts and broomsticks. He sought help from police and child welfare officials but got none. They interviewed the children only when the foster mother was present, he said.

Want to know more? Of course you do, so I'll let Rosenberg continue:

[Brown's] experience is the kind of story that tends to come to light only when a child dies. This one surfaced because [Brown] wrote about it (complete with useful tips for child welfare officials) for Foster Care Youth United, a bimonthly magazine written mainly by teen-agers in the system. The city's Administration for Children's Services, which is going through yet another reorganization, could learn a lot by paying attention to foster care authorities like [Bob Brown].

Well, Rosenberg writes on, weaving around more such tragic incidents a tale with a wider message about child abuse in New York City. And, what a *readable story* it is. Visualize the neck-of-the-vase structure, the Rosenberg approach, this way:

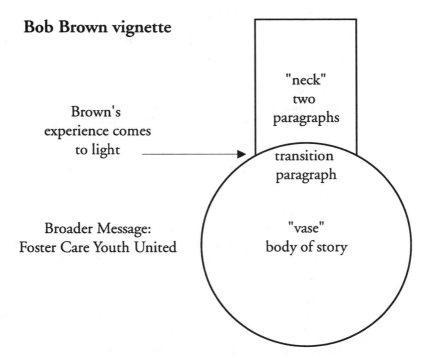

Figure 4.2.   Example of vase structure

How to write a successful neck-of-vase structure:

FIRST,

describe in your first paragraph or two, *a recognizable human being* readers can identify with—a 7 year old beaten by his mother with belts and broomsticks! That will capture readers as no dull recital of Welfare Department statistics ever could.

SECOND,

but don't let that opening vignette run too long. The Rosenberg piece is *not* about Bob Brown; rather, it's about child abuse. So, quickly get to the transition paragraph and widen your editorial to its broader meaning.

THIRD,

don't drop the personalized human element after the opening vignette. The Rosenberg commentary (which we don't have room to reproduce in full) is strengthened throughout by additional quick-shot vignettes—a girl who lived in 15 foster homes in 15 months, AIDS, alcoholism, drug-addicted parents. But Rosenberg doesn't overdo it, doesn't merely bottom-fish for dramatic impact. She writes:

> The stories are dispatches from hell, but their tone is not despair but triumph at having survived.[7]

The Personalized "You" Structure

One of the toughest challenges in editorial writing is *reducing the huge and complex to manageable simplicity*— translating, say, the national debate over the minimum wage into terms readers can grasp.

Billions of dollars and millions of families are affected by the debate, and who among us can sort out its complexities?

Well, an editorial writer for *USA Today* helped tremendously with a personalized "you" structure:

> How would you like to try to raise a family on $8,840 a year?
>
> That's what the federal minimum wage earns you for 52 40-hour weeks cleaning offices, serving food or caring for children—$1,135 less than a poverty-level income for a single parent and child.
>
> Outrage over that basic unfairness finally is bringing widespread change. Not in Washington, where Congress has left the minimum wage stuck at $4.25 an hour since 1991, but in communities and states tired of federal inaction.[8]

The "you" structure above has two strengths: First, addressing you, the reader, personalizes a vague, distant issue. *It invites you in for a chat.* Second, billions of dollars, a sum beyond comprehension, are reduced to $8,840, a figure each reader can grasp easily—and you almost can hear the readers' response: No! I wouldn't like to try raising a family on $8,840 a year.

However, your use of the "you" approach must be precise. You'll lose readers in a rush if they cannot readily identify with your "you."

For example, don't address an editorial to a "you" group so small it automatically eliminates the overwhelming majority of your readers:

How would you like to try feeding a herd of steers on $2.98 each a day?

That may be a legitimate "you" approach for the very few cattlemen in your reading audience. But most of your readers, who eat 'em rather than feed 'em, will go flying right on by your editorial. Make certain the "you" encompasses sufficient numbers of your readers.

Incidentally, note in the third graf of the *USA Today* editorial above the reference to outrage in communities and states tired of federal inaction. To back up that principal point, the writer follows with three examples set off by dashes ("dash matter," in industry parlance):

—Eleven states already mandate higher minimum wages than Washington. ...
—At least four municipalities also have acted on their own. ...
—Where lawmakers aren't acting, citizens are. ...

Two points about the *USA Today* example:
1. When you make a promise to your readers, ***deliver on that promise.*** *USA Today*'s third graf implicitly promises elaboration on that outrage angle. "Eleven states" ... "four municipalities" ... delivers on the promise.
2. For quick reading comprehension, nothing beats straight-forward listing of points—1, 2, 3—in dash matter. *USA Today* doesn't deliver poetry behind those dashes; it does deliver quick understanding.

In sum, the *USA Today* editorial above works nicely because it opens with a personalized "you," then translates billions of dollars into an understandable amount ($8,840) and, finally, backs up its opening thesis—there's "outrage" out there—with supporting facts in dash matter.

Now, *you* judge whether this "you" structure works:

Just when you thought sweeping health reform was dead, the biggest federal health benefit mandate ever is barreling out of the U.S. Senate.

That example above, also from *USA Today*, misses the mark, in my opinion.[9] Why? Because it assumes I—and all other *USA Today* readers—tumbled out of bed the morning it appeared, thinking that sweeping health reform was dead. Not only was I not thinking about whether it was dead, I wasn't thinking about health reform at all.

The Imagine-With-Me Structure

A close kin to the personalized "you" structure is a writing approach that draws a "picture" and invites readers to look at it.

Sometimes, the invitation is implied—the picture is drawn, and the writer assumes readers will look at it. Sometimes, the invitation is explicit:

> Imagine having a job that begins at 4:30 a.m. and ends at dark. Imagine working every holiday and weekend unless you could find someone competent enough to take your place. Imagine your business hinging on the weather, the cost of supplies and fickle marketplace for your goods.
>
> But this is not a bad job. Not at all. You'll witness thousands of sunrises and sunsets. You will know the pure joy of a bountiful harvest. You will witness and participate in life like no other man or woman.
>
> You will be a dairy farmer. And you will be proud of it.
>
> But things are changing rapidly for today's dairies, and we are to blame. Our governments are taxing their land to death. Our corporations are paying comparably nothing for the products farmers produce.
>
> We have taken the bounty for granted too long.[10]

The editorial above, published in the *Hornell* (N.Y.) *Evening Tribune*, illustrates noteworthy points:

FIRST,

the scenario readers are asked to imagine *is* memorable, though quickly sketched.

SECOND,

the editorial is not a fact-filled cry for specific action; rather, it's merely a cheer from the sidelines—simply a nice thing to say on a spring day in upstate New York to all the many dairy farmers who live around Hornell. There often is need to brandish a newspaper's institutional strength, to hack and stab with its sword of advocacy, the editorial. There also is need on occasion for a gentle word of encouragement, a little applause for your neighbors.

THIRD,

the editorial is short—and that alone draws attention in this era of so many overwritten, long, turgid exhortations bombarding readers from all directions. See Box 4-5 for one editorial writer's view on brevity.

| Box 4-5 | A Professional's Viewpoint |

Brevity is good. It is good if you are in a hurry. It is good if you do not have much to say. It is good if you are not being paid to write by the word. And the short editorial has one other attribute: It is usually read.

—Mark L. Genrich, deputy editor of *The Phoenix* (Ariz.) *Gazette*'s editorial pages, "Brevity is the Soul," *The Masthead*, Spring 1991, p. 22.

The Question Structure

Newspapers are in the business of *answering* questions, of course, but sometimes you can grab reader attention by *asking* one:

> Can the American people trust Attorney General Janet Reno to conduct a thorough probe of potentially illegal acts by her bosses in the White House?

Yes, of course, the question structure is another device for establishing a one-to-one relationship between writer and reader. The structure has these characteristics:

- It's *conversational;* it draws readers into a chat and doesn't bombard them immediately with your facts, your opinions, your answers.
- If you ask the right question you can achieve *immediate reader recognition.* When the editorial above was published in the *Roswell* (N.M.) *Daily Record,* the question about Reno was discussed widely in political and journalistic circles. Don't open with questions that have little—or-no-chance of engaging your readers. (Don't ask ranchers outside Roswell, "Can New Yorkers continue to pay such high apartment rents?")
- If you open your editorial with a question, you must answer the question or say you don't have the answer.

The *Roswell Daily Record* doesn't answer its own question outright, but it signals its opinion in this concluding graf:

> But the attorney general is curiously—and adamantly—opposed to seeking a special prosecutor to probe the campaign fund-raising scandal that has engulfed President Clinton, Vice President Al Gore and others in the White House. Her recent refusal once again to turn the investigation over to an outside counsel defies a mountain of evidence that laws were broken in the administration's lust for cash to finance the president's re-election bid.[11]

Note below how *The Washington Post* opens an editorial with three questions:

> What will happen if, at 12:01 a.m. on Jan. 1, 2000, computer chips and programs in everything from pace-makers to air-traffic computers begin to assume that it is Jan. 1, 1900, and calculate accordingly? Will there simply be massive confusion and inconvenience, followed perhaps by lawsuits, as citizens chase after their mysteriously canceled pension checks, and, for the hundredth time, reprogram their VCR clocks? Or will the stock market, the national defense and other unforeseen sectors screech to a halt? Nobody knows for sure.

Yes, of course, you guessed it: the writer didn't intend those questions literally; indeed, the writer didn't intend to answer them, let alone expect readers to do so. The question structure was simply a device to spark reader interest and state the proposition that would be examined later in the editorial.

For several hundred words, the editorial explores difficulties and costs sure to arise as computers are reprogrammed for the millennium, then concludes with a wry "kicker":

> The existing world stock of computers may be too dumb to navigate the millennium, but some fraction of their hard-headed human overseers are sure to figure out a way to do just fine.[12]

The We're-All-In-It-Together Structure

This structure gives you the same conversational intimacy gained in "you" structures or question intros.

However, in the "we're-all-in-it-together" structure you don't write to "you," the reader. Rather, you write about "us"—writer and reader, side by side, confronting what's out there in that crazy world of *ours.*

Note how easy it is to read the following, then say, "Ya, I agree ..." and find yourself willing to read more:

> Here we go again. Another cliffhanger of a trade dispute with China . . .
>
> *San Francisco Chronicle*[13]

> A few days ago we got a taste of the duplicity in Republican House Speaker Newt Gingrich's promises about campaign finance reform, which he and President Bill Clinton made a public vow to undertake. This week we learn that Clinton, who once pledged to end the use of so-called "soft money" in federal elections, is actually up to his Democratic ears in contributions from individuals and special interests groups with vital legislation pending.
>
> *Columbus* (Ga.) *Ledger-Enquirer*[14]

Note below how the *Dallas Morning News* opens with the "we" angle, then gets really chummy:

> 2030.
>
> We've all been mesmerized by now to believe that Social Security will be solvent until then.
>
> Listen to Shirley Chater, President Clinton's commissioner of Social Security: "Our Social Security system is soundly financed through 2030."
>
> Ha! If you're willing to swallow that sweet morsel of assurance, we've got some oceanfront land in Amarillo we'd like to sell you.[15]

You can be very effective by carrying the "us-against-them" tone throughout. For example, the Portland *Sunday Oregonian,* in a lengthy editorial on school funding, concludes this way:

> Our lack of a sales tax has always generated sort of a cockeyed pride among some Oregonians. It's up there with clean air and Tom McCall's legacy and rainy summers as something that distinguishes Oregon from the rest of the herd.
>
> It's time we looked, though, at whether we should be more proud of that than of our children and their schools.[16]

The Shock Approach

Sadly, much of what we write for newspapers is truly shocking news. When *you* do, these are your alternatives:

FIRST,
clean it up; sanitize the news, avoid any shocking language or word pictures—and leave the office confident you've not disturbed anyone (or, for that matter, stirred them to provocative thought, let alone action).

SECOND,
you can write 250 or so words of gory details and "milk" the shock value of bad news and thus ensure you're read.

THIRD,
you can use—selectively and with taste—the shock value of the news to pull readers into deeper, more meaningful thinking about an important issue.

Here's how *The Boston Globe* opened a thoughtful examination of child abuse:

> Every four days in Massachusetts, a child dies from abuse or neglect.[17]

The *Chicago Tribune* shocks—and catches—readers in commenting on U.S. Immigration and Naturalization Service guidelines for recognizing the persecution of women as grounds for granting asylum in this country:

> Fauziya Kasinga has been in jail for more than a year. She has been handcuffed, shackled, strip-searched and isolated.
>
> Her crime? At the age of 17, Kasinga sought asylum in the United States to avoid forced marriage and genital mutilation in her African homeland of Togo.
>
> But instead of asylum, she found an immigration system that treats certain foreigners seeking protection the same way it treats convicted criminals.[18]

The *Philadelphia Inquirer* doesn't pull any punches on this one:

> Philadelphia cops lied.

The Police Advisory Commission, established three years ago to investigate charges of police misconduct, came to that conclusion.[19]

Maintain Your Writing Momentum

It's not enough to structure a catchy or shock intro, then simply tack on fact and opinion and let your writing stumble toward a conclusion.

You must maintain writing momentum, leading readers gently through your editorial step by step. *Otherwise you'll lose your readers and, thus, any chance of communicating your message.*

Your best way of pulling readers along is to present them with reasonable, logical progression of your thinking. That, in turn, ties back to the validity of your underlying reporting and research.

Fancy writing won't paper over fundamental weakness in your reporting or reasoning. Readers are much too sophisticated these days to let you substitute a cute phrase for factual substance or clever writing for illogical reasoning.

However, clever writing *can* help you maintain that essential reading momentum. Let us look at examples. (We're all in this together, you know!)

Added Value

Transfusion of new, important information deep in an editorial can insert "added value" and pull readers ahead.

A *Los Angeles Times* writer, several hundred words into an editorial on domestic violence, inserts intriguing new information:

> Now, a new report says that more and more *women* are being arrested for domestic violence here in Los Angeles and around the country. The report ... [20]

The example above started out as a standard guy-beats-gal piece, then took that fascinating turn and pulled along readers (including me) who always thought of women as victims of domestic abuse, not abusers.

The Dramatic Quote

A *Boston Globe* editorial on gang violence starts this way:

> Youth gang violence in Boston strangles freedom. Residents are driven indoors. Commercial enterprises die or are never born. Active gang members fear for their lives when they venture a few blocks outside their territory. The old survive the young. Neighborhoods fade out and nothing comes in.

Now, the editorial explains to readers a Teen Empowerment program designed to help gang members find alternative lifestyles. Then, "housekeeping" details: A meeting will be held, 800 young people will attend, speeches will be given.

This editorial is beginning to slow down. So, the writer "juices" it with this paragraph:

> "My past still calls to me," said [John Jones] a 16-year-old former gang member who lives in the Bowdoin Street section of Dorchester, the site of several shootings in recent weeks. But intellectually, [Jones] has moved beyond the few streets that he was once so eager to "lock down." Now he studies and works as a Teen Empowerment coordinator at Madison Park High School. "There's hope," he said. "There are a lot of people who want to turn around."[21]

That paragraph above, with its dramatic quotes, renewed my interest and I was ready—willing—to read several hundred words that followed on the Teen Empowerment program.

The Jolting Paragraph

The *Chattanooga Times* publishes a lengthy editorial on educational level in the South. It opens this way:

> For decades after the Civil War, Jim Crow segregation—that overt manifestation of racism—combined with low-wage jobs, poor schools and exploitation of the region's bountiful natural resources to keep the South from reaching its full potential. Racial attitudes have improved since the 1960s, but racism is still evident, like a lingering virus.
>
> The South's robust economy, moreover, remains vulnerable to states' inability to provide the best education possible to their citizens. And to ensure they take advantage of it.

Now, in hundreds of words, the writer methodically presents facts and figures to support the *Times*' point that "education pays off." Frankly, it's heavy going—until the writer (wisely) inserts this "jolting paragraph":

> You don't need to be hit in the head with a two-by-four to get the message: Those shopping for a better life had better equip themselves with a good college or technical school education.[22]

In the example above, that jolting paragraph, with its slangy but sharp logic, somehow clarifies the point of the editorial. It focuses reader attention on the essential message: Education can lead to a better South, a better life for Southerners.

The Cute Phrase

The occasional cute phrase, the subtle play on words, little wisps of irony—

all can strengthen your writing and give readers that boost necessary to get them through editorials on even the most esoteric, difficult subjects.

For example, the *Columbus* (Ohio) *Dispatch* was just about to lose me after this opening paragraph:

> Ohio has 70 mega-livestock and poultry farms permitted to operate in various parts of the state, but only one consistently has earned a reputation for environmental and regulatory violations.

Then, a wonderful play on words opens the second graf:

> That bad egg is [Acme Inc.], the operator of a 2.5 million-hen egg farm at [Cripple Creek, Ohio].[23]

Enormously amused, I plowed dutifully forward until the writer made the concluding argument: A "substantive turnaround is long overdue" in how that company operates its affairs.

On that same *Columbus Dispatch* editorial page, I encountered this anecdotal opener:

> Most people will remember the woman who was awarded $2.9 million because the McDonald's coffee she spilled on herself was too hot. The award later was reduced to $640,000, which is not exactly chump change either.[24]

Did you like "not exactly chump change" in the example above? That slangy irreverence signals, "Hey, reader! This is an amusing little piece, so settle back and enjoy."

For several hundred uproariously funny words, the *Dispatch* writer describes ridiculous lawsuits filed for millions of dollars, (including one vignette about a guy who sued for $500,000 when he bit into a candy thinking it had a peanut inside ... only it didn't ... it had just chocolate ... and he "injured" his lip as a result).

See the point? The writing and the anecdotes *force* you to be interested and, importantly, to stick with the writer for the serious message: Let's stop these ludicrous lawsuits that are clogging our courts.

The Early Warning

You'll not be able to rely on mere clever writing to pull readers into some subjects that are important but difficult to understand.

Indeed, clever writing—the cute phrase, the wry hint—simply isn't appropriate for editorials on some subjects.

Such is the case with a *New York Times* editorial on U.S. policy toward the North Atlantic Treaty Organization. The editorial starts this way:

> The Clinton Administration is barreling toward an eastward expansion of NATO by the end of the decade without adequate discussion with the American people and Congress.

Now, even for the highly educated audience of *The New York Times*, this stuff is heavy going and, quite frankly, for time-starved readers, anxious to get to the rest of the *Times* and then to get on with their daily lives, this may be one editorial that can be skipped. But the *Times* writer, in the very next sentence, inserts this "early warning" (emphasis added):

> Though the issue seems remote and abstract to many citizens, and tends to come larded with the highfalutin terminology of the foreign-policy priest-hood, *it is exceedingly important*. NATO expansion would involve a crucial political and military realignment of Europe, the continent still most directly linked to the national security of the United States. The consequences are likely to be great and unpredictable.

There now follow 1,000 or so words of commentary on NATO and questions Americans should consider about its future.

The *Times* concludes:

> Tinkering with the balance of power on a continent that has been the site of so much conflict and violence should be done with great caution and a strong sense of humility.[25]

Lesson: In much newspaper writing, particularly in features, you have sufficient newshole to write indirectly, to entice readers, to hint and suggest—not to tell them but, rather, to let them discover. In editorial writing, you seldom can use the wordage that takes. Instead, you often must go directly to the point—reader, dear reader, this is important, so pay attention! That's the "early warning" intro—a writer saying, early in an editorial, "Take my word for it; you should read this."

Leave 'em Laughing

We all want—*need*—a little humor in our lives, and when your subject matter is appropriate, sprinkling your writing with a few chuckles or belly laughs can be extremely effective in drawing readers through an editorial.

Humor can be communicated in a few words or a stand-alone editorial. Here is how the *San Francisco Chronicle* put a smile on my lips with two words (emphasis added):

> The announcement by CBS that it will provide free TV time for presidential candidates in the final days of the campaign is welcome news, and may *even goose* the other two major commercial networks, ABC and NBC, to do the same.[26]

And here, the *Chronicle* really made me chuckle:

> Heart patients everywhere rejoiced at the good news yesterday that although there is a tiny chance of sexual activity causing a heart attack, it is well worth the risk.

After that opener, the *Chronicle* reports "straight-faced" that researchers determined that for heart patients having sex only narrowly increases odds of having another attack. The *Chronicle* concludes:

> Most of the 11 million Americans with heart disease can relax and enjoy sex if they want, according to the researchers, who found less enjoyable activities were far more dangerous for the heart. Sex is about as risky per episode as getting angry or waking up in the morning, while heavy exertion can be three times riskier than any of those activities.
>
> The message is: Have sex all you want, but don't get up in the morning, don't get mad and, certainly, don't exert yourself.[27]

Now, I don't know about you, but next time I pick up the *Chronicle* I'll be looking for that editorial writer with a sense of humor.

Summary

- Editorial writers and newswriters follow the same ethical standards, make the same judgments on what is news and use the same reporting techniques. But they differ dramatically in their writing.
- Newswriters, for example, report *what* the mayor's policy is and *why* it was formulated; editorial writers express opinion on whether the policy *should* be implemented.
- In addition to informing readers of the Five Ws and How, editorial writers must ask if their work passes the SEA test—does it Stimulate, Explain, Advocate?
- Staying close to the news lends strength to your editorial writing and adds timeliness, topicality and pertinence to your newspaper.
- Writing "precede" editorials acquaints your readers with details of an event before it is expected to occur—a hearing in Congress, say.
- A "follow" can be written for the day after an event, while it's still fresh in readers' minds.
- A "sum-up" editorial can look backward a week or more at a breaking story and summarize its importance for readers.
- Burl Osborne, publisher of the *Dallas* (Tex.) *Morning News,* says editorials help newspapers serve as "the honest broker in the debate of public issues."
- A basic structure for editorials is introduction (state subject), body (report details, alternatives) and conclusion (your opinion).
- The "neck-of-the-vase" structure is perfect for using a single individual or anecdote to lure readers into complex subject matter.
- The "you" structure permits personalized writing directed at "you," the reader.
- The "imagine-with-me" structure opens with a word "picture" the reader can "see," an effective means of communicating.

- Other effective writing structures include opening with a question directed at readers or shocking them with graphic detail.
- To maintain momentum in your writing, add new information along the way, insert dramatic quotes or a paragraph that jolts readers.
- Sometimes, you must put aside attempts to be cute or engaging in your writing and, instead, structure an "early warning" editorial that signals readers your material is important and should be read.
- When your subject matter is appropriate, leave 'em laughing. We all need a little humor in our lives, and editorial pages can be graced effectively with it.

Recommended Reading

Learning to write effective newspaper editorials is a two-step process: Read what the professionals write, then write, write, write until your fingers go numb.

To see what outstanding professionals write, see editorial pages of *The Wall Street Journal, The New York Times, Atlanta Constitution* and *Journal, Dallas Morning News, Chicago Tribune, Los Angeles Times,* among others.

For editorials with a light touch, watch the *San Francisco Chronicle, The New York Daily News.*

I discuss language usage and newswriting styles in *Introduction to Professional Newswriting* (New York: Addison Wesley Longman, 1998).

Notes

1. "Federal Spending Bill: Better Late Than Never," *The Los Angeles Times,* April 25, 1996, p. B-8.

2. "Ellen and 'Ellen' Come Out," *The New York Times,* national edition, May 1, 1997, p. A-20.

3. "The Court's Turn from Abortion," *The Los Angeles Times,* May 2, 1996, p. B-8.

4. "Use Canal Money Wisely," *The Daily Gazette,* Dec. 11, 1996, p. B-8.

5. "Georgians Produce Too Much Garbage," *The Ledger-Enquirer,* April 26, 1996, p. A-12.

6. Knight Ridder News Service dispatch for Sunday newspapers, May 4, 1997.

7. "The Real Foster Care Experts," *The New York Times,* Jan. 2, 1997, p. A-18.

8. "States Can Take Wage Lead While Washington Waffles," *USA Today,* April 17, 1996, p. 12-A.

9. "Out of Nowhere, a Major Health Reform Reappears," *USA Today,* April 23, 1996, p. 10-A.

10. This editorial in the *Hornell Evening Tribune* was reprinted as a guest editorial in the *Athens* (Ga.) *Banner-Herald and Daily News,* May 3, 1997, p. A-12.

11. This editorial in the *Roswell Daily Record* was reprinted as a guest editorial

in the *Athens* (Ga.) *Banner-Herald and Daily News,* May 3, 1997, p. A-12.

12. "Millennial Glitch," *The Washington Post,* March 27, 1997, p. A-26.

13. "China Trade Threat Reflects Policy Vacuum," *The San Francisco Chronicle,* May 10, 1996, p. A-26.

14. "Clinton Welshes on Campaign Reform," *The Ledger-Enquirer,* April 19, 1996, p. A-12.

15. "Social Security," *The Morning News,* May 5, 1996, p. J-2.

16. "The Next Step for Schools," *The Sunday Oregonian,* March 31, 1996, p. C-2.

17. "A Healthy Start for Newborns," *The Boston Globe,* April 23, 1996, p. 14.

18. "Practicing the Spirit of Asylum Law," *The Chicago Tribune,* April 10, 1996, p. 12.

19. "Trust in the Badge," *The Philadelphia Inquirer,* May 1, 1996, p. A-18.

20. "Domestic Violence: Let's Not Back Away from Reform," *The Los Angeles Times,* April, 30, 1996, p. B-8.

21. "Urban Peace Talks," *The Boston Globe,* May 4, 1996, p. 14.

22. "Educating the New South," *The Chattanooga Times,* April 20, 1996, p. A-4.

23. "Laying Blame," *The Columbus Dispatch,* Nov. 27, 1996, p. A-10.

24. "M&M Money," *The Columbus Dispatch,* op cit.

25. "Tinkering with Europe," *The New York Times,* Dec. 12, 1996, p. A-36.

26. "Free TV for Top Candidates," *The San Francisco Chronicle,* May 8, 1996, p. A-20.

27. "Heartening News on Sex," *The San Francisco Chronicle,* May 9, 1996, p. A-24.

Exercises

1. Examine today's lead editorial in your campus newspaper (or another newspaper your instructor designates) and put it to the SEA test.

Does the editorial stimulate, explain and advocate? If not, how would *you* write it so the SEA test would be passed successfully?

Write your answer in about 300 words.

2. Examine today's lead editorial in *The New York Times* (or another designated by your instructor) and, in about 300 words, analyze whether its writer stayed close to the news.

Did the editorial add timeliness, topicality and pertinence to the newspaper? If not, why not?

3. Based on front-page play in your campus newspaper today (or another newspaper your instructor designates) what type of "precede" editorial could you write on a matter of general, campus-wide interest?

What would be your central thrust? What "added value" reporting would you do?

Write your answer in 250 or so words.

4. Pick a subject from the news columns this week in your campus newspaper (or another your instructor designates) and write a neck-of-the-vase editorial.

Use an anecdotal intro, of course, then broaden your editorial with a clear-cut transition paragraph. Ensure your opening vignette is sufficiently drawn to spark reader interest but do not let the "neck" take over the editorial.

Do this in 400 words.

5. Read the editorials for one week in a newspaper selected by your instructor and discuss, in about 500-600 words, whether the publishing newspaper is serving as "the honest broker in the debate of public issues."

Do the editorials meet the standards set forth in the Burl Osborne question-and-answer in Box 4-4 in Chapter Four?

5 | Writing Magazine Editorials

ARE YOU wondering why Chapter Five turns to writing editorials for magazines as distinct from newspapers? After all, in many ways, magazine editorial writing resembles newspaper editorial writing. However, three factors require separate study of magazine writing:

First, *audience.* Magazine readers as a group are upscale in education and income. Meeting their needs requires special reporting and writing skills.

Second, *tailoring of content.* Many successful magazines focus content tightly to cover narrow information niches and serve readers who have a common interest. You need in-depth understanding of a magazine's niche subject to write about it with the required expertise.

Third, *frequency of publication.* Writing opinion on a weekly or monthly basis demands a rhythm quite different from daily writing.

Nobody knows exactly how many magazines are published in the United States. Hundreds of new titles are launched annually; hundreds fade away for lack of reader interest or advertiser support. But at least 11,000 magazines are out there, and we obviously must narrow our study. We'll concentrate on four types most important:

- *Newsmagazines,* such as *Time, Newsweek, Business Week* and *Forbes.* Most are published weekly, some monthly.
- *Thought leaders,* so-called for their serious treatment of the compellingly important social, economic and political issues of our day. *The Economist* and *New Republic* are two.
- *Consumer magazines,* a huge group of titles as varied as *The New Yorker, George* and *Cosmopolitan.*
- *Trade or special business magazines,* which are tailored narrowly for special interest groups—readers with common interest in a cer-

tain subject. Examples are *Editor & Publisher,* a newspaper industry weekly, and *Folio,* published monthly for the magazine industry.

First: Know Your Audience

As in writing for any medium, when writing for a magazine you first must consider the needs and desires of your audience.

What you want to say is important, of course, but it's service to your readers that must guide your selection of issues for comment, the reporting that supports your opinions, the timing of your writing, and the language and structure of your editorial.

Fortunately, we have excellent research on who reads magazines. Magazine Publishers of America, the leading consumer magazine industry group, provides this profile of the "average adult reader" of the "average magazine copy":

Median age	40.2 years (U.S. median, 41.2).
Education	35.7 percent high school graduates, 46.6 percent attended and/or graduated college.
Lifestyle	59.4 percent are married; 58.1 percent are heads of households; 67.5 percent own their homes, with median value of $92,878; 79.1 percent live in metropolitan areas.
Employment	55.7 percent are employed full-time; median household income is $37,161.[1]

We also have a pretty good fix on when, where and for how long magazines are read—and that signals *why* they are read.

For example, 78.9 percent of magazine reading occurs in the readers' own homes, according to the publishers' research; 61.6 percent of out-of-home reading occurs in someone else's home, at work and at a doctor or dentist's office.

Readers, that is, turn to magazines principally during leisure or spare moments (47 percent read after dinner or in bed) and take their time about it: On average, readers spend 52 minutes in reading time per magazine. Note this contrasts with newspaper readers, who read principally in the morning, before work, and who spend about 26 minutes on the *entire* newspaper.[2]

Lesson: Your magazine writing tone and structure should be selected for readers who are well-educated, upscale financially, who pick up magazines for lengthy periods, obviously searching for information, and who are willing to spend the time necessary to get it.

When you write for a magazine be sure to get demographic and psychographic information on its audience. It often is found in material published for advertisers, in a "marketing kit" or "advertising kit."

| Box 5-1 | A Professional's Viewpoint |

Recent surveys indicate that the majority of New York burglars prefer Crain's subscribers by a margin of 10 to 1.

With readers reporting an average household income of $245,000, that's not surprising.

> Advertising slogan used by *Crain's,* New York business magazine, in boasting about its upscale readers.

Write to Your Niche

Magazines cost more than newspapers. They publish less frequently, thus lack the timeliness of newspapers. So, what is a magazine's attraction to readers?

For many readers too busy for daily newspapers, a magazine's weekly or even monthly "catch-up" summary of events is a prime attraction.

Analytical writing—combined news and analysis of its meaning—is another draw.

Bold photographs and beautiful advertisements attract many readers, as well.

However, it's principally *narrowly tailored content* and in-depth treatment of a niche subject that draw many readers to magazines. Readers seek continuity in their magazine and focused coverage of specialized topics crucially important to them personally or professionally.

Such deep and continuing interest forces you to assume your readers have substantial expertise in the subject you're addressing. Lessons are obvious:

If you're writing for *Business Week*'s regular audience of business executives and investors you can assume they'll understand references to "prime rate" or "Federal Reserve Board." You couldn't make that same assumption in writing an editorial for the general audience of, say, the *Denver Post*.

No need to waste precious wordage explaining airplane flaps in an editorial for *Aviation Week & Space Technology,* whose readers are in aviation and space exploration. Don't assume *Denver Post* readers know what flaps are or what they do.

This does not mean you are ill-equipped to write for niche audiences if you are educated broadly in journalism or liberal arts or trained in general assignment newspaper reporting. In fact, that's *excellent* preparation for magazine writing. But it does mean any move into niche writing will require disciplined self-directed study of your specialized subject and rigorously accurate reporting for every editorial.

You must know—as your readers will—the meaning of, "The Fed raised the prime!" or, "Flaps didn't extend on landing!"

Publication Frequency and Your Writing Rhythm

Imagine walking across campus and encountering two friends. "What's new?" they ask.

Friend No. 1 you saw yesterday and the day before. In fact, you've talked daily with No. 1 for an entire week.

Friend No. 2 you haven't seen in a month. No conversations, no telephone calls, no letters.

Now, how do you answer their question?

Well, "What's new?" for friend No. 1 is simple—just relate quickly what's happened in the past 24 hours. This friend already is up to speed on your life.

Friend No. 2, of course, requires elaborate background on all that's happened in the past month. In fact, so much updating is required that you hardly have time to discuss what's really "new."

And so it is in writing opinion for magazines.

In writing for newspapers, you can establish special closeness with readers, touching base several times weekly or even daily on matters of compelling importance. Each day, your writing can assume a continuity of reader understanding that permits you to move into new territory, adding new information, to advance the conversation.

With less frequent contact, as in monthly or even weekly magazine writing, much of your opinion piece must be devoted to backgrounding and updating readers who, like Friend No. 2, are wondering, after your long absence, "What's new?"

Broadly, then, every editorial you write is divided into two parts:

1. The background and scene-setting detail your readers need to understand your subject even before they consider your opinions on it.
2. Your "added value" reporting of new information and your look-ahead opinion and analysis.

How much weight you assign to each part depends on your magazine's publishing frequency—how recently and consistently you've been able to chat with readers in your editorials.

Now, let's look at how these writing principles apply to different types of magazines.

Writing Editorials for Newsmagazines

In newsmagazines, opinion is all over the place—in institutional editorials, publishers' and editors' "letters" to readers, in columns and commentaries and even in "news" stories.

Some newsweeklies maintain traditional strict boundaries between news and opinion, and clearly label each writing form. Other magazines long ago broke down any separation between straight news, analytical writing and opinion.

The basic problem of newsmagazines, of course, is that if they go to press on a Friday in New York City they can't reach readers in Utah and elsewhere before Monday or Tuesday. That gives radio, television and daily newspapers three days to jump ahead in reporting "spot" news. So, newsmagazines cannot publish spot news or rely solely on summaries of last week's hard news, which *Time* and *Newsweek* originally stressed. Certainly, an opinion piece written on a Friday can be badly outpaced by events in three days.

Box 5-2 | A Professional's Viewpoint

That is the problem of modern news magazines. What can they bring to their readers that newspapers and TV haven't delivered days before?
—Kurt Andersen, "The Outsider," *The New Yorker,* March 31, 1997, p. 46

Consequently, newsmagazine opinion writers learn to identify news angles or "pegs" that, in industry parlance, will "stand" for several days—that is, remain valid no matter what news develops between press time in New York City and magazine arrival in Utah mailboxes.

For example, charges of sex scandals often erupted during President Clinton's administration with developments drawing newspapers into commenting each day on charges and counter-charges as they arose. Weekly newsmagazine writers had to avoid the daily rhythm of charge and counter-charge or risk being outdated by the time they reached their readers. For magazine writers, the writing angles had to be such things as trustworthiness in political life or a broadly based look at, say, morality in America.

Spotting the *institutional opinion* of newsmagazines is much more difficult than in years bygone.

For example, when led by co-founder Henry R. Luce (1898-1967), *Time* fairly reeked of ideology—Luce's right wing views. Today, under much less personalized leadership, *Time*'s corporate stance (as contrasted with personal opinions of columnists and analysts) is much more centrist.

In part, business considerations led *Time* and many other print media— newspapers included—to move away from ideological or political extremism: Broader reader appeal and, thus, advertiser support are found in the center.

It's easy for regular readers to catch over time the philosophical drift of columnists and analysts (whose writing we'll study in later chapters). But absent regular institutional editorials, *Time* doesn't clearly signal its corporate thinking on a weekly basis.

Newsweek, always much less ideological than *Time,* presents frequently the well-established and bylined views of columnists and analysts but is not regularly forthcoming on any corporate position.

U.S. News & World Report, featuring its "news you can use" format, expresses its institutional position through full-page commentaries by its owner, Mortimer B. Zuckerman.

At *Business Week,* there is no mistaking institutional thinking. Corporate opinion is published weekly—and clearly labeled the old-fashioned way, "Editorials." Writing is clever, engaging and always focused tightly on issues important to readers of business news.

For example, at a time of concern in the United States over economic growth, *Business Week* used three-quarters of a page, about 650 words, for an editorial counseling business and government leaders under the headline, "New Thinking About The New Economy." The lead:

> Is this a wonder economy, or what? Fast growth, dynamite profits, super-low unemployment, and tame inflation. We're sticking out our necks, but, as we've argued before, the good news is not just a one-quarter phenomenon.[3]

Note these characteristics of the intro:

- The question lead demonstrates again this useful writer's device for engaging reader attention.
- The bang-bang, almost staccato backup—"Fast growth, dynamite profits"—is designed to answer the question intro. (And you can almost hear readers thinking, "Yes, it sure is a 'wonder economy.' ")
- Willingness to take a stand—"We're sticking out our necks"—is shown on a question of considerable controversy: Is the good news about the economy truly long-term?
- Reference is made to being consistent with previously stated opinion—"as we've argued before ..." This *Business Week* writer is **chatting** with friends who drop in weekly to ask, "What's new?"

After that intro, the editorial broadens into added value reporting and analysis designed to support the writer's underlying thesis, that the U.S. economy has reached new heights of productivity and, "the implications are enormous." Cited are rising living standards, possible tax reductions, more jobs, perhaps redistribution of economic power in the world through information technology and globalization of business.

Then, a parting shot, a final word to friends who won't be checking in for a week: "Think about it."

In the same issue, *Business Week* examines balancing the federal budget, and its editorial is tough, filled with calls—demands—for action.

"Now it's time for politicians to get smart," says *Business Week*. And, "The tough work remains to be done ... politicians must find the backbone to do it."[4]

Another *Business Week* editorial uses an insider tone that assumes a high level of reader understanding, opening this way:

> The financial markets waited, as is their wont, with bated breath. Then, on the afternoon of May 20, they got the good news: The Federal Reserve's policy-setting Open Market Committee had opted to leave the key federal funds rate unchanged at 5.5%. Way to go, Alan! There's nothing happening in this economy that merits a rate increase right now: Wages are well behaved, companies have little pricing power, and economic growth is strong—but far from overpowered. It's a new world and a new economy.[5]

In the intro above, note:

- The look-back reference to May 20 that sets up the commentary that follows. Quickly, and in minimum wordage, readers are positioned. No need to use hundreds of words explaining to *Business Week*'s knowledgeable readers the significance of that unchanged interest rate.
- The exuberant compliment, "Way to go, Alan!"—a reference to Alan Greenspan, chairman of the Federal Reserve Board and a man well known in U.S. business circles.

The chummy, insider language of the intro is followed by a second graf opening this way: "The Fed's inaction holds out hope that even that august institution is coming around to the *Business Week* view that ..."

How's that for reminding readers that *Business Week* has a clearly-stated position on interest rates and, by golly, our pal Alan is coming around to our view!

Business Week, published by McGraw-Hill, a publicly owned company, keeps institutional opinion on that single page. Staff writers and contributors who write opinion do so elsewhere in the magazine under their own bylines.

At *Forbes*, a prestigious biweekly business news magazine owned by the Forbes family, Editor in Chief Steve Forbes writes for each issue, "Fact and Comment," a two-page collection of short (100-200 words) position statements on political and economic issues. His writing follows the conservative position Forbes adopts in his active Republican political career.

| Box 5-3 | Professional Viewpoints |

You may not always like what we say, but you always know where we stand.

Editor James W. Michaels of *Forbes*, to readers in his column "Side Lines," July 7, 1997, p. 14.

You can build the authority of your magazine with the editor's column. Too often, this page is squandered on a bland recap of the table of contents.
Make the most of the opportunity to write editorials that challenge conventional wisdom, sound the alarm, or otherwise stake out a strong position. In the process, the editor can give a magazine more personality by becoming its face and its voice.

—Frank Finn, magazine consultant, "Better Editorial For Less Money," *Folio*, April, 15, 1993, p. 33.

Caspar W. Weinberger, *Forbes* chairman and a well-known Republican, writes a full-page commentary under his own byline for each issue. But his writing is more personal than an attempt to represent a *Forbes'* corporate view.

In addition to appearing in Steve Forbes' column, that corporate view shows up in what might seem to be straight news stories.

For example, Robert Lenzner, senior editor, and David S. Fondiller, staff writer, take readers through a dispassionate and objective profile of Charles Munger and Warren Buffett, who have made fortunes in stock market investing through Berkshire Hathaway Co.

The writers note both investors are philanthropists and conclude the article with this:

In *Forbes'* view, the social conscience Munger expresses is part and parcel of his investment success, as is Buffett's. And so these complex, aging prodigies carefully tend their compound interest machine, a joint creation of two exceptional personalities. Others may try to duplicate Berkshire Hathaway but they won't be able to duplicate these two exceptional minds.[6]

You make the call: Does that concluding paragraph belong in a straight news story? Is "*Forbes'* view" the view of two writers? Of Steve Forbes? Of Forbes and Weinberger? Of an editorial board?

So goes opinion writing today in newsmagazines.

Writing Editorials for Thought Leaders

In some ways, "Thought (or Opinion) Leaders" are close kin to newsweeklies. For example, two we'll look at, *The New Republic* and *The Economist*, are published weekly. Both stick close to the breaking news. Both feature strong, insightful writing.

However, both *The New Republic* and *The Economist* give readers much heavier doses of **institutional opinion** than do *Time*, *Newsweek* or *Business Week*.

The New Republic, founded in 1914, advertises itself as, "A weekly journal of opinion"—and lives up to that slogan. Each week, the magazine opens with a full-page institutional essay that usually applies liberal social, economic and political ideas to a major news event of the preceding week. Long-time readers easily recognize ideological consistency in these essays, and for those who don't, *The New Republic* provides frequent reminders that it has a long-standing corporate position on the way the world works—and that it sticks to that position.

For example, this is how the magazine opens a full-page analysis of talks in Washington about balancing the federal budget:

> This magazine spent the 1980s and early 1990s counseling fiscal restraint. We did so because the huge, chronic budget deficits racked up by the Reagan and Bush administrations and the Old Democratic Congress stunted long-term economic growth and symbolized the inability of the voting public to accept, or their elected representatives to demand, sacrifice for the common good. We believed that balancing the budget was necessary to assuage these blights. We think so still, generally speaking, but last week's budget deal was a reminder that necessary is not the same as sufficient. ...

Now, *The New Republic* essay broadens into thoughtful, detailed examination of the budget debate's pros and cons. Writing exhibits these characteristics:

- Emphasis is on insightful, thoughtful writing, not clever, pandering attempts to pull in reluctant readers. Readers not deeply interested in the subject will find this writing tough going. Only once in the full-page essay does the writer employ a device standard in much magazine (and newspaper) writing—translating a complex idea into kitchen-table conversational terms. In discussing investment that "boosts economic productivity and hence makes it easier to support future retirees," the writer adds, "(The more workers produce, the more they can afford to give Grandma.)" Mostly, *The New Republic* essay is serious stuff for serious readers.
- The essay surrounds the previous week's news in an historical context almost impossible to force on time-starved readers attracted to the faster, crispier writing style of, say, *Time* or *Newsweek* or, certainly, daily newspapers. *The New Republic* reaches back decades for comparisons and precedents, thus offering added value in a broader perspective not available in all weekly or daily publications.

- After thorough discussion of the issue, the writer concludes with a hard-hitting prescription fully consistent with *The New Republic*'s established ideological position: Democrats are showing growing "and overdue" recognition of budgetary realities. ...

> But Republicans make no such concession to reality. They continue to believe they can balance the budget while refusing to ask their political base to sacrifice what it loves most: tax cuts. They continue with the fiction that the only ones who need to belt-tighten are faceless bureaucrats. "Under this budget agreement, official Washington must learn to make do with less, while Americans will keep more of what they earn," crowed Majority Leader Trent Lott. This is the opposite of the correct lesson. The long-term deficit crisis will only abate when the American public realizes that it, rather than some nebulous, bureaucratic other, must ultimately bear the cost of fiscal stability. The budget pact postpones that day of reckoning.[7]

As if to let gasping readers up for air, *The New Republic* follows each week's lengthy institutional essay with short, crackling, sardonic mini-essays in a feature titled, "Notebook." The heavy discussion of budget deficits cited above was followed by delightful pokes at right-wing attitudes on the sexual revolution, Saddam Hussein and his Iraqi dictatorship, the National Rifle Association, *The Washington Post* and *Newsweek*—and all with a wry tone and ideological slant expected by long-time *New Republic* readers.

Like *The New Republic*, *The Economist* is a journal of opinion. It, too, is published weekly. But similarities end there.

The Economist has been published in London for more than 150 years and has enormous international reach and influence. About 80 percent of its 600,000 circulation is outside Britain, much of it in the United States.

Among journalists, *The Economist* (which actually describes itself as a "newspaper") is highly respected for the subject and area expertise of its staff writers and contributors around the world. If you want to write for *The Economist*, bring expert reporting knowledge, as well as writing skill.

Each week's *Economist* opens with as many as five or six institutional editorials, each running hundreds of words, on current news. One endorsed re-election of Britain's Conservative (Tory) government, although the magazine acknowledged the Labour opposition likely would win overwhelmingly (as indeed it did.) Why should *The Economist* be so out of synch with voters? *The Economist* noted:

> To understand our predilections, and our attitude, a little history may be helpful.
>
> Except in the late 1840s when our founder, James Wilson, entered politics as an MP [Member of Parliament] and then a minister in a Liberal government, *The Economist* has never had a party-political affiliation in Britain, or anywhere else. Ideas rather than parties are what guide our

endorsements. Liberalism expressed through freedom of choice, political equality, free trade and limits to the discretionary powers of the state, has always been our creed. For much of the 19th century, that led us to favour the Liberals, a choice followed more loosely until the 1940s. Having been oddly (and wimpishly) neutral in 1945-51, the paper then endorsed the Conservatives in 1955 and 1959 before, for the first and (so far) only time, endorsing Labour in 1964. Since then, the Tories have had our vote.[8]

The thought leaders, then, stake out ideological ground and stick to it, and in that way develop audiences with commonality of interests and, in the case of both *The New Republic* and *The Economist*, audiences of deep loyalties to the magazines.

Writing Editorials for Consumer Magazines

Opinion writing in this magazine category, the largest in the industry, is marked by two characteristics:

First, many consumer magazines take no strong, consistent corporate position on economic, political or social issues. These magazines challenge readers with niche or specialized content and columnists (often *very* opinionated) but don't preach as institutions.

Second, many consumer magazines that do take institutional positions do so in editor's letters or publisher's notes designed to inform readers which topics are being covered by articles in the current issue. Often, these notes to readers tie corporate opinion to articles being published.

Magazines in this category include widely varied titles: *The New Yorker, Cosmopolitan, Good Housekeeping, Sports Afield, Redbook, Harper's Bazaar, George, Mother Jones* and others. Their handling of opinion writing is as varied as their content.

For example, although it has a definite ambiance or tone, *The New Yorker* has no regular corporate editorial page or column, no "*New Yorker* position," as does, say, *Business Week*. Instead, *The New Yorker* makes its statement through the totality of its content.

That is, articles, columns, analysis, reviews—even cartoons and advertisements—create cutting edge commentary on books, movies, theater, fashion and a host of other subjects important to sophisticated "with-it" readers or, just as importantly, readers who *want* to be sophisticated and with-it.

The New Yorker perhaps comes closest to an institutional editorial with a column titled, "Comment," that leads each week's issue. "Comment," signed by different writers, sticks close to the news, and, as you know, in a weekly that takes agile writing.

For example, it was ***mandatory*** that *The New Yorker*, famed for its movie and television reviews, weigh in on the Oscar award ceremony the year that the entertainment industry was all agog about a gay television star who "came out" during a TV sitcom. (*The New York Times*' treatment of that event was covered in Chapter Four.)

"Comment," signed this time by Hendrik Hertzberg, chose a look-ahead angle:

> At about the time this issue of *The New Yorker* opens wide, as they say on the multiplex circuit, a billion or so television viewers will be tuning in, with the usual mixture of excitement and resignation, to the world-wide broadcast of the annual awards of the Academy of Motion Picture Arts and Sciences. No doubt there are surprises in store. At this writing, though, it's safe to predict that (a) the show will be long, (b) the production numbers will galumph, and (c) no Oscar will go to a leading man or leading lady who is openly gay, because in the Hollywood bestiary no such animal exists.[9]

Note two points about that intro:

1. There is no specific reference to the television sitcom so widely discussed at the time (and, in fact, neither the program nor gay actress is named anywhere in the column). Yet, the subject—gays in entertainment—resonates because of the ongoing discussion (in *The New York Times* and elsewhere) about gay entertainers.
2. In just one paragraph, the writer twice notes his inability to provide spot news or commentary that is tied to an event ("At about the time this issue of *The New Yorker* opens wide" and "At this writing ...").

In all, writer Hertzberg is masterful in providing added value by using the much-discussed television sitcom as his writing peg but then advancing beyond that to a more general discussion of Hollywood's attitudes toward gays and gay themes. And, Hertzberg stays right on the cutting edge despite the obvious disadvantage of writing for a weekly.

George, immediately a "hot" magazine after launch in 1995, creates its editorial stance principally through the overall effect of articles and advertisements it publishes. Overt statement of corporate position is limited to "Editor's Letter" signed by John F. Kennedy Jr., son of the late president, co-founder of the monthly and its editor in chief.

Kennedy's "Editor's Letter" neatly combines his thinking on a political or social question with a "come-on" reference to an article on that question in the current issue. For example, here is one of his intros:

> If Americans seem cynical about politics, they seem even more skeptical about the institution of marriage when it comes to public figures. Despite the Clintons' 21-year union in an era when almost half of all marriages end in divorce, much of the populace continue to doubt the sincerity of their bond. For some reason, when both halves of a couple are high-powered, the public assumes their marriage is a calculated power merger rather than a love story.

Kennedy then discusses the strain political life can put on marriage, commenting that the husband usually gets all the attention, "while the wife is expected not only to give up her career but gaze adoringly during every photo opportunity." It's a nice low bow to modern women that acknowledges the problem many have in combining marriage with their own career aspirations. And that, of course, puts Kennedy and *George* right on the wavelength of an important audience segment sought by advertisers.

Box 5-4	A Professional's Viewpoint

Don't be afraid to reveal yourself to your readers. Remember that they are friends. Many writers believe that the best editorials are highly personalized—the more personal, the better. Readers who feel they know and like you because of what you've written are an asset to any magazine.

—Anne Graham, executive editor of *Internal Auditor*, "Write On The Mark," *Folio*, Nov. 1, 1996, p. 55

Kennedy notes several marriages in U.S. history that survived the strain of White House living, then personalizes his column with a reference to his mother, Jacqueline, and concludes with:

> In "The Power of Two" (page 130), *George* features some of the great romances in an age when marriage has become not only a personal but also a professional partnership.[10]

Kennedy's personal involvement with the magazine created much of the widespread interest accompanying its launch. And, he personalizes his column at every opportunity, avoiding the impersonal (and cold) "we," "us," "this page," "this magazine" that marks much institutional opinion writing. For example, note this intro:

> In the winter of 1980 I was going door-to-door in New Hampshire distributing literature for Senator Kennedy's presidential campaign. I was having limited success—states that love Pat Buchanan have little room in their hearts for politicians named Kennedy.

Kennedy then recalls knocking on a door, having it opened by a young woman with a baby on her hip—and having it slammed ("roughly") by her husband, who said, "We're votin' Reagan this year." Kennedy writes that he learned that was not an uncommon occurrence in those days—men making the decisions in American life.

Then, another low bow to the new American woman:

> In this issue we bring you our choice of the 20 most fascinating women in politics. Some of those we chose are in elected office. Others are not, but are nonetheless shaping public issues in important and personal ways.[11]

Lessons in this form of opinion writing:

- Personalized references ("I was going door-to-door ...") nicely warm up the "Editor's Letter." Kennedy's writing tone says, "Lemme tell you a story ..."
- Anecdotal illustrations—home-bound mom, overbearing husband—show Kennedy's support for the liberated American woman better than would a thousand words about social trends, demographic research and historic male domination of women.
- The writer's vehicles in *George*—in Kennedy's opinion piece and other articles—are the *personalities* in American politics, rather than profoundly deep discussions of issues alone.
- Kennedy's monthly letter gently ties his thinking to *George*'s content. He's a "pitchman" for his magazine, but only subtly.

Mother Jones is an example of magazines that overtly take strong editorial positions and clearly tie the *explanatory journalism* of articles to *advocacy calls for action.*

Mother Jones was founded in 1975 to, it says, "educate and empower people to work toward progressive change." Packages of articles and opinion pieces address social issues that *Mother Jones* raises under that mission statement.

For example, *Mother Jones* published a "take-out" of thousands of words on the theme that the Christian right "has become an unparalleled force in national politics." Accompanying that was a three-page "Editor's Note" thundering against "the religious right" and demanding separation of government and religion. The package of article-plus-comment included names, addresses, telephone numbers and e-mail addresses of watchdog groups readers can contact.[12]

Among many consumer magazines, much gentler advocacy is the general practice. For example, *Macon Magazine* practices obvious but gentle "boosterism" of the good life in Macon, Ga., Editor Joni Williams Woolf, in her regular opinion column, "From the Editor ...", notes an election is coming up and local politicians are quarreling with each other. She points out:

> This must change if Macon is to attract new businesses, which translates into more jobs—a connection Maconites don't always make. Technology has changed the investigation and selection process so dramatically that prospective companies already know, before they come to visit, about the illiteracy rate, the sub-standard housing rate, the voter percentage in local elections, the lack of support for public education—all of our flaws. They know the good things too, but geographic location, interstate access, historic homes and a stable water supply don't always make up for the glaring deficits. Maybe those of us who've been here a long time just don't see them anymore.

Like Kennedy in *George*, Woolf in *Macon Magazine* teases readers into her principal article:

> This issue begins with a story about a vision for Macon. Actually, it's the vision of 10 of Macon's leading citizens, but so many common threads run through their responses that it amounts to a single vision.

Pull together, Woolf tells her readers; elect the right officials and Macon's future "could, indeed, be grand."[13]

Writing Editorials for Trade Magazines

Broadly, two approaches mark editorial writing in this magazine category:

- Unabashed boosterism of the industry that trade magazines cover (and from which they get their advertising support). Such uncritical comment on an industry is little more than public relations "spin" writing and, thus, outside the purview of this book.
- Discerning editorial comment that criticizes as well as compliments, that guides and counsels as well as applauds.

This discerning approach is taken by some editors so seriously that they prefer their magazines be known as "special business magazines" in belief that signals their more objective, dispassionate stance.

Make no mistake: For magazines depending on advertising support from the industry they cover, being critical—or even objective—can require courage.

For example, *Advertising Age* ran considerable risk of reader and advertiser anger when it called on R.J. Reynolds Tobacco Co. to get rid of its Joe Camel symbol, then under attack as aimed at selling cigarettes to children. Throughout the advertising industry there was (and is) strong support for advertising freedom in the sale of any legal product.

Yet, *Ad Age,* a weekly published by Crain Communications Inc., repeatedly called for Joe's end, and, when the Federal Trade Commission got into the act, the magazine hit hard in an editorial:

> ... there's nothing to gain in fighting on for Joe. Even if he beats the rap at FTC, he will be "guilty" in the eyes of the public. Joe was a great ad idea, but a terrible choice to represent a product that supposedly is for grown-ups only. It will be a gift to the rest of the ad business if RJR calls off the lawyers and brings Joe to a well-deserved, and long overdue, end.[14]

In the same editorial column (titled "Viewpoint"), *Ad Age* was highly complimentary about another advertising slogan, this one from Christian Dior Perfumes for a new hair product. The slogan was, "A stroke of brilliance for the hair." *Ad Age* commented:

Make that a stroke of genius. Everyone talks about product innovation and spends millions trying to achieve it. Dior was just out for some fun but, much to its credit, recognized an original when it saw it. Other marketers, regardless of what they make, would do well to take note.[15]

There, in that *Ad Age* straddle—a slap on the wrist, a compliment—is the best in special business magazine editorial writing. No one—not reader, advertiser or media critic—can doubt *Ad Age*'s independence, its objectivity. And all that builds the single most important asset a magazine can have—credibility.

| Box 5-5 | A Professional's Viewpoint |

Most editors, in the business press, especially, probably feel they're already walking a fine line when it comes to running stories about advertisers and their products. Trade editors must constantly battle the notion that advertisers dictate editorial content. ... Every editor who's been on the job more than a month has had to deal with an advertiser who is irate over something associated with the magazine. ...

... The real question, regardless of whether we're on the consumer or trade side, is still this: Who are we here to serve? Our readers, of course ...

—Lisa E. Phillips, "Editor's Note," *Folio*, May 1, 1997, p. 7

If they *sometimes* slap their own industry's wrist, business magazines *nearly always* can be counted on to defend against attack from outside.

For example, *Folio* (self-billed "Magazine for Magazine Management") took on convenience chain stores that refused to sell magazines deemed "anti-family." *Folio* also attacked the Defense Department for ruling *Penthouse* unfit for sale on military bases. *Folio* commented:

Bad enough that retailers act as unwanted filters, but worse yet that our government wants into the business of magazine censorship, too.[16]

Support of First Amendment rights runs through magazines covering the media. *Editor & Publisher*, which covers the newspaper industry, campaigns against State Department restrictions on news organizations setting up bureaus in Cuba.[17] *Broadcasting & Cable* lets few weeks go by without editorials calling for more deregulation of broadcasting and non-interference by government in broadcast advertising.[18]

Lessons to Ponder

Let's say you have no in-depth understanding of, say, Afghanistan but want to pontificate a bit on that faraway country so unknown to Americans.

Using a little journalistic smoke and mirrors, you could do an opinion piece built around a few facts drawn from *The World Almanac,* a bit of current history from *New York Times* clips and some impressions drawn from recent news coverage by *The Economist.*

With deft writing, you might pull it off for a general audience of newspaper readers or consumer magazine subscribers.

Now, let's say you have no background in computers and want to write opinion for *Computerworld.* Or you know nothing about trucks and your muse moves for *Heavy Duty Trucking.* Or you want to write for *Indiana Prairie Farmer* and the closest you ever got to a farm was driving by one on the interstate.

You *do* face special challenges in writing opinion for trade or special business magazines (and for many specialized consumer magazines, too).

FIRST,
you're writing for *insiders*—readers who know your subject (and who sometimes know more about it than you do). *Staying on the cutting edge* is imperative for a writer. *Computerworld* readers follow trends in computer technology; *Indiana Prairie Farmer* readers know what's new in farming. You better know, too.

SECOND,
you'll need much *sharper reporting skills* to back your opinion writing for insider readers. Write that Afghanistan borders on Pakistan but not on China, which it does, and not every newspaper reader or consumer magazine subscriber will catch your error. But comment on Hereford milk production, when you mean Holstein, and you won't get by readers of *Indiana Prairie Farmer.*

THIRD,
because of their expertise, readers of trade and special business magazines demand a *high level of authority and credibility* in your writing. You build that by avoiding generalizations and, instead, riveting facts and figures to the structure of your opinion piece. Strongly reported and believable detail must be the foundation.

FOURTH,
you must believe in the industry you're covering. That does not require slavish, unthinking boosterism; it does require that you believe, for example, in the underlying marketplace and societal validity of advertising if you want to write for *Advertising Age.* If you're entirely unsympathetic to the American family farm, don't try to write for *Indiana Prairie Farmer.* You (and your readers) would be miserable.

FIFTH,
guard against dull writing. Some trade magazine writers believe the message is all that counts and that however ponderous and dense their writing, read-

ers will plow forward patiently. Not true. Even though they principally seek factual and informed opinion, readers of trade and special business magazines cannot be force-fed—no "castor oil journalism." ("Here, gulp this down; it's good for you!") Engaging and light-footed writing will win every time over heavy, obtuse writing.

| Box 5-6 | Writing That Grabs |

Whether writing opinion for newspapers or magazines, you'll not get your message across unless your writing catches readers. Note how the following writers write to grab!

Defending paparazzi this week would be like press agenting for pit bulls. ...

Journalism by its nature is intrusive. If paparazzi are the sleazy underbelly of the photojournalism trade, and you'd get no argument from us this week, they still cannot be censored without doing damage to the practice of serious journalism, which can also enrage, intimidate and embarrass its subjects (and sometimes save lives and right wrongs in the process) ...

We're sick of voyeurism masquerading as reporting, and of the public's seemingly insatiable appetite for it. We welcome a ground swell of public and professional revulsion aimed at the "stalkarazzi." The answer is for publications—print and broadcast—to just say no.

Broadcasting & Cable, commenting on Princess Diana's death, in "Stalkarazzi," an editorial, Sept. 8, 1997, p. 82.

I never thought I'd say this, but I'm tired of sex.

I have eros-fatigue.

We have been so awash in lurid details about sexual misadventures between men and women in New York, Hollywood, Washington, Aberdeen, Minot and Little Rock that it's made me long for some old-fashioned, deadly earnest policy stories.

Columnist Maureen Dowd, "Eros, Schmeros," *The New York Times*, June 11, 1997, p. A-25.

In the same week that an Army general with 147 Vietnam combat missions ended his career over an adulterous affair 13 years ago, the news broke that a New Jersey girl gave birth to a baby in the bathroom at her high school prom, put it in the trash and went out to ask the deejay to play a song by Metallica—for her boyfriend. The baby is dead.

Welcome to morality in late 20th century America, where what's right and what's wrong is anyone's guess on any given day. ...

> *The Wall Street Journal,* an editorial, "Modern Morality," June 11, 1997, p. A-16.

He may be the only quarterback in history who could stand on his own two-yard line, trailing by five with less than two minutes to play, no time-outs left, wind-chill -5 degrees, and cause the opposing coach to mutter, "We're in trouble."

> —Rick Reilly, senior writer, *Sports Illustrated,* on Denver Bronco quarterback John Elway, "Rick Reilly on ..." in "Inside Track," 1997, p. 2.

Summary

- Magazine opinion writing requires special touch because of magazines' upscale audiences, tailored content and weekly or monthly publishing rhythms.
- Four types of magazines are most important to students of opinion writing—newsmagazines, the so-called "thought leaders," consumer magazines and trade or special business magazines.
- Writing to your audience is extremely important, and students of opinion writing must understand magazine audiences are upscale in education and income.
- Magazine readers on average spend 52 minute per issue and read principally in leisure moments at home.
- Readers buy magazines for many reasons but principally for narrowly tailored content and continuity in coverage of specialized topics important to them personally or professionally.
- You must report and write with insider understanding of your magazine's tailored content and the news niche interests of your readers.
- Writing opinion on a weekly or monthly rhythm, rather than for daily newspapers requires careful judgment on how much of a single editorial must be devoted to bring readers up to speed on recent developments and how much to new, "carry-forward" material.
- Newsmagazines vary greatly in how they present institutional or corporate opinion; many long ago broke down barriers between editorial and straight news writing.
- *Business Week* is one newsmagazine that presents its institutional thinking the old-fashioned way: on a page labeled "Editorials" and in strong, advocacy language.

- "Thought leaders," such as *The New Republic*, are principally journals of opinion and are sought out by readers familiar with the ideological positions taken by the magazines week after week.
- Many consumer magazines take no institutional or corporate position editorially; instead, they create an *editorial tone* through the totality of their articles and advertising.
- Personalized opinion columns—for example, the "Editor's Letter" signed by John F. Kennedy Jr., editor in chief of *George*—are popular with many consumer magazine editors for blending opinion with information on articles in current issues.
- Trade or "special business" magazines are divided roughly into those that are unabashed and uncritical boosters of their industry and those that offer discerning and sometimes critical editorial comment on their industry.

Recommended Reading

A couple hours at the magazine rack of your local supermarket will give you fascinating insight into the many types of American magazines and their varying approaches to opinion writing. The supermarket manager won't mind (at least, I've never had a problem).

In my *Inside the Media* (White Plains, N.Y.: Longman, 1990), I take you on a tour of the magazine industry and inside *U.S. News & World Report*. My *Introduction to Magazine Writing* (New York: Macmillan, 1994) looks at the industry and magazine writing in general. *Gale Directory of Publications and Media* (Detroit: Gale Research, Inc., 1996) lists most magazines of consequence.

For beginning writers, watching how the pros do it can be enormously helpful. I recommend you regularly read opinion in *Business Week, The Economist, Forbes, Advertising Age* and, to see how it's done in an industry magazine, *Folio*.

Notes

1. "The Magazine Handbook," Magazine Publishers of America, 919 Third Avenue, New York, NY, 10022, p. 15-16.
2. Ibid, p. 48-49.
3. "New Thinking About The New Economy," *Business Week*, May 19, 1997, p. 150.
4. "This Budget Doesn't Tackle Entitlements," *Business Week*, May 19, 1997, p. 150.
5. "The Mark of a Cool-Headed Fed," *Business Week*, June 2, 1997, p. 158.
6. Robert Lenzner and David S. Fondiller, "The Not-So-Silent-Partner," *Forbes*, Jan. 22, 1996, p. 78.
7. "Big Deal," *The New Republic*, May 26, 1997, p. 7.
8. "Labour Doesn't Deserve It," *The Economist*, April 26, 1997, p. 13.
9. Hendrik Hertzberg, "Oscar's Closet," *The New Yorker*, March 31, 1997, p. 7.

10. John F. Kennedy Jr., "Of Bedfellows And Birthdays," *George*, October 1996, p. 12.

11. John F. Kennedy Jr., "Editor's Letter," *George*, September 1996, p. 14.

12. This package was led with "Editor's Note: What Is Sacred" and the principal story was Adele M. Stan, "Power Preying," p. 3 and p. 32, respectively, *Mother Jones*, November/December 1995.

13. Joni Williams Woolf, "Winds of Change Are Blowing," *Macon Magazine*, November/December 1995, p. 4.

14. "'Old Joe' in the Dock," *Advertising Age*, June 2, 1997, p. 28.

15. "Dior's Winner," *Advertising Age*, June 2, 1997, p. 28.

16. Anne M. Russell, "Free Speech's Weakest Voice," *Folio*, March 1, 1997, p. 1.

17. Note, for example, "Bureaus in Cuba," *Editor & Publisher*, Feb. 22, 1997, p. 4.

18. Note, for example "Born-Again TV," *Broadcasting & Cable*, Dec. 2, 1996, p. 90.

Exercises

1. Study the lead story in your college newspaper (or another paper your instructor selects) and describe what approach you would take in writing an editorial on the subject of that story for a) a daily newspaper and b) a weekly newsmagazine.

In about 250 words, detail the writing "peg" you would use in each editorial, the type of background you would include, what the rhythm and structure of your writing would be, and the general conclusion you would reach.

2. In about 300 words, discuss whether magazines should maintain separate and distinct editorial pages, as does *Business Week*, or incorporate institutional opinion in news analysis and interpretation, as *Forbes* sometimes does.

Is there ethical need to label *all* opinion as such? Or, do you think the demands for analysis and interpretation are so great that *all* magazine writing should contain guidance for readers in the form of opinion? Are newspapers old-fashioned in maintaining distinction between news and editorial columns?

3. Your instructor will discuss with your class the leading news story on campus, be that crime, enrollment, tuition levels, the football team's record or whatever.

In about 300 words, write an editorial on that subject for a *weekly newsmagazine* tailored for students on your campus.

This is a take-home assignment. Your deadline is Friday of the current week. Your "magazine" will reach student readers only on the following Monday. As you write, remember that news developments can break on Saturday and Sunday, after your deadline.

4. Examine the current issue of *The New Yorker* (or another magazine selected by your instructor) and, in about 300 words, discuss the overall editorial tone of the magazine.

What "ambiance" is created by the magazine's totality of content—its signed commentary, reviews, articles, advertising? Do you detect a commonality of journalistic thrusts? What impressions do editors want readers left holding?

5. Examine the editorial page of this week's *Business Week* (or another magazine selected by your instructor) and, in about 350 words, discuss these questions:

- Are editorials structured and in language appropriate for "insiders" or general lay audiences?
- Do the reporting and writing indicate the writer has deep understanding of the subject? How is that indicated?
- Do you think the writing and reporting are "pitched" at appropriate levels of reader understanding?
- How would you *improve* the editorials? Be specific.

PART THREE

Writing Personal Columns

L ET'S TURN to one of the most coveted jobs in all of print journalism—writing personal columns.

Writing your own column on the op-ed page or elsewhere frees you from the institutional position of your newspaper or magazine. Under your own byline (and, often, your photo!), you can write it *your* way, put *your* spin on the world of ideas, reach out and touch *your* readers one by one.

That is, we turn now to a writing form distinct from editorials. The views of two pros:

> I know editorials are read by movers and shakers. I try to look at life from the perspective of the moved and shaken.
>
> Therefore I tend to think of the editorial page as institutional, while the column can be rebellious. I think of the editorial page as stable, stately, and consistent, while the column can be quick, mischievous, and unpredictable.
>
> The editorial page speaks; the columnist responds. If the editorial page packs a bigger wallop, the columnist has more fun.
>
> —Clarence Page, *Chicago Tribune,* syndicated columnist

> Because its readers are usually well-informed, hurried, and opinionated themselves, the op-ed page must be the light cavalry of literary forms, an 800-word argument striking quickly and sharply.
>
> —H. George Hahn, *The Masthead*[1]

Being a columnist is so attractive that some of our most talented journalists labor for years in hard news to develop reporting and writing skills that qualify them for a column. Competition for a column is fierce in any newsroom.

However, there is good news for you aspiring writers: Newspapers and magazines offer more jobs to columnists than ever before. There are two principal reasons:

- Editors know they must offer readers analysis and personalized interpretation of the hard-news stuff we display on front pages—politics, foreign affairs, business, war and peace. In this complex world of ours, simply shoveling hard news at readers can leave them befuddled unless we provide analysis, too.
- Editors also know readers are drawn to the personalized writing in columns, and that nothing else in the paper or magazine establishes quite the same one-to-one intimacy between writer and reader. Columns are great for building loyal readership.

In Part Three, we'll look at three dimensions of column writing:

Chapter Six, "Commentary That Hits Hard," discusses column writing that sticks close to the news, helping readers make sense of the compellingly important stories of the day.

Chapter Seven, "Amusing, Entertaining or Making 'em Cry," looks at columns that bypass the day's hard news and, instead, focus on the amusing, the wry, the *human* dimension of life.

Chapter Eight, "The Fun and Business of Sports," examines

one of the most popular features of all newspapers—columns on prep, college and pro sports. Many of our most loyal readers visit our pages principally for sports, and sports columnists, in turn, offer those readers much of our very best writing.

6 | Commentary That Hits Hard

JOIN THE CROWD around the (ahem!) water fountain at the National Press Club in Washington and before long you'll hear something like this:

"Did you see Broder's angle today?"

"*Where* does Safire get that stuff?"

"Clarence Page rang the bell again this morning at the Trib."

Wherever journalists gather—in Washington, at the Overseas Press Club in New York City or at press clubs nationwide—newspaper talk often turns to the same subject: the impact on American politics and national policy achieved by columnists such as David Broder of *The Washington Post,* among the best non-partisan political columnist operating out of the capital; William Safire of *The New York Times,* a conservative on a liberal op-ed page and a "scoop artist" who regularly breaks important news stories; and Clarence Page of *The Chicago Tribune,* a black social commentator who shadows hard-news developments, particularly in racial matters.[1]

All three are syndicated, appearing in newspapers worldwide and are widely respected among journalists.

And readers? They love or hate columnists. All columnists learn this when they read their mail.

> If you write opinion for a living, you get mail, some of it pretty vicious.
>
> Hate mail, unfortunately, seems to go with the territory. The trick is to keep your sense of humor when someone is calling you "scum" or worse.
>
> One column-writing colleague used to keep the hate letter she received stashed in a file labeled "Fan Mail From Hell," a sort of grab bag of reflections from the criminally insane. The letters I have come to cherish tend to be written in crayon and rely heavily on exclamation points.
>
> —Sue Ryon, *The Milwaukee Journal Sentinel*[2]

How do columnists write to arouse such interest—such passion—among newspaper readers? We'll explore that as we turn in Chapter Six to the art of column writing.

The Columnist's Tool Chest

Whatever their subject or the tone of their column, successful columnists are experts with the tools of their trade. Read columnists for major newspapers and magazines or those syndicated in many newspapers nationally and you'll see these tools in use:

- *Strong basic reporting skills*, developed mostly in years of intensive hard-news reporting for daily newspapers.
- *Intimate knowledge of their subject*, be that politics, economics, foreign policy or whatever.
- *Knowledgeable and authoritative sources*, strategically placed to yield "insider" perspectives.
- *Cutting edge instincts*, a firm grasp of precisely where the news is in a developing story, and how to advance the story into virgin territory.
- *Writing ability* of, roughly, two kinds: (a) businesslike style that translates complex matters into terms easily understood by readers or (b) dazzling keyboard artistry that yields fluid and beautiful—and thus, irresistible—prose.

Let's look more closely at these tools.

| Box 6-1 | A Professional's Viewpoint |

George Melloan is deputy editor (international) of *The Wall Street Journal* and longtime columnist for its highly-respected op-ed page. Here are his hints on how you can approach column writing.

Obviously, the first requirement for opinion writing is to have opinions. But that doesn't disqualify many people. Finding a publisher willing to print one's opinions is a harder task.

Four questions will occur to a publisher weighing qualifications of the would-be columnist: Are the applicant's opinions interesting? Are they informed? Can I afford another columnist? Do I have space for another column?

Those questions narrow the market for opinion writers quite substantially. Yet there is a market for writers who have developed the skills that apply to all forms of good journalism. To name three:

— analytical ability.
— some talent for stringing words together in ways that are both engaging and grammatically correct.

— and enough curiosity about how the world works to dig hard for the underlying truths behind events in the news.

Most opinion writers approach ideas and events armed with some underlying philosophy, usually one that doesn't fit the hackneyed "liberal" and "conservative," that have become the common currency of American politics. Probably most opinion columnists think of themselves as populists, originally defined as defenders of the right of all people to have a voice in how they are governed.

The judgments of opinion writers vary widely on what is good or bad for the community they are addressing, but I think most believe they are arguing for what best serves the public weal, or what policies deliver the most good to the most people.

My own venture into column writing came after many years at *The Wall Street Journal*, as a reporter, page-one rewriteman, foreign correspondent and finally as an editorial writer. I launched a column called "Business World"in 1987, and then in 1990 another new column called "Global View," which coincided with moving my base of operations to Brussels. I combine column writing with supervising editorial pages of *The Wall Street Journal Europe* and *The Asian Wall Street Journal,* now once again from New York.

My daily work with copy generated abroad eases the task of taking a "global view" each week. I get much information that stimulates my thoughts about what might make an interesting and informative column. I have telephone and e-mail conversations with *Journal* editorial page writers abroad, scan six newspapers, various magazines, the newswires and the flow of reports and studies from think tanks, agencies of various governments and individual correspondents. The *Journal* editorial page has a steady stream of visitors from around the world, most with some role in their home governments.

But each column needs to be independently researched, just as any good news story or feature article must be. A column about high-stakes politics surrounding the huge Caspian Sea oil and gas deposits necessitated interviewing an adviser to the president of Azerbaijan, some Republic of Georgia parliamentarians who happened to be passing through, the president of an oil company developing deposits in the region and a Washington consultant knowledgeable in business and political risks involved. I searched the Dow Jones News Retrieval data bank to see what others had written, collected special studies on the Caspian oil play and in the end had a pile of documents a couple inches high. Out of this I distilled my allotted 23 column inches of copy discussing Russia's neo-imperialism and U.S. foreign policy.

In other words, I did a lot of reporting, something *The Wall Street Journal* expects of all its writers, including editorial page writers. An opinion columnist is expected to take a position, but unsupported arguments won't contribute much to reader understanding of issues or add to the quality of public debate. Even supported arguments may not arrive at good public policy choices, but they are more likely to do so than mere wool gathering backed only by superficial knowledge of the issues.

Do opinion columns in major publications like *The Wall Street Journal* influence policy? Here, I think, modesty is becoming. Many voices, in and outside the press, clamor for the attention of policy-makers. Politics has a logic of its own that doesn't always correspond to the cool analytical reasoning of an observer not directly engaged in the fray. Politicians think of the interests of their constituents and that doesn't always shake out as support, for example, of free market economics.

But, it is clear from visits I have nearly every week with policy-makers from around the globe that many have read my column or *Journal* editorials and are responding by offering us their own arguments. They obviously seek support for their positions in print. Sometimes we agree with them and sometimes we don't. These discussions are the most interesting part of my job and I assume people who visit us see value in trying to influence what we write.

But in the final analysis, a columnist's influence is only as good as the power and persuasiveness of his arguments. That is achieved not only by skillful and forceful use of words but also through the hard work of digging out and trying to understand the many facets of public issues. The growing complexity of the world we live in will, I believe, continue to provide work for writers who learn early the importance of doing their homework.

Report for Your Column

Before launching into opinion writing, most truly great columnists develop strong hard-news reporting skills. Look at David Broder's experience before he became a syndicated political columnist for *The Washington Post*:

- Three years in general assignment reporting for *The Bloomington Daily Pantagraph*, a medium-size daily in Illinois farm country.
- Five years reporting in Washington for *The Congressional Quarterly*, which immersed Broder in political affairs.
- Five years reporting for *The Washington Star*.
- Two years in the Washington bureau of *The New York Times*.
- Nine years in political reporting for *The Washington Post*, which won a Pulitzer Prize, among other awards.

And now? Broder *still* calls himself a reporter. Here is how he opens a column after covering the British elections:

> Washington—A reporter returning home from London to the miseries of the American political scene ... [3]

"A reporter ..." is Broder's clear signal to readers that he regards his principal task as digging for facts, interviewing authoritative sources and then—*only* then—delivering a columnist's overlay of analysis and interpretation.

His obvious belief that reporter credentials are essential for a columnist led Broder into a strong attack on one columnist who began opinion writing without reporting experience—William Safire of *The New York Times*.

Broder wrote:

> Safire is part of the trend in the past couple of decades for people to achieve prominent places in journalism not by working their way up from routine beats to more responsible tasks in the newsroom, but instead by vaulting the wall from politics and government straight into punditry. He was not the first, but since Safire moved directly from speech-writing and flackery for Richard Nixon and Spiro Agnew onto the op-ed page of the *Times*, dozens of others have followed his route and tried to emulate his success.
>
> They carry over from their former roles as political *consiglieri* the habit of giving advice to politicians. ... [4]

Broder was commenting on a Safire column which gave political advice to House Speaker Newt Gingrich. A columnist's role, Broder wrote, is reporting that helps the public understand complex issues, not advising politicians.

In a subsequent column, Safire responded:

> Broder and I have for decades debated the virtues of inside experience in analyzing politics. Although many fine journalists grump about pols who "cross the street" into the land of lucrative purity and newsies who gain power as press secretaries, I think that's healthy cross-pollination.
>
> Broder is right about the clear conflict in journalists giving private advice to politicians. When the speaker calls me, however, and I drop an unexpected opinion on him, get a reaction plus a revealing financial fact, and promptly write all about it, that's not just my living—that's my role in political life.[5]

Whatever their differences in backgrounds, Broder and Safire share journalistic commonalities. Both travel widely, reporting under datelines throughout the United States and world. Both have powerful, well-placed news sources. Both write in fresh, "newsy" styles close to the cutting edge of what's on front pages and the evening news. Both provide added value reporting that enables them to break news stories, not simply comment on stories broken by other reporters.

| Box 6-2 | A Professional's Viewpoint |

We substituted door knocking and shoe leather for the random sample and for the number of interviews that a professional pollster would use. Those techniques can work. One of the best ways to report a campaign is to park yourself in a particular community long enough to find out who is for whom—and why. It is reporting, not polling. But when done well—with some luck added—it can tell you as much about the dynamics of a particular election as any poll.

> —David Broder, describing how he covered a key primary during a presidential election, in *Behind The Front Page,* (New York: Simon & Schuster, 1987)

Thus, Broder reports under a Cleveland dateline on a conference of U.S. mayors, which physically removes him from journalistically incestuous Washington *and* takes his reporting down to grass-roots level.

In this single column, Broder names 11 mayors and sources on the problems of struggling cities. Broder's attributions are those he learned as a cub reporter on the *Bloomington Daily Pantagraph:*

- Indianapolis Mayor Steve Goldsmith "spoke here ..."
- Philadelphia's Ed Rendell "noted on a 'Meet the Press' broadcast from here ..."
- Mayor Hal Daub of Omaha "told me ..."

Broder's *reporting* leads readers through a description of fiscal tension between Washington, cities and their suburbs. Then he concludes with a single paragraph of *opinion:*

> Perhaps the fiscal squeeze from Washington and the state capitals will force suburban voters to realize that they are in the same boat as city dwellers. The change can't come too soon for these hard-working mayors.[6]

Like Broder, *The New York Times'* Safire often puts on reporter's shoes for extensive travel outside his home base, Washington. On-site reporting freshens Safire's writing.

For example, Safire travels to Israel and, under a Tel Aviv dateline, breaks fresh ground with inside reporting on political maneuvering by Prime Minister Benjamin Netanyahu. This is his opener:

> Tel Aviv—You think Yasir Arafat and Israeli Prime Minister Benjamin Netanyahu don't trust each other? You think Ehud Barak, the opposition Labor Party's new top man, and "Bibi" don't trust each other?
>
> Those fierce feelings are as nothing compared with the depth of distrust felt for one another by Bibi and almost all the longtime leaders of his own right-wing coalition.

For hundreds of words, Safire describes ins and outs of Israeli politics. Even considering widespread U.S. interest in Israel and the *Times'* large Jewish readership in New York City, the detail is a bit much. Then this:

> Why have I taken the American reader—interested mainly in Israel's "peace process"—through the delicious, back-biting minutiae of Israeli right-wing politics?
>
> My purpose is to illustrate what happens when one voter-friendly political leader dares to try and turn a parliamentary system, built on the British model, toward a presidential system adapted from the American constitutional model.[7]

Incidentally, did you note Safire's second-graf reference to the nickname "Bibi" for Prime Minister Netanyahu? That's Safire's signal to readers that he's inside the political loop in Israel and is on intimate terms with important people there; in fact, that he knows "Bibi" himself.

Many are the writing devices columnists use to lend authority to their writing!

| Box 6-3 | The Viewpoint of Professionals |

Columnists have a huge advantage over editorial writers: They can humanize their writing by using personal anecdotes to lure readers into a serious subject they might otherwise avoid. Here is how pros do it:

Davos, Switzerland—Before the Nazis shot him, my grandfather, Jacob Glass, was one of Poland's richest men.

> —Andrew Glass, Washington bureau chief for Cox Newspapers, writing about Swiss banks holding money deposited by Holocaust victims during World War II. "Forgiveness and Forgotten Funds," *The Atlanta Journal* and *Constitution,* Feb. 11, 1997, A-11.

In 1973, Edward Bennett Williams's law partner, Paul Connolly, gave me my first news tip as a neophyte *New York Times* columnist: that Vice President Spiro T. Agnew was the target of a grand jury inquiry for being on the take while Governor of Maryland.

As a former Nixon speechwriter who had nattered a few nabobs, I had unique access to the V.P., and sent in a query: True? The answer came back: No. Believing the lie, I wrote nothing and was beaten on the story.

> —William Safire, "A Heartbeat Away," *The New York Times,* national edition, Sept. 19, 1996, p. A-21.

When you go to war with a guy, even one you don't admire or like very much, you and he ever after have a special bond.

I liked and admired Mack Allen enormously.

> —James Brady, on the death of a friend from Korean War days. "A Gentleman From Virginia," *Advertising Age,* June 24, 1996, p. 24.

This is not the column I intended to write.

That column was a response to a Miami professor who was critical of an essay in which I used government statistics to debunk the myth of black criminals preying on white victims. ...

I was all over this guy like white on rice. Like stupid on Dennis Rodman. I had expert testimony, numbers on top of numbers to prove him wrong.

Too many numbers, as it turned out. The boss said it gave her a headache. She sent it back for a rewrite.

—Leonard Pitts of the *Miami Herald*. "A Temple in My Own Good Time," guest column, *The Atlanta Journal and Constitution*, May 8, 1997, A-19.

∽

In nearly 34 years of column writing, never before had I faced such concentrated attack from all points on the political compass. My sin: I reported March 6 that Louis Farrakhan, head of the Nation of Islam, was knocking on the Republican Party's door, and suggested some response might be appropriate.

With that report and that suggestion, I touched a political untouchable.

Syndicated columnist Robert D. Novak, "Farrakhan And Me," *The Washington Post*, March 27, 1997, A-27.

∽

Casablanca, Morocco—The frigate U.S.S. Carr pulled into Casablanca harbor last week and the U.S. Embassy held a reception on board, replete with Budweiser and chicken fingers, for local dignitaries. I dropped by and soon was conversing with a senior Moroccan official.

—Thomas L. Friedman, "Parlez-Vous U.S.A.?", *The New York Times*, national edition, Feb. 26, 1997, p. A-15.

But the single most important lesson of the Broder and Safire examples is this: Whether you develop your journalistic skills as a street reporter (Broder) or as a politician-turned-pundit (Safire), *reporting* is the difference between columns that attract readers with added value content and columns that turn readers away with mere manipulation of words and somebody else's ideas. Knowledgeable readers spot the difference immediately!

Eileen McNamara, who switched from reporting to writing a column for *The Boston Globe*, puts it this way:

I learned long ago as a reporter that there is no greater privilege than to have people share their stories with you. I tell those stories now to make a point, my point, but it is a point I'd better be prepared to defend with something more than opinion. Readers are a lot like my father, I've learned. They'll heed or dismiss me, depending on how well I support my case.[8]

Know Your Subject

Nothing is more readily apparent (or insulting) to readers than columnists who don't know what they're writing about—columnists who pontificate without understanding.

Readers are increasingly well-educated and sophisticated; they are adept at sorting through the literally thousands of media and advertising messages that bombard them daily; they quickly dismiss bunk!

Lesson: Don't write beyond your competence. Stick to subjects you understand. You're a student? Write about student affairs, not the United Nations, Afghanistan or another subject distant.

Obviously, however, columnists, like reporters, often must write about subjects on which their personal understanding is shallow. When that happens to you, fall back on the "Broder Technique"—traveling to Cleveland, interviewing mayors and pretty much sticking to what *they* say about the ills of U.S. cities.

Happily, columnists frequently can write from positions of strength, basing their opinions on personal experience or insider knowledge.

Clarence Page, a black columnist syndicated by *The Chicago Tribune,* does this in a piece on racism. He sets up his readers with this intro:

> Racial discrimination has declined. African Americans are gaining power and prominence in areas of American life in which we could not even get a job 30 years ago. Has the time come for us to stop viewing ourselves as "outsiders"?
>
> The question stunned my audience, a well-tailored, intelligent-looking group of young black professionals— "buppies," in today's parlance—from up and down the East Coast. The weekend conference, convened by the regional chapter of the National Urban League, had asked me to speak on the future of black professionals at the dawn of a new century. I delivered, but the question I raised was more than some had bargained for.

Note in the above intro Page's use of "we" and "I"—clear signals to readers that his reporting is coming from the inside. Page continues that personalized approach in a passage that (to me, anyway) is irresistible:

> "I seriously question your premise that racial discrimination has declined," said a young lawyer in a dark blue pinstripe suit. "I don't think we've made progress. Discrimination has only become more subtle."
>
> He went on to describe how his law firm, a major one in the nation's capital, has only four black lawyers, who don't get enough respect from the rest.
>
> "If I was white, I'd probably be a partner by now," he said.
>
> "Shoot, if I was white, I'd probably be a publisher by now," I said.
>
> That broke the ice. Everyone, including the young lawyer, got a laugh.
>
> My point was that, no, discrimination has not disappeared and it probably never will. But four lawyers in his firm is a lot better than zero and, moreover, the overall trajectory of history is pushing ahead, despite occasional setbacks, toward more progress.
>
> "Who knows?" I said. "You're a young man. I have faith that you're going to be a partner yet." Either at his current firm or someplace else.
>
> But, first, you've got to have faith. ...

Page now quotes from a Yankelovich Partners Inc., survey on the economic status of blacks, quotes a black sociologist from Harvard and slides in Jesse Jackson's view. ("No one can save us for us, but us.")

Page returns to personalized writing with this two-graf "kicker":

> To take advantage of new opportunities, one must be optimistic about one's ability to succeed. Perhaps my optimism is a sign of my age. As one who struggled through college at the end of the 1960s, I marvel at how far African Americans have come in a short time. When opportunities opened up, my generation was happy to get a boarding pass. Today's younger generation is looking for an upgrade. Good for them.
>
> No matter how wide the doors to opportunity open, we black Americans are reluctant to think of ourselves as "insiders" in a system that has rejected us for so long. But if we're going to do any good for ourselves or our children, we had better start thinking about it.[9]

What makes Page's writing so authoritative? What signals his knowledge of his subject?

First, of course, Page makes clear throughout that he is a black writing about black affairs (just as you, if you're black, could write authoritatively about black affairs on your campus; just as you, whatever your race, could write authoritatively about campus politics, about students' music, about virtually any student-oriented subject).

Second, Page uses dialogue ("I said" ... "he said") to, in effect, tell readers, "I was there for you; I got the goods for you." *Never* neglect to inform readers of your on-site reporting; let them see what gave you first-hand, eyewitness understanding.

Third, Page does what all great reporters do: He quotes authoritative sources—Yankelovich, the Harvard sociologist, Jesse Jackson. A common failing among young columnists is thinking that everything they write must flow through their minds alone, through only their vocabularies. Yet, nothing strengthens writing and underscores its authoritativeness more than quoting qualified sources.

It doesn't take much to insert a ring of authority in column writing:

> "As Secretary (of State) Shultz remarked to me ... ," Thomas L. Friedman, two-time Pulitzer Prize winner of *The New York Times*.[10]

> "On recent trips to Europe, I heard ... ," Jim Hoagland, *The Washington Post*.[11]

> "I entered south Lebanon in the wake of an Israeli invasion ... ," Trudy Rubin, *The Philadelphia Inquirer*.[12]

> "In conversations this week with three former top Clinton administration officials ... ," Albert R. Hunt, *The Wall Street Journal*.[13]

"I checked in with Michigan Republican Congressman Pete Hoekstra... ," Walter Shapiro, *USA Today*.[14]

"McGann has finally agreed to have a drink with me ... ," Margaret Carlson, *Time* (on interviewing Eileen McGann, wife of presidential adviser Dick Morris.)[15]

And walk away from this one—if you can:

Midway through the White House Correspondents' Association dinner, a friend came up to the head table and asked President Clinton how he was doing.

"Better than I deserve," laughed the president, who is sitting atop a 20-point lead in the polls as he seeks the second term that once seemed as unlikely as snow in August.

Mr. Clinton's comment epitomized the generally jovial mood surrounding the annual affair, over which I presided as the association's outgoing president. ... [16]

—Carl Leubsdorf, *The Dallas Morning News*

Bottom line: The strongest columns are strongly reported *and* their writers let readers *see* the reporting out of which flows authoritative writing.

For example, here is Ralph De La Cruz, Long Beach (Calif.) *Press-Telegram* columnist, describing himself on the job:

Through the back window of the ambulance, by the light of intermittent red flashes, I can see a crowd is gathering fast.

People are ringed around a secured area, morbidly curious, a little scared. As our small group climbs out and scrambles roward the house, I can feel their eyes examining my clothes, my face, hoping to spot some clue about the condition of the young man on the ground.

But I'm not a paramedic. And they don't stare long because it's obvious I know less about what's going on than just about anybody there.

I'm a columnist with the *Press-Telegram* of Long Beach. A pair of paid eyes. I'm here to document the impact of a gunshot on one individual and several communities; the victim's family, friends, taxpayers, caregivers, police and firefighters.

It's a project called Path of a Bullet. ...[17]

Sharpen Your Cutting Edge Instincts

When news is in the wind readers, listeners and viewers lean into it, feeling for its meaning, trying to detect its importance to them and their lives.

Newspaper and magazine sales soar, sometimes dramatically; TV and radio station news ratings rise.

Experienced editors understand this cause-and-effect relationship and quickly turn their newspages and newscasts into the wind, to catch the full benefit of billowing public interest.

Smart columnists turn into the wind, too, and if you want your column—your byline—to attract and hold readers you also will need sharp instincts on precisely where the news story is, what it is and how strong is public interest in it.

An example of how the pros sniff the wind:

A British general election promises defeat for Conservatives and victory for Labour, led by Tony Blair. Because of the "special relationship" between the United States and Britain, news coverage is heavy in the American press. Columnists jump on the story.

Britain's election will be held on a Thursday. *On the preceding Sunday,* Jane R. Eisner, editor of *The Philadelphia Inquirer*'s editorial page, is in print with a signed column that opens with five grafs describing how Conservatives won power in 1979. Then, in her sixth graf, Eisner pegs the column to the election four days hence:

> Labour hasn't held the reins of power since.
>
> That may change on Thursday. If Labour holds onto its substantial lead in national elections and is back in power for the first time since Jimmy Carter was president. I offer a modest plea to the new prime minister ... [18]

Eisner, who was *The Inquirer*'s London correspondent from 1985 to 1987, then advises Labour against assuming centrist positions on political issues if it defeats John Major's conservatives. (Incidentally, note how nicely Eisner *characterizes* how long Labour has been out of power—"since Jimmy Carter was president." For American readers, that's an excellent historical yardstick.)

With the election duly held on Thursday, Jim Hoagland is in *The Washington Post* three days later, on Sunday:

> Elected on Thursday, Tony Blair took office at 10 Downing Street on Friday possessing one giant advantage over a newly elected American president. The British prime minister does not have time after his election to ponder what he intends to do with power and with whom he intends to do it.
>
> Like most leaders in Europe—only more so—the British prime minister has to arrive in office with an established agenda and already knowing his cabinet ministers and the roles he expects them to play. A 24-hour transition such as the one Blair and John Major have just accomplished does not permit the extended agonizing over personnel and policies that the American system encourages, complete with unpleasant surprises.[19]

Note Hoagland's angle: The immediacy of Tony Blair's challenge—what Blair must do now, today, tomorrow.

Now comes *Forbes* magazine, a biweekly whose columnists cannot write weeks later with Hoagland's emphasis on election results or Blair's challenge today. Rather, the *Forbes* writing pitch *must be ahead,* moving the story forward into broader meaning and laying down analysis that daily newspapers, television and radio haven't emphasized. *Forbes'* Steve H. Hanke does that this way:

> With the elections of Tony Blair in the U.K. and Lionel Jospin in France, the left controls the governments in 13 of the 15 countries in the European Union. Does this portend a new swing to the left in Europe? Not really. It simply reflects voter disillusion with the so-called right. Left or right, the European political elites embrace the welfare state and the European Monetary Union. The economic debate in Europe, to the extent that there is one, is limited to haggling over details. The voters simply chose a change of faces, not a real change in policy. ... [20]

For Hanke, the British election, held weeks earlier is only a *news peg*— a point of reader recognition—on which to hang discussion of a larger economic debate in Europe.

You can get even closer to the news and maximize your column's impact if you get in print in tandem, the same day, with an editorial or news story on the same subject. This requires more than simple instinct on what the story is; you also must closely coordinate with editors to learn what's being planned for newspages, editorial columns and op-ed pages.

For example, *The Atlanta Journal and Constitution* decides to turn over most of its Sunday op-ed page to Dexter Scott King, youngest son of the late Rev. Martin Luther King Jr. He writes how his family, through the King Center, has a right to copyright his father's books and speeches and profit from ownership of his "intellectual property."

It's a hot topic in Atlanta, where Martin Luther King Jr. is a hero to many and where debate is raging on the family's profit-oriented tactics. In a column printed *adjacent* to the King article, Cynthia Tucker, editor of the *Constitution*'s editorial page, lashes out:

> Since the Martin Luther King Jr. Center for Non-violent Social Change opened in 1980, it has proved steady at only one thing: providing jobs for members of the family of the slain civil rights leader. At various times, the center has provided employment for King's widow, Coretta Scott King, their second son, Dexter Scott King, and nephew Issac Farris.
>
> The family no longer needs the work. On Jan. 8, Time Warner Inc. announced a multimillion-dollar joint venture with the King estate: a deal to publish King's books, speeches and sermons in media both old and new ... the King estate should be worth between $30 million and $50 million within three to five years. ...
>
> Perhaps the family will now relinquish the King Center to less self-interested stewards. They have done little with it. The center has never lived up to its promise.
>
> Ostensibly founded to perpetuate King's legacy of nonviolent social transformation, the King Center ought to be the leading authority on conflict

resolution and the first-line resource for civic activists seeking to quell the violence that continues to decimate poor black neighborhoods across the country. It ought to be the spontaneous gathering place for citizens struggling with the violence unleashed on an Oklahoma federal office building in April 1995 or an Atlanta family planning clinic last Thursday. It is not.

Nor is there any guarantee that the bonanza from the Time Warner deal will be used to enhance the work of the cash-strapped, nonprofit King Center. While family members are given to glossing over the distinction between the King Center and the King estate—perhaps because they see the King Center as a family business—the money from this commercial venture will be theirs to use as they see fit. The handsome profits from this deal could end up purchasing more luxury cars and Armani suits. ...

Tucker now discusses the elder King's determination during his lifetime to avoid profiting from his civil rights activities. She suggests the King family turn over the King Center to a college or the National Park Service, which might "convert it into an impressive civil rights museum."

Tucker concludes with this kicker:

Or must the family profit from every scrap of King's legacy?[21]

Note these characteristics of the Tucker column:

- It ties directly, with same-day impact, to the op-ed piece that expresses the family's view. Readers get both sides of the controversy immediately, without journalism's usual delay of days (or weeks!) between point and counterpoint.
- Tucker doesn't simply criticize; she offers alternatives: convert the King Center to a civil rights museum. Make it a "gathering place" for Atlantans.
- Above all, Tucker writes with courage, hitting hard at tactics of a family well-established in the Atlanta social hierarchy and persons—by name—regarded by many as custodians of a revered memory.

Time similarly links point with counterpoint in side-by-side presentations on new technology. A news story discusses "smart-car technology" that promises automated driving and anticollision devices. In an adjacent "Viewpoint" column, J. Madeleine Nash opines that there is a downside to new technology. Her lead:

Imagine waking up one morning and discovering an ungainly metal tower, 150 ft. tall, looming above the trees in your front yard. No, such a contraption—a stout monopole topped with a crown of antennas—doesn't yet mar my leafy corner of suburb. But it will soon, unless I do something about it. ...[22]

Nash now describes how she and her neighbors are churning out a "torrent of letters, petitions and telephone calls" to stop construction of the tower, planned by a communication company.

Lesson: With down-home, front-yard realities, Nash's column counterbalances the news story's gushy promises about the benefits of future technology.

Use *your* column to bring larger issues down to your (and your fellow students') front yards. National debate rages on, say, tenure for college faculty? Discuss the impact on your campus. The national press covers the rising cost of college educations? Write for your student readers on costs at your college.

Even if you can't achieve side-by-side publication, your commentary can have great impact if you get into print quickly after a news story breaks. *And,* it helps to refresh reader memories on which news story sparked your analysis.

The New York Times does this after one of its reporters breaks a story on financial contributions to President Bill Clinton's legal defense fund. The *Times'* lead *editorial* opens this way:

> Facing an avalanche of new disclosures about White House fund-raising, Attorney General Janet Reno continues to maintain that there is no credible evidence of illegal behavior by senior officials that would require appointment of a special prosecutor. But Ms. Reno's narrow interpretation of the law cannot obscure the fact that someone in Washington—the Federal Elections Commission, the Justice Department or the appropriate committees in Congress—needs to get busy. For journalistic reports make it clear that President and Mrs. Clinton, the Administration and the Democratic National Committee were involved in a finance system that was running amok throughout 1996. Money was being harvested while benefits ranging from jobs on obscure Presidential commissions to nights in the Lincoln Bedroom were being handed out like candy. ...

In an op-ed piece on the same day, *Times* columnist William Safire pegs his writing to the original news story: "Now, thanks to Steve Labaton of *The New York Times,* we learn that ... "

Safire, a Nixonian conservative who counterbalances the *Times'* generally more liberal editorial stance, attacks in harsh language:

> Never in the history of the White House has so much influence been for sale for so much money to so many foreign connections.
>
> In olden times, we had some invitations to state dinners and places on the Kennedy Center board going to campaign contributors. But it took shameless Bill Clinton to put a $100,000-per-night price tag on sleeping in the Lincoln Bedroom. ... [23]

Safire's choice of language shows he regards his corner of the op-ed page as *his turf,* where he can say what he pleases, how he pleases. Safire's column refers to "the sinkhole of money-grubbing that the Executive Mansion became" and accuses the President of "the sale of access to the Oval Office." Safire points to "White House greed" and "cover-up."

The *Times'* one-two punch this day gives readers, in the editorial, a broader and more moderate outline of how fund-raising should be investigated and, in Safire's column, one political partisan's bitter view. That's effective commentary.

Linking your commentary to a news event helps readers put your analysis in an overall context; it shows them the connection between objective fact and your subjective opinion. And, this sometimes takes just a few words. Examples (emphasis added):

> Mexico dressed herself up for Bill Clinton *this week*. She put on a parade of cavalry and glinting swords and ornamental cannon; she hid her blemishes behind a thick layer of security goons, who kept poor people out of sight. Mr. Clinton, *on his first visit to Mexico* as president, responded gallantly ...
> —"Lexington," *The Economist*[24]

> In explaining his abrupt withdrawal *last week* as President Clinton's nominee for director of the Central Intelligence Agency, Anthony Lake issued a scorching lament about the loss of civility in Washington, saying that the place had gone "haywire" ...
> —Jane Mayer, *The New Yorker*[25]

> The unacknowledged but ever-present issue in our politics these days is standing. I don't mean standing to sue, which is the legal version. I mean standing to speak, or, more precisely, standing to be listened to—standing to be taken seriously on a subject. *I got to thinking about this not long ago while reading news reports* about an aging former KGB agent who was denouncing as unjust the death sentence imposed on Julius and Ethel Rosenberg for espionage nearly half a century ago. ...
> —Meg Greenfield, *Newsweek*[26]

> Jerusalem—Hours after a truce was declared Friday, quieting the guns that had rocked Lebanon and northern Israel for 17 days, two Israeli friends were still locked in a battle of their own on a West Jerusalem street corner. ...
> —Alan Sipress, Sunday *Philadelphia Inquirer*[27]

> Has someone kidnaped Newt Gingrich and put an impostor in his place? Many who witnessed his return from self-imposed exile at a dinner with Republican activists *last week* were left wondering where the real Gingrich had gone. ...
> —Arianna Huffington, *The Los Angeles Times*[28]

Caution: Yes, close to the news is where readers often are found, and linking your writing to a breaking story can pull some your way. But you have unique freedom in column writing. Use it sometimes to roam off the beaten path, away from the journalistic herd that too often stampedes in the same direction, in pursuit of the same story.

Polish Your Writing

Just as you are free to search for off-beat subjects for your column, so are you free to stretch for new, exciting ways to write it.

In column writing you're not restrained by tight bonds of objectivity that tie much newswriting into dense structures and dull language. Nor are you burdened by your publication's institutional position, which suffocates much editorial writing.

As noted by *The Chicago Tribune*'s Clarence Page early in this chapter, columns *can* be "quick, mischievous and unpredictable." Add to that, "And *should* be well-written."

Two reasons compel my addition:

First, to succeed, columns must differ from the writing in straight, dispassionate news coverage and the institutional opinion of editorials. The way you write—subjectively, colorfully—can be the leading reason why readers turn to your column after scanning the news stories and editorials.

Second, your writing, if lively and insightful, can help readers sort through the terribly complex, convoluted news of the day. Good writing invites readers in, then leads them by the hand; poor writing is virtually a "No Trespassing" sign hung atop your column.

| Box 6-4 | A Professional's Viewpoint |

Question: Would you call yourself a reporter or a columnist?

Answer: I'm both. I write informed editorials, pieces that have a point of view but are reported. I do the same thing any reporter would do. I call up the other side because I believe in fairness. But fairness is not the same thing as objectivity, and one of the reasons modern journalism is in disrepute with many people is that objectivity is not possible. Objectivity is like the unicorn; it's a marvelous creature, wonderful to behold, but not to be seen on this planet.

—John Fund, *The Wall Street Journal,* interviewed by *George* magazine.

Need for good writing is a message of this entire book, of course. But it requires special mention in three dimensions of hard-hitting commentary:

- In leads, which must be specially crafted to catch readers racing through newspapers or magazines (in about 26 minutes on average for the former, a bit longer for the latter).
- In "juice" or "jolting" paragraphs inserted lower in your column to maintain reader momentum by feeding in a cute turn of phrase or a tantalizing tidbit of information.
- Or, all cute phraseology aside, simply to settle down and do a straight, professional job of writing, in simple language, a column that flows easily toward reader understanding of a complex subject. Doing that and doing it well is an art in itself.

Leads That Catch Readers

Mortimer B. Zuckerman, editor in chief and owner of *U.S. News & World Report,* catches me with this lead on his regular column:

> The international community's two most famous political alcoholics, the Israelis and the Palestinians, have fallen off the wagon again, drunk on a cocktail of suspicion and resentment. ... [29]

Want to read more about the independent counsel's investigation of President Clinton? No? Okay, but can you resist the following?

> In every poker game there's a moment when money's on the table, cards are dealt and you have to show your hand. For Kenneth Starr, the Whitewater independent counsel, the moment is here: Put up or shut up. Starr has spent $22 million and 22 months. If he has the goods on the first couple or on White House confederates, it's time to hammer out indictments. Or to make a final report to the three-judge panel that appointed him. Time for closure. ...
>
> —Sandy Grady, *The Philadelphia Daily News*[30]

And, walk away—if you can—from Tom Teepen, national columnist for Cox Newspapers:

> Alabama's politicians have found God again, and they are shaking him down for all he's worth. They do that every few years.
>   This time the issue is a federal court ruling that Etowah County Court Judge Roy Moore must remove a Ten Commandments plaque from his courtroom. It violates church-state separation.[31]

James J. Kilpatrick, Universal Press Syndicate columnist, catches readers with this type of writing:

> Jacqueline Montanez was 15 years old on the night she murdered Hector Reyes. That was four years ago this month. Now her case is pending before the U.S. Supreme Court on a petition for review.[32]

Michael Gartner shows, in his regular *USA Today* column, why he won a Pulitzer Prize for editorial writing in the small-town *Ames* (Iowa) *Tribune:*

> Ames, Iowa—Here are facts to think about as you play with your toddlers before they go to bed tonight:
> There are five countries in this world where 1 of every 4 children dies before reaching age 5, another dozen or so where 1 in 5 dies, and nearly 50 nations where 1 of every 10 children dies before his fifth birthday. (In the United States, it's one in 100). ... [33]

Steve Forbes uses his *Forbes* column to put in perspective a battle between man and machine:

> The loss by world chess champion Garry Kasparov to Deep Blue, the IBM computer, is about as significant as an Olympic gold medalist's losing a weight-lifting content to a crane or a forklift.
> Computers are becoming ever more helpful tools for managing businesses and improving the quality of our lives. But they are no more capable of colluding on their own and taking over the world than are, say, Labrador retrievers. [34]

And, don't you find the following leads irresistible?

> You probably didn't notice, because it involves such a small amount, but the Pentagon and the congressional Republican leadership are pushing to add $15 billion to the budget for military weapons.
> —Robert Scheer, *Los Angeles Times*[35]

> Washington—Twenty-nine weeks out, Sen. Christopher Dodd of Connecticut is a happy man. In fact, if euphoria were a crime, the chairman of the Democratic Party would be in chains.
> —Mary McGrory, syndicated columnist[36]

> Betty Crocker—America's most-beloved baker—has been recoiffured, tanned, face-lifted, nipped, tucked, liposuctioned and outfitted in new clothes for her 75th birthday.
> —Bill Maxwell, *The Sunday Oregonian*[37]

> The reward for information leading to an arrest and conviction in this month's gruesome on-campus bludgeon murders of a University of Miami football player and his date is $10,000.
> The reward for information leading to an arrest and conviction of whoever is responsible for the bludgeon and torch murders of four homeless per-

sons in Miami over a short period is $11,000.

And the reward for information leading to an arrest and conviction of the person who tortured, hanged and burned a pet dog in Miami last week is beyond $12,000—and growing.

Something doesn't make sense.

—Howard Kleinberg, Cox News Service[38]

| Box 6-5 | A Professional's Viewpoint |

Tom Teepen, national correspondent for Cox Newspapers, is an acknowledged wordsmith who clearly has fun writing his column. Even readers who hate his message love his style!

Some thoughts about writing columns of the opining sort, in no order at all:

Be fair but don't use fairness as an excuse to shun vigor or conviction. Remember, you are being fair to someone who is dead wrong.

If you find yourself writing, "On the other hand ... ," quit the business. Or at least go out for a drink. Even-handedness works better with self-abuse than with column-writing, to whatever degree there's a difference.

Don't pretend astonishment at the self-evident—you'll look the fool to anyone with common sense—but don't altogether neglect the obvious. You'd be surprised how many need to have it called to their attention.

Foremost, what you owe your readers is your absolute intellectual honesty. Don't play games you think will get you poll points. And whatever your political lean, don't be afraid sometimes to push against it. If you just play to the claque, soon that's all you'll be playing to.

If you have nothing to offer except your endorsement of the conventional, you have nothing to offer.

Honor the old saw: Say what you mean and mean what you say. (OK, and don't banish cliches; just avoid them.)

Taking your work seriously doesn't mean taking yourself seriously. Propound by all means, persuade if you can, preen if you will but, for God's sake, don't pontificate.

Respect English but have fun with it, too. Your affair with the language is a life-long fling. Enjoy it. Your writing should entertain even the readers who hate its message. If you aren't having fun writing, readers won't have fun reading what you have written. Don't shrink from the off-beat word if it would be telling or just delightful.

It helps to know what you're writing about, but hide the research in the prose.

And read all other columnists. They need the love.

"Juicing" Your Writing Along the Way

Face it: Hard-news columnists frequently must write about stuff that's dull and heavy—but very important.

Your challenge is to write that dull stuff in a lively manner, *not to inflate the message beyond its intrinsic value but to communicate its true importance.* And even if you capture readers with a lively lead, you'll lose them—fail to communicate—if later in your column your writing slows or stumbles into dense thickets of meaningless verbiage.

Thomas L. Friedman of *The New York Times,* half way through a column on Hong Kong, brightens things considerably with this:

> In other words, Hong Kong's return to China is not just a slice of the West being given back to the East, it is a slice of the future being given back to the past.[39]

I am having difficulty understanding Paul A. Gigot's explanation, in his *Wall Street Journal* column, of why two heavyweight politicians were added to the senior White House staff. Then Gigot gives me this:

> Both recruits are better at cutting up opponents than at cutting deals. They're black belts in the Clintonian black art of offensive defense.[40]

Frankly, I once swore I'd never read another column on the technological revolution. Then, Robert Landauer gives me this in the Portland *Sunday Oregonian*:

> Smell the future: the technological revolution. You can sense it—like sailors who feel land long before they see it.[41]

Molly Ivins of the *Fort Worth Star-Telegram,* syndicated in many papers nationwide, sometimes stuffs her column smack in a reader's eye, and I read her entire column waiting for it. This, deep in a column on uneven administration of the death penalty in Texas:

> ... A retarded, mentally disturbed guy who was living across the street from a convent in Amarillo raped and killed an elderly nun. Can't get worse than that. But this sorry citizen barely had the IQ of a Labrador retriever. Did he realize what he had done? We're not even sure he knew his own name. The fellow nuns of the murder victim asked that the man not be put to death; the pope asked that this perp not be put to death. But we put him to death anyway. ...
>
> Want some more? In this state, we fry 'em even if they're not all there, mentally speaking. For years, the state used a famous "expert witness" who invariably testified that the perp was of sound mind and fully understood his actions, even if the guy was running around in circles on all fours barking. ...
>
> We are especially apt to fry 'em if a black perp offs a white victim—and if you even blink at that, you're too ignorant to be in this discussion. ... [42]

George F. Will shows how even a single word can juice a sentence (emphasis added):

> John Silber, the *sandpapery* president of Boston University, might have been governor of Massachusetts—he was the Democratic nominee in 1990—were he not given to speaking his formidable mind as bluntly as he did when ... [43]

You also can put sparkle in a column with *judicious* insertion of a little personal background, as Cynthia Tucker does in her *Atlanta Journal and Constitution* column on debate over Confederate symbolism in Georgia's state flag:

> As a Southerner who traces her lineage to slave and slave owner alike, I want the entire story of the South told.[44]

Katharine Q. Seelye of *The New York Times* inserts herself in a piece about Bob Dole losing his bid for the White House. Note how she adds to a reader's understanding of the man and the moment. She writes of Dole's complaints about *Times* coverage of his candidacy. Then this:

> So, on Monday, no one was more surprised than I when, somewhere between Houston and Lafayette, La., word filtered to the back of the plane that the Senator wanted to see me.
>
> I walked up the aisle, reporters on both sides clearing a path, and saw Mr. Dole waiting. When I was about five feet away, I asked, "Is it safe for me to come up there?"
>
> He smiled and stretched out his hand. When I reached his side, he put his arm around me and said, "Don't believe everything I say."
>
> It was at once tender and cynical and revealing. By then he clearly knew the race was over, and I think part of him was relieved. Now he could be the kind of person he wanted to be and the kind of person many reporters had known him to be. ... [45]

Note above how *The Times'* Seelye demonstrates a tender touch at the keyboard. Juicing your writing with cheap shots at politicians is easy—and can create a misleading impression of *all* public officials.

Like Seelye, *The Washington Post's* Broder can be tender and balanced, as well as tough. In 1997, Broder received the National Society of Newspaper Columnists' Lifetime Achievement Award, and spoke of a columnist's responsibility to differentiate for readers the good and bad among politicians:

> There's so much distrust and contempt out there for politics and politicians. We have to help people make distinctions between the crooks and charlatans and the people doing their jobs.[46]

Sometimes: Avoid the Cute Stuff

Sometimes, a columnist's subject is simply so dreadful that cute writing is inappropriate. That was Dan Lynch's obvious opinion as he wrote his column in *The Albany* (N.Y.) *Times Union* about a local bombing and subsequent tension between police and reporters:

> Reporters tend to be suspicious and nosy. That's the way we are.
>
> Cops tend to be suspicious and secretive. That's the way they are.
>
> Sometimes, when we deal with one another, this slight but significant difference in perspective can present a huge problem. Take, for instance, this crazy bombing case in Clifton Park last Christmas Eve.
>
> [Jim and Mary Smith] had returned to home to find a package addressed to them in their mailbox. When their 10-year-old daughter, [Jane], opened the thing on the kitchen table, it blew up. ... [47]

Note above the open, straight-forward approach taken by the *Times Union*'s columnist. No fancy footwork is needed; the story tells itself.

In his *Boston Globe* column, Jeff Jacoby, laboring through a complex story about housing law, uses typographical devices—paragraphing and a colon—to set off and thus emphasize an important point:

> There is much to be said about City Hall's latest assault on the people who supply housing for Boston tenants, but the most important observation is this:
>
> It's illegal.[48]

Still, a clever turn of phrase can make a serious point in a column on serious matters. Here is Maureen Dowd of *The New York Times* on a reported attempt by Republicans to oust their own party's House speaker (and note how she uses a movie scene to draw a word picture for readers):

> Newt Gingrich's bumbling lieutenants Dick Armey and Tom DeLay, who helped foment the coup but now say they were just gathering intelligence so they could foil the plot, were hilariously reminiscent of the scene in "Blazing Saddles" where the sheriff holds a gun to his own head and takes himself hostage.[49]

So much for cute and clever writing designed to communicate serious information. Let's look, in Chapter Seven, at writing ***designed to be clever for clever's sake***—to entertain and amuse, as much as inform.

Summary

- Column writing is one of the most coveted jobs in print journalism and competition to become a columnist is fierce in newsrooms.
- However, more column-writing jobs are opening because editors increasingly use columnists to analyze hard-news stories that require interpretation.
- Successful columnists achieve special intimacy with readers that's achieved by no other offering in most newspapers and magazines.

- The best columnists have strong basic reporting skills developed in years of intensive hard-news reporting.
- Intimate knowledge of their subject is a characteristic of successful columnists.
- Columnists dealing with the important stories of our day must have knowledgeable and authoritative sources who yield "insider" perspectives.
- To attract and hold readers, columnists must have strong cutting-edge instincts—a firm grasp of precisely where the news is in a developing story and how to advance the story into virgin territory.
- Successful columnists write well, developing workmanlike styles that translate complex matters into terms easily understood by readers, or creating dazzling keyboard artistry that yields fluid and beautiful prose.
- Columnists have a big advantage over editorial writers: They can humanize their writing by using personal anecdotes to lure readers into serious subjects they otherwise might avoid.
- Insert an authoritative ring in your writing by, for example, quoting expert sources, just as you would in writing hard news.
- Writing on a hot topic in the news can strengthen your appeal to readers, but sometimes use your freedom as a columnist to roam elsewhere in search of off-beat stories.
- Seek ways to "juice" or enliven your writing, but only to communicate the true importance of your message, never to inflate the message beyond its intrinsic value.

Recommended Reading

Aspiring columnists must develop ability to locate and "work" authoritative sources—to go behind the front-page story for deeper meaning and significance. These books will show you four of the greatest hard-news columnists of our time at work: David Broder, *Behind the Front Page* (New York: Simon & Schuster, 1987); James (Scotty) Reston, *Sketches in the Sand* (New York: Alfred A. Knopf, 1967); Arthur Krock, *Memoirs: Sixty Years on the Firing Line* (New York: Funk & Wagnalls, 1968); C.L. Sulzberger, *A Long Row of Candles* (New York: The Macmillan Company, 1969).

Notes

1. Clarence Page, "Sassy Pages Add Spice to Bland Paper," *The Masthead,* Winter 1995, p. 5; Prof. H. George Hahn, "A Field Guide to The Op-Ed War Zone," *The Masthead,* Winter, 1996, p. 11.

2. Sue Ryon, "Fan Mail From Hell," *The Masthead,* Winter 1993, p. 5.

3. Column for April 29, 1997, published that day in "Elections English Style," *The Atlanta Constitution,* p. A-7.

4. Column for Jan. 7, 1997, published that day in "Policy-Makers in Print," *The Atlanta Constitution,* p. A-7.

5. William Safire, "Notes on Ethics and Duty," *The Atlanta Constitution*, Jan. 7, 1997, p. A-7.

6. David Broder, "Crossing the Boundaries," *The Chicago Tribune*, June 26, 1996, p. 15.

7. William Safire, "Politics in Israel," *The New York Times*, June 22, 1997, p. 15.

8. Eileen McNamara, "The Reporter Turns Columnist," *Nieman Reports*, Summer 1996, p. 91.

9. Clarence Page, "Why Do Blacks Who Have Made It Feel Shortchanged?", *The Los Angeles Times*, April, 25, 1996, p. B-9.

10. Thomas L. Friedman, "Gardening with Beijing," *The New York Times*, national edition, April 17, 1996, p. A-15.

11. Jim Hoagland, "The Euro Challenge," *The Washington Post*, May 1, 1997, p. A-23.

12. Trudy Rubin, "Israelis Should Aim Their Ire at Syria," *The Philadelphia Inquirer*, May 1, 1996, p. A-19.

13. Albert R. Hunt, "For Clinton, Trust Issue Is a Time Bomb," *The Wall Street Journal*, June 27, 1996, p. A-17.

14. Walter Shapiro, "Art With a Dab of Politics: This Is Not a Pretty Picture," *USA Today*, June 20, 1997, p. 4-A.

15. Margaret Carlson, "Public Eye," *Time*, Jan. 27, 1997, p. 36.

16. Carl P. Leubsdorf, "Polls, Not Treatment, Bolster Clinton," *The Dallas Morning News*, May 9, 1996, p. 31-A.

17. Ralph De La Cruz, "Press-Telegram Tracks Bullet's Tragic Impact," *Knight Ridder News*, Spring 1997, p. 10.

18. Jane R. Eisner, "Picking Up America's Bad Habits," *The Philadelphia Inquirer*, April 27, 1997, p. E-7.

19. Jim Hoagland, " ... And the Transition," *The Washington Post*, May 4, 1997, p. C-7.

20. Steve H. Hanke, "Right Wing, Left Wing: What's the Difference?", *Forbes*, July 7, 1997, p. 52.

21. Dexter Scott King, "Guarding the Estate," and Cynthia Tucker, "A Leading Role for King Center," both in *The Atlanta Journal and Constitution*, Jan. 19, 1997, p. R-5.

22. J. Madeleine Nash, "Viewpoint," *Time*, Nov. 4, 1996, p. 78.

23. The editorial was, "Clinton Money Mysteries, Again," and Safire's column was, "Clinton's Dirty Money," both in *The New York Times*, national edition, Dec. 9, 1996, p. A-29.

24. Lexington, "Excelentisimo Clinton," *The Economist*, May 10, 1997, p. 30.

25. Jane Mayer, "Tony Lake Is Missing," *The New Yorker*, March 31, 1997, p. 33.

26. Meg Greenfield, "The Last Word," *Newsweek*, April 21, 1997, p. 86.

27. Alan Sipress, "Cease-Fire in Lebanon Fans Peace Hopes Anew," *The Philadelphia Inquirer*, April 28, 1996, p. D-1.

28. Arianna Huffington, "Column Right," *The Los Angeles Times*, April 28, 1996, p. M-5.

29. Mortimer B. Zuckerman, "Sobering Up in the Middle East," *U.S. News & World Report*, Oct. 21, 1996, p. 100.

30. Sandy Grady, "Know When to Fold," *The Philadelphia Daily News,* May 15, 1997, p. A-19.

31. Tom Teepen, "The Latest Christian Soldier," *The Atlanta Constitution and Journal,* April 20, 1997, p. R-3.

32. James J. Kilpatrick, "How and Why Did Child Go So Wrong?", *The Greenville* (S.C.) *News,* May 12, 1996, p. 3-F.

33. Michael Gartner, "The World Again Is Killing Its Young," *USA Today,* May 7, 1996, p. 11-A.

34. Steve Forbes, "So What?", *Forbes,* June 2, 1997, p. 28.

35. Robert Scheer, "Column Left," *The Los Angeles Times,* April 23, 1996, p. B-7.

36. Mary McGrory, "Democrats See Smooth Sailing Past Whitewater," *The Boston Globe,* April 20, 1996, p. 15.

37. Bill Maxwell, "Betty Crocker Whips Up Some Ethnic Health Food," The Portland *Sunday Oregonian,* April 7, 1996, p. F-5.

38. Howard Kleinberg, "Big Reward for Dog Doesn't Make Sense in Human Terms," Cox News Service, April 26, 1996, p. A-9.

39. Thomas L. Friedman, "What the Goose Eats," *The New York Times,* Dec. 15, 1996, p. 13.

40. Paul A. Gigot, "New Clinton Recruits Know How to Smite," *The Wall Street Journal,* June 30, 1997, p. A-18.

41. Robert Landauer, "Technology Rules the Classrooms," The Portland *Sunday Oregonian,* April 7, 1996, p. F-3.

42. Molly Ivins, "Executive Weakened by Overkill," *The Atlanta Constitution,* June 11, 1997, A-13.

43. George F. Will, "Column Right," *The Los Angeles Times,* May 2, 1996, p. B-9.

44. Cynthia Tucker, "Fly an Inclusive Flag, and See Who'll Salute," *The Atlanta Journal and Constitution,* Feb. 16, 1997, p. R-5.

45. Katharine Q. Seelye, "The Nation," *The New York Times,* national edition, Nov. 10, 1996, p. 14-E.

46. David Astor, "David Broder Gets a Lifetime Award," *Editor & Publisher,* July 5, 1997, p. 32.

47. Dan Lynch, "Bomb Case Secrecy Adds to Suspicions," *The Albany (N.Y.) Times Union,* June 29, 1997, p. D-1.

48. Jeff Jacoby, "New Tortures for Landlords," *The Boston Globe,* May 2, 1996, p. 17.

49. Maureen Dowd, "The Ides of July," *The New York Times,* July 19, 1997, p. 19.

Exercises

1. Study the top hard-news story that broke on your campus for *today*'s newspaper (or another story designated by your instructor). In about 500 words, write a signed column on that story for *tomorrow*'s paper.

Stick close to the news in this assignment, but consult sources not mentioned in the hard-news treatment of the story. And be sure to give your readers "added value" reporting.

2. In this assignment you must plan a *magazine* column on the hard-news story covered in Exercise 6-1. Your magazine story will be published two weeks from today.

In about 350 words, explain how you will carry the hard-news story forward, using the intervening two weeks to develop new sources, new angles.

Remember: You cannot stick close to the news in this column; rather, you'll have to plan how to broaden the subject to create a column that will "stand," or being journalistically valid, two weeks hence.

3. Study a single column by your favorite hard-news columnist (or one designated by your instructor) and, in about 300 words, address these questions: Does the column demonstrate the writer has strong reporting skills? Does the author obviously have intimate knowledge of the subject matter? Are authoritative sources quoted? Is the column on the cutting edge of news and reader interest? Is the writing strong or weak?

If you are critical of the column or author be certain to suggest alternative reporting or writing styles that should have been used.

4. Study George Melloan's "Global View" weekly column in *The Wall Street Journal* and, in about 300 words, discuss whether it meets the reporting and writing standards he lays down for column writing in his "Professional's Viewpoint" contribution to Chapter Six.

Does Melloan practice what he preaches? Is his column "independently researched," as he says any good column must be? Does it demonstrate analytical ability and "some talent for stringing words together"?

5. In about 400 words, discuss the quarrel between columnists David Broder of *The Washington Post* and William Safire of *The New York Times* over the reporting background a columnist should have.

Is Broder correct in saying, as he does in Chapter Six, that columnists must come up the hard-news reporting ladder, working their way through newsroom jobs to qualify for a column?

Or, is there merit in Safire's position that valuable "cross pollination" can result if political operative moves directly into opinion writing and carry with them the insider knowledge they gained in politics?

Do *you* trust columnists, such as Safire, who write from such partisan viewpoints? Do you think Safire, who was a speechwriter for President Nixon and other Republicans, can be balanced in writing about President Clinton, a Democrat?

7 Amusing, Entertaining or Making 'em Cry

BY READING this far in this book you've worked through heavy stuff: social responsibilities in opinion writing, deep-dig reporting, commentary that hits hard.

Now, let's kick back a bit and have some fun discussing columnists whose missions are to amuse and entertain readers or, on occasion, pull a tear or two from them.

You and I deserve a break, don't you think? And, that thinking—that readers need a break—is precisely why editors value highly those columnists who can throw a smile or two into the daily front-page news mix of war, flood and famine.

Even the sober *The New York Times*, a great newspaper but nobody's choice for laugh-a-day journalism, has a fine humor columnist, Russell Baker (described by columnist James Brady of *Advertising Age* as "the one and only columnist of *The New York Times* officially permitted to be funny").[1]

So, let's treat this chapter as light-hearted conversation, a brief interruption in our serious mission of preparing serious students for serious column writing.

Readers flock to light-hearted columns. Readership research always accords high rankings to columnists such as Baker, Dave Barry, Art Buchwald, Tony Kornheiser, Ellen Goodman. Before dying in 1997, Mike Royko was worth thousands of subscriptions for *The Chicago Sun-Times*, then *The Chicago Tribune*—and for more than 600 newspapers around the world that printed his syndicated column.

When Herb Caen wrote in his column for the *San Francisco*

Chronicle that he had inoperable lung cancer, 5,000 letters arrived at the newspaper; 75,000 people turned out for Herb Caen Day, honoring the man whose column was better read than the *Chronicle*'s front page.

And here is what a reader wrote *U.S. News & World Report* about its beautifully wry and sarcastic columnist, John Leo: "His essays alone are worth more than your subscription price."[2]

So, there's a serious side to this business of writing funny.

Now, Be Serious for a Minute

One dismal pre-dawn, long after both of us should have been home abed, I encountered Hal Boyle, the most famous humorist to ever write for The Associated Press, at the Overseas Press Club in New York City.

"Hal," I exclaimed, "what are you doing up and around at this hour?"

"Looking for an idea," he mumbled, "looking for an idea."[3]

In those days, Boyle was writing a daily humor column for AP's afternoon papers and, his deadline just hours ahead, he wandered off through the streets of Manhattan, searching for an idea for that day's column.

Writing funny might look easy, but it isn't.

By his 25th anniversary with AP, Boyle had written more than 6,000 columns that appeared in over 800 newspapers across America, and he had suffered daily torture meeting each deadline. (For a book of his columns, Boyle chose the title, *Help, Help! Another Day!*)[4]

Saul Pett, an AP colleague who, like Boyle, won a Pulitzer Prize for essays, describes the columnist at work:

Awake or asleep, Harold Vincent Boyle spends 22 hours a day thinking, worrying about his column and two hours actually writing it. Boyle at the typewriter is a study in terror. It is the time, he says, when "you just take a cold chisel, put it to your head, and start quarrying."

Boyle at the typewriter, with 60 or 90 minutes to go, is taut, silent, stiff, intense, measuring each word carefully for content and sound, writing, X-ing out, rephrasing, sweating out the sentences through a jungle of alternatives, bringing them finally out into the light in shining simplicity.

He can't work without chewing murderously on his cigar, stopping compulsively to comb his hair or taking a deep breath like a pitcher nervously eyeing the batter and that small strike zone. Boyle never forgets how small that strike zone is.

This is the Boyle who sees nothing, hears nothing, hasn't a friend in the world, is a child alone in a dark forest. This is where all retreat, all delay, all distractions must end. This is the wall, and Boyle writes every morning with his back to it.[5]

Boyle isn't the only columnist ever worn down by the daily need to be entertaining.

Howard Kurtz of *The Washington Post* recalls interviewing Mike Royko after that Pulitzer Prize winner had been a columnist for three decades:

> ... his last years were rough. ... He had been writing a column since 1963, and he was clearly tired of it. He said he kept going to support his two small children with his second wife.[6]

And, read James Thurber describing the tortures Harold Ross went through as founding editor and publisher of the light-hearted, wry, amusing, entertaining *The New Yorker*:

> From the first day I met him till the last time I saw him, Ross was like a sleepless, apprehensive sea captain pacing the bridge, expecting any minute to run aground, collide with something nameless in a sudden fog, or find his vessel abandoned and adrift.[7]

Now, if you *still* are serious about writing funny stuff, let's look at a couple clues on how to start.

Box 7-1	Professional Viewpoints

Beyond the conviction that humor provides not the slightest comfort to the man on the gallows, I cling to no thoughts on the subject worth writing down.

Columnist Russell Baker of *The New York Times* when asked to comment on the role of humor on editorial pages. Letter to Sue Rayon in response to her request for a piece for *Masthead*; see, "Humor on The Editorial Page," *The Masthead*, Summer 1991, p. 5.

Think of satire as another tool in the toolbox, a versatile tool. Editorial writers are pretty much limited (or think they are, which amounts to the same thing) to one voice: the voice of consensusized, conglomerated reason and responsibility. With satire, editors have a choice of voices, because satirists can choose: What's the best way to tell this story? A fable? A verse? A bit of dialog? A memo that smells almost real? One-liners stretching to the horizon?

Syndicated columnist Rick Horowitz, "Call Me Irresponsible," *The Masthead*, Summer 1991, p. 8.

Few subjects resist rational discussion so persistently as humor does. You can't analyze humor because, like beauty, there's no standard of measurement. No one can say what's beautiful. We know it when we see it, but we

can't put our finger on what causes us to think so. Same with funny. ... You can't ask someone to write funny Monday, Wednesday and Friday. At its best, humor is a by-product. It comes up in the course of something serious. Almost every time someone sets out, deliberately, to write something funny, the effort falls flat. There are only three or four writers in America who can be funny with any regularity, and the best of them fail half the time.

—Andy Rooney, syndicated columnist and CBS humorist, "Editorial Pages Are Better Off Without Humor," *The Masthead*, Summer 1991, p. 9.

Stay Close to the News

As I write this, U.S. scientists have put an unmanned exploratory vehicle on Mars. The amazing feat dominates front pages and evening newscasts. Everybody's talking about it.

In New York City, where some very witty people labor for the tabloids, *The New York Post* and *The New York Daily News*, the moment is not lost.

"Earth Invades Mars!"
"Earthlings to Martians: Give Up!"
"Earth to Mars: Anybody There?"

Those are some of the lines being thrown around, and their broad slapstick humor is just right for the occasion *because the timing is right.*

Meanwhile, if past performance is any measure, aspiring humor columnists at college newspapers across America are ignoring the Mars probe and everything else on the front pages or in the public consciousness. Instead, they're laboring to write funny about something narrowly introspective, something dragged from their own tight little closet of private memories, something so intensely personal that readers, who are on another wavelength, in another world, are left bewildered.

Big mistake.

With Mars all over front pages, a column pegged to "Earth Invades Mars!" needs no elaborate explanation, no 200 words of background to bring readers up to speed. A college humorist, trying to be funny with a distant and intensely personal childhood memory, can't build on such reader understanding.

Take a tip from Will Rogers, one of the first syndicated humorists. He said that when he couldn't think of anything funny to write about he'd just pick up a newspaper and see what Congress was doing that day.

Art Buchwald, syndicated internationally by the Los Angeles Times Syndicate, is a master at hitching his good humor wagon to the news. Here is how he opens a column and sets up readers with a "news" intro:

A federal judge in Greensboro, N.C., ruled that the Food and Drug Administration can regulate tobacco products but cannot have any control over advertising and promotion of the product.

It is an interesting decision, since cigarettes are now considered a dangerous drug, but the producers can advertise and promote it so more people will use it.

Now, with just 56 words devoted to the set up, the *real* Buchwald is off and running:

As soon as the decision was announced, the advertising agencies went into full throttle.

Allen, Allen & Zagreb, who have the Choke Cigarette account, brought ideas for a new campaign into the Choke offices. ...

It's a great spoof on ad agencies, tobacco, the whole crazy idea of advertising a product which, doctors say, will kill you if used as directed. At one point, Buchwald has adman Mike Zagreb pitching a campaign to his colleagues:

Zagreb holds up another poster. "In this one, a little boy is saying, 'The reason I smoke Chokes is that theirs is the only cigarette pack displaying a picture of a Foreign Legionnaire kissing a Camel on the lips.' "

Buchwald kicks around such delightful ideas for a couple hundred words, then exits with a kicker tied to another event in the news at the time—President Clinton (who said he once tried marijuana but didn't inhale) injures a knee falling on a staircase:

One executive said, "Let's hit this thing head-on. Why don't we have a death's-head on the package with a President Clinton look-alike in the ad saying, 'The reason I fell down those steps is that I smoked a Choke cigarette—it wouldn't have happened if I had inhaled.' "[8]

The front page of *The Washington Post*'s news section reports the tobacco advertising dispute, and—bang—the next day, Buchwald nails 'em in his column.

Leaf through Buchwald's many book collections of his columns and you'll see how quickly he jumps on a news angle. For example, look at Buchwald's *Lighten Up, George* (New York: G.P. Putnam's Sons, 1991):

- Congressional hearings are held on gun control, and Buchwald is on it. ("I sought guidance from Milton Hammer, a pistol aficionado who once told me at a picnic, 'I may not agree with what you say, but I will shoot to death anyone who tries to stop you from saying it.' ")
- A U.S. Supreme Court ruling on abortion doesn't settle the question of when life begins, and Buchwald zeros in. (" 'If men didn't make love, the justices wouldn't have to decide when life begins,' a nice lady snarled. An-

other woman added, 'Everybody knows that life begins when the guy says, 'How about it?' and the girl says, 'Okay.' ")

- It's revealed that television news shows simulate news events, and Buchwald pounces. ("TV news is getting more exciting than ever. The reason is that there has been a breakthrough. It is now possible to simulate a news story that is as good as or even better than the real thing.")[9]

Well, you get the point: Buchwald goes for humor in the "big story" that people are talking about across the kitchen table (and he sometimes uses across-the-table informality, opening with, "It was in all the papers ...").

Sometimes, though, you can have special impact by heading *away* from the "big story."

Play Counterpoint: Think Small

Ever read the front pages or watch the evening news shows and think, "They're all obsessed with the same story"?

Lots of readers and viewers think that, and you can gather in many of them by ignoring the big story and, instead, heading for the small things in life—the little irritations, little pleasures, the stuff that's actually nonessential but, nevertheless, on the minds of many people.

Like terrible airline food, for example.

That set off Andy Rooney, a CBS humorist for "60 Minutes" and a syndicated columnist. At a time when front pages—and editorial pages and op-ed pages and, it seems, all columnists—were obsessed with Whitewater investigations of the White House ("Whitewatergate"), Rooney got very sore about airline food. And, he wrote about it (*The Atlanta Constitution* played his column under the headline, "Not Quite Cookiegate"):

Last week, I flew to Cincinnati from New York on an early-morning Delta flight. Delta has fallen on hard times and you can see it in the pennies they pinch. "Breakfast" on the flight consisted of coffee and one plastic-wrapped biscuit two-thirds the length of a stick of gum and about twice the thickness of one. The label said it weighed three-sixteenths of an ounce. You know how heavy an ounce is? This was less than a quarter of that. Not a hearty breakfast. Delta was not serving up scrambled eggs, toast and bacon, or even pancakes and sausage with maple syrup.

By now, this nationally syndicated column has caught me, for I, too, am a victim of many such airline "meals," as are thousands, maybe millions of readers. Then—and get this, it's hilarious—Rooney writes about getting on the telephone and tracking down the company that makes the biscuit!

First, he finds out the damned thing, advertised on its wrapper as "all natural," is made in part from "partially hydrogenated vegetable oil." He wonders about that.

Second, Rooney learns he can buy a box of 200 for $9.90, and he calculates Delta spent "a little less than a nickel each" for biscuits served as "breakfast" to hungry travelers out of Cincinnati that morning.[10]

You know, it's strange: That column on the cheapskate breakfast fed to Rooney sticks in my mind; I remember nothing else that was in the paper that day.

Front pages and his own magazine are consumed by Bosnia, Africa, White House politics—and John Leo of *U.S. News & World Report* heads in another direction:

> Women all over America are paying $5.99 for a very thin paperback telling them they can attract the mate of their dreams by being elusive and reticent. The book (note the stern title, the semi-ironic subtitle) is *The Rules: Time-tested Secrets for Capturing the Heart of Mr. Right.*
>
> There are 35 rules, but the general idea is to hang back and play hard to get. Let the male take the lead and carry the conversation. Be honest but mysterious—men like a challenge. Don't return all his calls, and never stay on the phone with him longer than 10 minutes. Always be the one who ends a date or a phone call. Don't date too much too early in the relationship, don't split the check or pick it up yourself, never accept a Saturday date if he asks later than Wednesday. Break off the relationship immediately if no gift arrives on your birthday or Valentine's Day.

Leo notes *Rules* "received the ultimate accolade in our Oprahfied culture: an appearance by the authors on Oprah's show." Well, that certainly was intriguing so, "I walked over to B. Dalton's on Fifth Avenue the other day and purchased 14 self-help books, about one-tenth of 1 percent of the store's vast collection of books on self-improvement and the inner me."

On rambles Leo, quoting hilarious guidance *Rules* gives women on how to catch a man. Leo doesn't need to pump life into this one; he simply quotes from the book:

> Even more shockingly, the authors voice one of the forbidden thoughts of the 1990s: that men and women are actually different. "Biologically, the man must pursue the woman," they write, advising *Rules* wives and girlfriends to let their men make all sexual overtures.

Then, Leo exits with this kicker:

> Of course, the plan has a flaw or two. Strong women may have some difficulty converting themselves into passive monitors of male pursuit. And the plan presumes large numbers of males willing to keep chasing women who don't say much, never arrange a social occasion, don't return phone calls, rarely say thank you for presents, and get all their dating behavior out of a book. Lots of luck *Rules* girls.[11]

Does Leo's essay address a compellingly important social issue? Nah! Will it win a Pulitzer Prize? No. So what does it do? It entertains, amuses and provides wonderful relief—counterpoint to the day's hard news. And that's plenty.

Walter Shapiro, normally a big story guy, plays counterpoint in his *USA Today* politics column ("Hype & Glory"):

> The charge is, of course, ludicrous. The very idea that the media elites are out of touch, that columnists don't understand the daily struggles of ordinary Americans. It's sheer balderdash.
>
> Column writing is hard work, as anyone knows who has seen me out there in teeth-chattering cold, laboring away with my pickax, chiseling opinion from the rock-hard surface of fact. After a long day at the word mines, maybe I don't get back to Main Street USA as much as I used to.
>
> So, the other day I set out to do something guaranteed to make me feel exactly like your typical American in mid-December as the days grow short and the Christmas lists grow long. As a way of demonstrating my Clinton-like empathy for others, I obligingly came down with a bad case of the flu.

Then Shapiro asks a question probably asked at one time or another by tens of thousands of his readers (certainly, it's one I have asked):

> I won't dwell on the nobility of my suffering, nor the Stoic-like grace with which I have accepted my symptoms. I must say, in passing that it does seem darned unfair that I've been afflicted like this. I floss, I use alcoholic beverages responsibly, I don't talk loudly on cell phones in crowded restaurants. So what have I possibly done to deserve my fate as the malady lingers on?[12]

Airline breakfast biscuits, the flu—the little (but important) things in life can resonate strongly with readers.

In campus journalism, how about a humor column on the agonies of computer sign-up during registration? Or riding crowded buses to class? Or eating cafeteria food that's not quite like mom's?

Lesson No. 1: Yes, follow the news because, as in hard-news column writing, that's where readers are found. But play counterpoint and break away on occasion and strike a blow for the little person—and bigger biscuits!

Lesson No. 2: When going for the little things in life, pick those likely to affect many readers. Each of your readers can identify with a column on the flu!

And that's key, too—*writing as if you are speaking to a single reader,* a real person, an individual and not a crowd. Bring the dialogue down to one-on-one. Chat about what each of us fears, loves, hates, respects, disrespects.

How about human vs. computer? Or, each of us pitted against telephone solicitors, or each of us wrestling with computerized answering services. ("Press one if you're going crazy.") Think in those personal terms and you'll write a humor column that scores!

In times bygone, editors told young writers, "Write it for the Kansas City milkman."

Get Your Own Slats Grobnik

> Like all kids, Slats had to find out one day that there was no Santa. He still remembers.
>
> He was awakened during the night by the sound of somebody moving about in the kitchen.
>
> Slats crept from his bed, hoping at last to catch a glimpse of Santa.
>
> But there, by the kitchen stove, stood his father in his long underwear, his arms loaded with gifts.
>
> Slats bounded through the kitchen to his parents' bedroom howling:
>
> "Ma, get up quick—Pa's filching every damn present Santa left for us!"[13]

That's Slats Grobnik of Chicago, of course, learning life the hard way, the way Mike Royko learned it when he grew up in a Polish neighborhood in Chicago. Royko talked with Slats all the time in his column.

With Slats, Royko reduced the compellingly important social, economic and political issues of the day to the working stiff's level, in everyday language. They chatted over a couple of beers in a neighborhood bar, Billy Goat's Tavern, at the ball park, on a street corner.

And for millions of readers worldwide who followed the pair through Royko's Tribune Media Services column, Slats became real, not just a writer's foil skillfully created. (To this day, I can "see" in my mind the tavern where Royko and his imaginary pal met.)

For Slats, the deal was wonderful: He became internationally famous and he had only to chat and listen while Royko drove straight to the heart of a lot of things bugging hell out of a lot of everyday Americans.

For Royko, Slats grew and grew as the perfect vehicle for a message. So, Royko brought in others in the Grobnik tribe:

> My attitude toward [banks] is the same as that of Mrs. Grobnik, who was Slats Grobnik's mother.
>
> "A good bank," she always said, "should look like a jail, except the bank's walls should be thicker."
>
> Whenever she made a deposit—and she never made withdrawals—Mrs. Grobnik would walk around the lobby to see if they had hired any new guards. If she found one, she would ask him:
>
> "Are you a good shot?"
>
> They always said yes, so she'd ask:
>
> "Who have you shot?"
>
> If they hadn't shot anybody, she would go to the chief cashier and ask why they were hiring inexperienced people.[14]

Royko (and the Grobniks) didn't always try to be funny. (Royko once wrote, "Show me somebody who is always smiling, always cheerful, always optimistic, and I will show you somebody who hasn't the faintest idea what the heck is really going on.")[15]

Royko could be hard, sharp, sarcastic, wounding:

- Gun control is all the rage, and Royko writes that he loves pistols and considers "the phallus to be a pistol symbol" and "I have always felt sorry for women because they don't have a pistol symbol."
- Political correctness sweeps American universities and Royko calls it, "stupid ... really kind of dumb."
- Gov. Jerry Brown of California propounds far-out social policies, and Royko dubs him "Gov. Moonbeam," and it sticks to Brown forever—as does "President Sneaky," for Richard M. Nixon, and "President Palooka" for Gerald Ford, who fell down a lot when in the White House.
- Chicago aldermen are "alderboobs" and one—by name—has a "pea-sized intellect."
- Women's clothing designers change fashions, forcing women to dress, in turn, "like a hooker"; then "a frump"; then a "gypsy fortune-teller" and a "farm wife ... and every time the pimps of fashion give the word, all these enlightened female persons obediently trudge to the clothing stores. With that attitude, they might as well be fetching a pipe and slippers."[16]

Talk about playing counterpoint! It all led Howard Kurtz to write in *The Washington Post*:

> He was cantankerous, soft-hearted, infuriating, earthy, bullheaded, funny. He was loved. He was hated. He was read.
>
> Mike Royko, who died Tuesday at 64, was more than a Chicago legend, more than a throwback to the days when columnists smoked, drank, hired legmen and chased dames. He was a writer who made people mad, a rarity in today's buttoned-down, ironically detached, cappuccino-sipping journalistic culture.[17]

Box 7-2	A Professional's Viewpoint

Question: What do you owe your readers?

Answer: I'm not sure. In the past, I'd be sitting in a restaurant and someone would come up and say, "I don't like your column on this or that." I'd hand him 35 cents. That was what the paper cost then. The refund on the product. He'd get upset. Well, that's one attitude I have. Today it's a half a buck. What can you buy for half a buck? Do I owe them something that will be worth reading a hundred years from now? I don't think so. Do I owe them something of the quality of Mark Twain? Naaaa. Not for 50 cents.

I guess what I owe them is that when I write something, it's what I think. No editor told me to write it. I'm not doing it because the *Tribune* editorial page will like it, or not. So they can be quite sure that they're getting what I think at the moment.

Syndicated columnist Mike Royko in interview with WBEZ-FM, Chicago. Extended excerpts from the transcript are available in "Perspective," a special section in *The Chicago Tribune* on Royko's death, published May 4, 1997.

But, no matter what critics (or angry clothing designers) said, Royko always had Slats Grobnik, and Slats always understood.

On occasion, Royko wrote about "the sharp-eyed blond with whom I live." Keying off a spouse is a favorite device other humor columnists use for getting into a subject.

Here's Art Buchwald warming up:

- "My wife is a strong women's rights advocate. She will fight for any kind of equal opportunity, except when it comes to large public restrooms." (It's Buchwald's way of striking at "them"—the nameless, faceless but always threatening "them"—who "build a theater for two thousand people and a women's restroom for two.")[18]
- " 'I'm toying with the idea of running for president of the United States. How would you like to be First Lady?' I asked my wife" (and off he goes, lampooning life for the First Lady).[19]
- For a piece on Romania, Buchwald talks to "a Romanian Gypsy violinist who plays at the Georgetown Tea Room down the street." For perspective on Donald Trump's divorce, Buchwald checks in with, "My friend Debby, who has been The Other Woman several times, ..."[20]

Erma Bombeck, who entertained millions with her tales of serving as mom, wife, car pool driver and harried shopper, liked to bring in her husband for extended conversations about life in suburban America.[21]

For Ellen Goodman, syndicated *Boston Globe* columnist, mom was there when Jacqueline Kennedy Onassis's clothing and personal effects were auctioned for astronomical prices:

Hot Damn. I should have saved the dress my mom wore to the wedding. But who knew?

For years, my mother maintained one wry claim to fame. She was the only woman who changed for the wedding of Jack and Jackie in the restroom of a gas station just north of Newport, R.I. Put that on the record. ...[22]

Here's one of your challenges as a humor columnist: Although hard-news columnists can interview sources in the news, you cannot; you must create a vehicle—your Slats Grobnik?—to carry your column forward. If you create your own Slats Grobnik, keep this in mind:

- Your fictional character must be real enough, developed enough, to be recognizable, to have continuity of views, to become a friend not only to you but also to your readers.
- However, your Slats Grobnik must not take over your column, must not obscure your message, your thinking. Make your Slats Grobnik real, but not dominant.

Listen to Your Readers

As do all writers one time or another, AP's Boyle sometimes found his own creative well empty. Dig though he did, Boyle sometimes *really* was stumped for an idea.

Then, Boyle would look at his mail and, sure enough, somewhere in that huge pile of letters was The Idea—maybe just the sniff of one but enough to get Boyle going.

His column would open, "What a columnist wouldn't know unless he opened his mail ..." and maybe would be nothing more than excerpts from articles carefully clipped and sent him or facts contributed by readers. But it answered his plea, "Help! Another Day!"

His mail told Boyle what many Americans were thinking about. That's important for you as a columnist, because travel, talk and read as much as you can, and you *still* will be in danger of intellectual isolation, of being different from and distant from those for whom you write. And if that happens, your *column* is distant.

Remember our discussion in Chapter Six of David Broder's reporting technique—travel, talk, investigate, *then* write. His hard-news column stays fresh because he listens to folks. Keep your humor column fresh by listening to your readers.

Buchwald gets readers into his act even when they clearly have *not* written. For example:

> I have received many queries about whether I would print my Super Bowl Quick Weight-Loss Diet this year.[23]

Now, if you've ever seen a picture of the more-than-slightly-overweight Buchwald atop his column you know nobody ever would ask about his "Quick Weight-Loss Diet." But that doesn't matter, it's all a ploy to get you into his column, which reports, among other things, "Scientists now know from studying rats that most weight gain takes place in front of television sets during sports events."

Royko was ingenious in getting raging quarrels going with letter-writing readers. He'd give them column space to rant and rave—calling him "one of those right-wing pro-life religious nuts" ... "homophobic" ... a "racist" ... "cold-blooded." Then, while his many delighted readers waited expectantly, Royko would strike back.

For example, Royko took an anti-abortion stance, which brought in furious letters, including one from a Florida woman: "The problem is, neither you nor these other men have a clue as to what is involved in carrying an unwanted child, nor will you ever do so."

Royko responded harshly:

True, a man doesn't know what it is like to bear a child. On the other hand, I don't know of any woman who knows what it feels like to have a hole poked in the base of her skull and her brains sucked out, although some talk as if they might have experienced it.[24]

Other times, Royko's fistfight-by-mail ploy was on gentler subjects, if not in gentler terms. For example, Royko once got a thing going about which were the best Westerns ever made by Hollywood. He brought in writer Garry Wills on the subject, and that drew a response from a reader I'll call "Al Smith":

Al Smith, Chicago: Regarding the greatest Westerns: "Big Jake"? Garry Wills is nuts. Agree with most of your list. "Magnificent Seven" is among the best ever—only "Blazing Saddles" (which may belong, too) has more great lines. "Shane" is wonderful. Wills' knockdown of "High Noon" makes no sense— and you're absolutely right about "Red River." The only terrific moment in that one is the start of the drive. But "True Grit" is pure crap. It's unwatchable. Even the song is crap. So there.

COMMENT: Mr. Smith, I have good news. Because of your bold stance on "True Grit," members of the Great Western Gang have unanimously voted you in as a full voting member of the club. They did this for the pleasure of immediately voting to throw you out because of your bold but bubble-headed views on "True Grit." So there to you, too, bucko.[25]

Know something? I'll bet Al Smith clipped that column and carries it in his wallet and will show it to you next time he sees you at a barbecue picnic. Even the Florida woman who got slam-dunked on abortion probably brags how she got her name in Mike Royko's column.

Get your readers—by name—in your column.

One of Boyle's best columns is an open letter to a woman dead two years. Boyle, who truly worked at his job round the clock, talked to everybody he met, as do all good journalists. Only, Boyle heard things the rest of us didn't.

So, Boyle heard The Idea one "crisp, clear autumn morning, the kind that makes a music in your veins." He caught a taxi in New York City and the driver, Max, started talking about his wife, who died of cancer two years earlier. ... Max was still in love with Sarah, and he told Boyle how she worked and saved to make a home, to be a good mother.

Boyle, who learned his trade the tough way, as a war correspondent and street reporter, stayed tender, nevertheless. He was moved to write:

New York—Dear Sarah.

You have been in your grave two years. You never heard of me in your life, and I never heard of you until an hour ago. I am taking this way of letting the world know what a wonderful wife you were.

Then, Boyle lets Max talk, and Max tells about "marrying you 19 years ago. He told about the first years when all you often had to eat was bread and milk and coffee, and how cheerful you were."

At the end of his ride, Boyle paid Max, and Max "drove away smiling, still thinking of you."

> Signed
> Sincerely,
> *Hal Boyle*[26]

Play the Goat

We all love hero stories—firefighters rescue children, good-guy cops catch bad-guy robbers.

But, we love as much the *goat story*—the guy who can't make anything work, the suburban soccer mom overwhelmed by household duties and crabgrass in the lawn.

Goat stories are especially good if you—the writer—are the goat.

Want to poke fun and get readers to chuckle? *Poke it at yourself.* You don't need Slats Grobnik; you've got yourself!

Tony Kornheiser of *The Washington Post*:

> I don't like to brag, but last week's tender column about my elderly father's eccentricities got a huge reader response. People ate it up.
>
> And, um, then they threw up.
>
> "You are an intellectual dwarf," wrote an 80-year-old woman from Washington. "I'm glad you're not my son."
>
> An 86-year-old man from Virginia thinks me "insensitive, heartless, humiliating and demeaning."
>
> And those were some of the nicer responses. Letter writers apparently felt that I was unkind in general to old people and in particular to my father, whose eyesight and hearing might not be what they used to be, but he is still a human being deserving of respect, affection and dignity.

Now, Kornheiser describes how misunderstood he is. He actually feels terrible, doesn't want readers to dislike him and certainly doesn't want anyone to think he is a bad son because he really loves his father.

But, Kornheiser *still* can't get it together:

> The first thing I did was telephone my dad in Florida, to make sure he wasn't offended. This is our conversation, verbatim.
>
> "Hello?" he said.
>
> "Hi, Dad. It's Tony."
>
> "WHAT? WHAT? HELLO?"
>
> "It's me, Tony. How are you?"
>
> "WHAT??? I CAN'T HEAR YOU!"
>
> "Dad?"
>
> "LOOK, I DON'T WANT ANY." Click.[27]

Now, the Kornheiser angle wouldn't be funny if he was squealing on a friend or a friend's father. But Kornheiser gets chuckles on this because he sets up *himself* in self-deprecating, goat-like terms.

Andy Rooney makes a very good living by whining in his column and on "60 Minutes" about not being able to open aspirin bottles since they were child-proofed, about being overwhelmed by junk mail, about being helpless when confronted by conflicting road signs or automated telephone answering services. ...

Poor Andy Rooney; helpless in a fast-moving bewildering world!

Hal Boyle "goated" himself all the time, often in the third person. For example:

> New York—One of the daily miracles of our times is how a middle-aged man manages to get up and face life every morning.
>
> And particularly on the mornings he has to go to work.

Now, Boyle describes what happens "in the kind of home many of us know." In comes his wife:

> A spectral, yawning figure steps to the bedside of the middle-aged man and holds the noisy alarm clock silently before his shuddering face.
>
> "Call 'em at the office and tell 'em I've got a summer cold, dropsy, neuritis, bursitis, inflammation of the esophagus, a pain in my chest—and a sore elbow," the man mutters feebly.
>
> "You had all those things last month," says the wife. "They won't believe you. You've run out of ailments."
>
> She goes away and returns two moments later.
>
> "Do you want me to starve?" she asks dramatically.
>
> The question interests the middle-aged man. He half-lifts himself to inquire, "How long will it take?"[28]

Note Boyle hangs his goat spoof on something we all understand—the pain of rolling out of bed some mornings. Don't goat yourself on some private little hang-up readers won't understand; *bring them into the scenario.*

One of Art Buchwald's problems is that people always ask him difficult questions. During the U.S.-led Gulf War against the Iraqi regime of Saddam Hussein, Buchwald is put on the spot:

> The question I am asked more than any other is, "Why don't we just blow away Saddam Hussein and be done with it?"

Well, Buchwald mulls this over, and it occurs to him that maybe the Mafia would be interested in taking on the job.

> I went to see my friend Lucky Rico to ask him if he thought that the Mob might be interested in doing one of its celebrated hit jobs on the infamous Saddam.

So, we readers get the picture of poor befuddled Buchwald wandering around muttering to mobsters and not really understanding when Lucky says:

> We're not certain that we want the job. The Mafia has always believed that dictators should be strung up by their own people—the way Mussolini was.[29]

Sometimes, of course, Buchwald has the answers to those difficult questions:

> Friends often ask me if I can remember exactly where I was and what I was doing when the first shot of the French Revolution was fired. I recall it well.
>
> I was working for *People* magazine at the time, and they sent me to France to do another feature on Marie Antoinette. ...
>
> Well, things didn't work out for Marie. She was sent to the guillotine and. ...
>
> I didn't photograph Marie again until October 16, 1793, and as I was a foreigner, I had a front seat at her execution. On October 20, 1793, *People* ran its last cover photo of Marie Antoinette. It was a head shot.[30]

Erma Bombeck was always goating herself because she worried:

> I've always worried a lot and frankly I'm good at it.
>
> I worry about introducing people and going blank when I get to my mother. I worry about a shortage of ball bearings; a snake coming up through my kitchen drain. ... I worry about what the dog thinks when he sees me coming out of the shower, that one of my children will marry an Eskimo who will set me adrift on an iceberg when I can no longer feed myself. ... I worry about scientists discovering someday that lettuce has been fattening all along. ...[31]

Ridiculous worries, too far out for a column? Not at all. Bombeck knew she was giving a chuckle to millions who also worry too much—particularly her favorite reader-targets, housemoms.

Ellen Goodman has fun goating herself on serious subjects. This time, it's America's obsession with fat-free foods. She describes frantically shopping for hours to find a totally fat-free Thanksgiving menu for her family, then escaping the market and announcing "rebelliously in the parking lot" that she has succeeded; her Turkey Day will be fat-free. Then:

> But as I utter this Thanksgiving proclamation, somewhere from deep in the culinary culture a small voice whispers a warning in my ear: Fat chance.[32]

| Box 7-3 | A Professional's Viewpoint |

A lot of columnists write words to end up in the Congressional Record, or on the President's desk or at the Pulitzer Committee's door. But Erma

Bombeck went us all one better. Her words won her the permanent place of honor in American life: the refrigerator door.

> —Ellen Goodman of *The Boston Globe*, in an April 25, 1996, column marking the death of fellow columnist Erma Bombeck.

Open With a Joke

Ever notice how friends lean in to listen when you say, "Did you hear the one about. ..."

Everybody loves a good joke, as Steven Chapman knew in writing a *Chicago Tribune* column on suggestions in Georgia that candidates for state office be given drug tests. Chapman's opener:

> A few years ago, when Democratic Sen. Ernest Hollings was running for re-election in South Carolina, his opponent had the bright idea of demanding that he submit to a drug test. Hollings disposed of the issue with a succinct reply: "I'll take a drug test if he'll take an IQ test."[33]

And, what could Jonathan Power of *The Boston Globe* possibly do with the enormous challenge of getting readers into yet another column on impoverished India and dictatorial Pakistan? Open with a joke, of course!

> Two dogs met on the Indo-Pakistan border. The Indian dog was making for Pakistan, and the Pakistani dog heading for India. "Why are you going in the other direction?" They asked each other. The Indian dog replied, "I need to eat." The Pakistani dog said, "I need to bark."[34]

Want readers to "lean into" your column? Tell 'em a joke—even an old one.

You're Not Paid to Write by the Yard

Ever watch really good comedians telling jokes? Jokes are short, snappy, the dialogue swift. It's into a story, quickly out—and on to the next one.

Comedians, even the good ones, can't hold an audience in *telling* long, complicated, convoluted jokes. Neither can you, in *writing* humor.

It's worth repeating: On average, readers give about 26 minutes to an *entire newspaper.* Your column is just one of many stopping points as they hurry through the pages. You can't waylay them for long.

Buchwald, a real pro at this column-writing business, *writes short* (in industry parlance). His column on his "Super Bowl Quick Weight-Loss Diet," cited earlier, ran about 490 words. Buchwald picks a single theme and gets quickly into it, which he normally can do easily because his subjects are in the news and, thus, fresh in readers' minds. Then, Buchwald moves swiftly, with single-minded discipline, to a snappy conclusion.

Hal Boyle did that Sarah column in 720 words. He, too, knew how to get in and out quickly.

Some humor columnists write longer, of course. Dave Barry, Russell Baker and Tony Kornheiser often run a full newspaper column or more. Their styles are *to entertain by having an amusing conversation* with readers, not snap off quick jokes one after another. Still, even their fans might agree lengthy columns that wander here and there, though pleasantly, often lose zest and momentum.

When *you* turn to humor writing, write to your subject matter—to the end of the joke, then stop; to the end of your funny story, then stop.

Write, Rewrite, Then Rewrite Some More

Do you think great lines like the following just drop out of the blue?

> In war, as in love, it is your first campaign that stays bone deep in your memory. And Tunisia was our introduction to the sweetheart with the lipless kiss.
>
> —Hal Boyle, The Associated Press, recalling his World War II reporting.[35]

> It's just my own personal observation, but I don't think God ever meant for man to do his banking, order food, or mail a letter from the driver's seat of the car.
>
> —Erma Bombeck, in *Four of a Kind*[36]

> What's next?
> A statue of Thomas Jefferson surrounded by slaves?
> U.S. Grant waving a cigar and a whiskey bottle?
> Adding wooden false teeth to portraits of George Washington?
> Recasting Abraham Lincoln's homely, melancholy mug so Abe looks as cheerful as Steve Forbes?
>
> > —Sandy Grady, *The Philadelphia Daily News*, on arguments that to be historically accurate a statue of Franklin Delano Roosevelt must show him in a wheelchair.[37]

> In the old days husbands and wives murdered each other. Now they hire hit men to do it for them. This is surely the final disgrace of a society corrupted by its own riches.
>
> Before the big money rolled in few couples could afford to hire somebody to clean house, much less a hit man.
>
> > —Russell Baker, *The New York Times*, on new stories about husbands and wives hiring hit men to bump off their spouses.[38]

In reading those examples you've answered the question that opened this section: No, great writing doesn't drop out of the blue. It flows from the agony of writing and rewriting, then rewriting again. Want to be a great humor writer? Let your agony begin. Go to the keyboard. Now.

Summary

- Editors value highly those columnists who can throw a smile or two into the daily front-page mix of war, flood and famine; readers flock to entertaining columns.
- Writing funny is difficult, and many humor columnists get tense and exhausted over the challenge of coming up with good ideas.
- As in writing hard-news columns, humorists often score by sticking close to the news and writing about what's on front pages.
- Great columnists, such as Art Buchwald, write about what's in the news because they can "set up" readers with background in minimum wordage, then devote their column to a punchy spoof.
- You can score by playing "counterpoint," avoiding "big stories" and writing about life's little irritations, little pleasures—stuff that's nonessential but on the minds of many readers.
- For aspiring college humor writers, column ideas are in computer foul-ups during registration, crowded buses, cafeteria food that's not like mom's.
- Syndicated columnist Mike Royko created an imaginary friend, Slats Grobnik, with whom he discussed life at the working stiff's level, in everyday language. Create your own Slats Grobnik.
- When using a fictional character as the vehicle for your column be sure the character is developed enough to be real, recognizable and a friend your readers can identify with—but not so dominant that the character obscures your message, your thinking.
- Great columnists listen to—and respond to—readers, who will tell you what many Americans are thinking.
- Everybody loves a hero story—firefighter rescues child—but we love as much the "goat story," the bumbling fumbler who can't get anything right; it's even better if you make yourself the goat!
- If you know a good joke, tell it; sometimes even a good old joke is a great column-opener.
- And always remember you're not paid to write by the yard. Write to the end of the joke, to the end of your story, then quit. Like this. With a period.

Recommended Reading

Again, the lesson is in disciplined reading—in reading the great columnists, such as Russell Baker in *The New York Times*, Art Buchwald and Tony Kornheiser in *The Washington Post*, Ellen Goodman in *The Boston Globe*. All are syndicated and thus can be read in other papers. Note, too, John Leo each week in *U.S. News & World Report*.

The aspiring humor writer will be rewarded by spending hours (yes, *hours*) in collections of great columns. Of Art Buchwald's many books, you'll find a wealth of writing lessons in *Lighten Up, George* (New York: G.P. Putnam's Sons, 1991). Many of Hal Boyle's best columns—and some are very good—are in *Help, Help! Another Day!* (New York: The Associated Press, 1969). Be *certain* to read Erma Bombeck, *Four of a Kind: A Suburban Field Guide* (New York: Galahad Books, 1985). And, for an amusing, entertaining look at the creative genius behind the humor of *The New Yorker*, read James Thurber, *The Years with Ross* (Boston: Little, Brown and Company, 1957).

Notes

1. James Brady, "Get Used to Witch Hunts Resulting from Clinton's PC Military," *Advertising Age*, June 23, 1997, p. 13.

2. Letters, *U.S. News & World Report*, Oct. 31, 1994, p. 6.

3. I was an AP colleague of Boyle at the time and marveled with others as Boyle performed day after day under such deadline pressure.

4. Hal Boyle, *Help, Help! Another Day!* (New York: The Associated Press, 1969.)

5. Saul Pett, "The View from the Next Desk," prologue to Boyle's *Help, Help! Another Day!*, p. 13.

6. Howard Kurtz, "Mike Royko: Columnist, Curmudgeon, Character," *The Washington Post*, May 1, 1997, p. C-1.

7. James Thurber, *The Years with Ross* (Boston: Little, Brown and Company, 1957), p. 9.

8. Art Buchwald, syndicated column for May 1, 1997, published that day in "Still Puffing Their Products," *The Washington Post*, p. C-1.

9. These syndicated columns are in *Lighten Up, George* on, respectively, p. 19, 63, 64.

10. Andy Rooney, "Not Quite Cookiegate," *The Atlanta Constitution*, May 9, 1997, p. A-17.

11. John Leo, "On Society," *U.S. News & World Report*, Oct. 21, 1996, p. 38.

12. Walter Shapiro, "From Fog of the Flu, Some Indoors Insights," *USA Today*, Dec. 11, 1996, p. A-9.

13. This column, originally published Dec. 26, 1969, in *The Chicago Daily News*, is excerpted in "Perspective," a special section of *The Chicago Tribune*, published May 4, 1997, to mark Royko's death.

14. Ibid, "Perspective," *Chicago Tribune*, May 4, 1997 (column was published originally in *Chicago Daily News*, June 18, 1970.)

15. Ibid, originally published in *Chicago Tribune*, March 17, 1987.

16. Ibid.

17. Op cit, Howard Kurtz, *The Washington Post*.

18. Op cit, Art Buchwald, *Lighten Up, George*, p. 223.

19. Op cit, Art Buchwald, *Lighten Up, George*, p. 17.

20. Op cit, Art Buchwald, *Lighten Up, George*, pp. 118 and 175, respectively.

21. Erma Bombeck, *Four of a Kind: A Suburban Field Guide* (New York: Galahad Books, 1985).

22. Ellen Goodman, column for May 1, 1996 published that day in "Camelot Yard Sale Unbelievable," *Greenville* (S.C.) *News*, p. A-11.

23. Op cit, Art Buchwald, *Lighten Up, George*, p. 301.

24. Mike Royko, column for March 25, 1997, published that day in, "Readers' Reproaches, Replies Draw Retorts from Royko," *The Athens* (Ga.) *Banner-Herald*, p. A-8.

25. Ibid.

26. Op cit, Hal Boyle, *Help, Help! Another Day!*, p. 264.

27. Tony Kornheiser, syndicated column for Feb. 21, 1997, published that day in, "Sorry, Older Readers; I Didn't Mean to Offend," *The Atlanta Constitution*, p. D-1.

28. Op cit, Hal Boyle, *Help, Help! Another Day!*, p. 286.

29. Op cit, Art Buchwald, *Lighten Up, George*, p. 317.

30. Op cit, Art Buchwald, *Lighten Up, George*, p. 53.

31. Op cit, Erma Bombeck, *Four of a Kind*, p. 159.

32. Ellen Goodman, column for Nov. 27, 1996, published that day in, "Thanksgiving Cook Decides to Shed Guilt," *The Columbus* (Ohio) *Dispatch*, p. A-11.

33. Stephen Chapman, "Test Canceled by Court Order," *The Chicago Tribune*, April 17, 1997, p. 11.

34. Jonathan Power, "Change in Pakistan and India Must Come from Below," *The Boston Globe*, May 4, 1996, p. 15.

35. Op cit, Hal Boyle, *Help, Help! Another Day!*, p. 50.

36. Op cit, Erma Bombeck, *Four of a Kind*, p. 229.

37. Sandy Grady, column for April 25, 1997, published that day in "FDR Furor," *The Dallas Morning News*, p. A-35.

38. Russell Baker, "After the Magic Dies," *The New York Times*, July 8, 1997, p. A-17.

Exercises

1. Study today's *The New York Times*' hard-news coverage (or coverage in another newspaper designated by your instructor) and outline four ideas for humor columns that tie to events in the news.

Describe each column idea in no more than 150 words. Demonstrate how you would tie the column to **student interests**. How would you "set up" each column? What would be the vehicle (a fictional character?) used to pull readers through your column?

2. In this exercise you must "think small," as described in Chapter Seven. Avoid the hard-news content of today's newspapers and TV newscasts, and outline four ideas for humor columns that tie to the small, insignificant stuff of *everyday student life on your campus.*

Limit each story idea to 150 words. Be certain your ideas will resonate with your fellow students. Don't reach into your own tight little closet of memories for a column idea that your readers will not understand.

3. In this exercise you will describe, in about 500 words, your own "Slats Grobnik." Sketch the personality, characteristics, social and economic status of a fictional "friend" you could use as Mike Royko used Slats Grobnik to take his column down to the working stiff's level.

Would you bounce your column off a roommate? A professor? Write the who, what and how of this character who could be your vehicle in writing that will resonate with fellow students.

4. For the next three days (or for a period designated by your instructor), listen carefully to your fellow students. What are they talking about? What's in the public consciousness of your campus? What's the topic on all lips?

Then write a humor column—*in no more than 700 words*— zeroing in on what your fellow students are talking about. Be certain you write on a student wavelength, in terms that will resonate with students.

5. Play the goat in this exercise, writing a column that pokes fun at yourself. Make certain your topic will be readily recognizable to your fellow students—your poor study habits, your money problems, your love problems (all subjects familiar to most students).

Write this column in no more than 600 words. Try for the short, snappy approach Art Buchwald uses so effectively.

8 | The Fun and Business of Sports

WELL, WE had a couple lighthearted moments in Chapter Seven, and I hope you enjoyed them. But now we must get serious again.

Serious? About *sports*?

You bet. For millions of readers and the editors of thousands of newspapers and magazines, sports indeed is serious. Note:

- Among adult newspaper readers, 88 percent of men and 68 percent of women read sports.[1]
- Of the hundreds of new magazines launched each year, sports magazines are second-most numerous (new sex magazines always are No. 1).[2]
- For all electronic media, particularly the more than 500 online services offered by newspapers, sports results, statistics, commentary and analysis are important offerings.[3]

Significantly, sports *readership* is growing apace with sports *viewing* on television. Sports fans want to read about what they've seen (true in general news, too). Fans turn particularly to analysis and commentary for (1) explanation of something they saw but don't understand but also (2) simply to see if a columnist's view of what happened confirms their own!

In this chapter, we'll address principally five factors that should influence your entry into writing opinion about sports:

- Remember, it's a business and many—perhaps most—of the biggest stories are off the field or court, not on it.
- You must know the game, just as business writers must know Wall Street, as Washington commentators must know politics.

- Great sports commentary gets *deep into the story*, beneath simply who won, who lost, and always is written with TV competition in mind.
- Sports is about people and their competition against other people, against their own personal best performance, against the odds and the record books.
- In no other newswriting do writers achieve quite the intimacy with readers that's achieved by great sports columnists. We're talking here about writing that's often down home, shoes off, over a beer.

First, The Business of Sports

Here, young writer, is a scenario for you:

A famous Washington Redskins running back is driving 133 miles an hour in a 55 mph zone, chased by police. His Ferrari slides off the road and into a tree. He is intoxicated, police say.

After the player regains consciousness, there is great relief at Redskins headquarters. The player suffered "just some scratches on his elbow, that's all," one official says, and he'll be in training camp as scheduled.

Now, young writer, let's say you're writing sports commentary on the Redskins. You now have two general angles to take:

First, you can take the official Redskins line that boys will be boys; the incident is nothing to get excited about; the important thing is that *our* top running back will be in camp as scheduled.

Or, second, you can use your column to shout, "Time out! What's going on here?"

If there is a single point of departure between how sports commentary was written in days bygone and how top professionals write it today, you're at it: In days past, sports writers generally drew one-dimensional portraits of athletes, writing about on-field performance and ignoring off-field misdeeds. Hero status was conferred on even despicable characters simply because they could run fast, hit balls, score points.

Today, sports analysts—and sports readers—are liberated from that unabashed boosterism nonsense. For example, William C. Rhoden of *The New York Times,* in his column, "Sports of The Times," explodes after the Washington Redskins incident:

> Scratches on his elbow? Terry Thomas Allen nearly killed himself last Saturday and we hear about scratches and how happy everyone is that he'll report to camp today.

Rhoden goes to the larger issue of sports as a business:

This is where we are on the eve of a new millennium: the perfection of damage control and spin moves.

Minimizing everything "bad" and blowing up everything "good" reflects a deeper problem that sucks the last drops of meaning from a cherished institution. In fact, next year sports will no longer be an institution. The Bureau of Labor Statistics will officially confer industry status on sports.

And so the final obliteration of the heroic instinct will occur, for where the institution nurtures and cultivates, the industry refines and processes. Where the institution protects the individual, the industry protects raw material.

Rhoden now brings in an icon of clean amateur sports, the highly respected Joe Paterno, Penn State football coach:

If we're not careful, we're going to be actually hiring gladiators ... we're getting ourselves lost in what sports are. The phenomena of sports were in today is very young. Television, the money, the agents, free agents; we're going through a whole transitional period. We're all trying to adjust to this fantastic explosion of exposure and of information. None of us quite understand how to manage it.

Finally, writer Rhoden, ends on a bitterly critical note:

Perhaps athletes need to organize their own Million Man March, gather to affirm, reaffirm, repudiate, once and for all what they thought they stood for, what they do in fact stand for.

Fans grow increasingly hungry for thrills, but continue to long for the vanishing American hero. The inspirational guide. A hard-working athlete like Allen builds himself up, scales a mountaintop, then tumbles and "scratches his elbow." In the process, Allen lost more than his consciousness last week, he lost credibility.[4]

You may think, Well, that critical stuff is written by a New York columnist about a Washington player. How do columnists handle damaging information about the *home team*?

This is a question many college sports writers *fail to answer correctly*. Too many young writers pull their punches on their home-town college teams, fearing that tough commentary will cost them access to coaches and players but often simply because they grew up worshiping the team they're covering.

Writing what must be written about your favorite team—negative news as well as positive—isn't treason; it's good journalism.

In Big League sports commentary, boosterism—the uniformly uncritical support of the home team—is as outdated as leather helmets. The *news* is what successful commentators analyze for their readers.

For example, Larry Felser, sports editor and columnist of *The Buffalo News,* visits training camp where coach Marv Levy is getting the Bills ready for the fall season. For his reader-fans, who are enormously loyal to the home team, Felser focuses his column on brawls between players, one of the most disruptive factors in any football team's drive for a winning year:

> So how to judge the 1997 Bills? We know that the boys are cranky. There has been more physical stuff, to say nothing of brawling, than at any time in the Levy era. We also discovered that linebacker Damien Covington can clean and jerk Glenn Parker. ...[5]

Fighting between players isn't what coach Levy—or the Bills' business office—wants publicized. But to columnist Felser *it is the news.*

Dave Anderson, widely-read *New York Times* columnist, is up-front on the business of sports and public relations spin doctors in charge of it. He *opens* a column this way:

> Cleveland—After four months of hype and $12.8 million of faith in his fast-ball, the Yankees will finally put their Japanese import, Hideki Irabu, on the mound at Yankee Stadium tomorrow night against the Detroit Tigers.[6]

At *The Washington Post,* the sports editor invites in *Post* humorist Tony Kornheiser (our hilarious friend from Chapter Seven) to *lead* the sports section with a column under the headline, "Even Overseas, It's Show Me the Money."

Kornheiser has been reading sports stories about how foreign basketball players are recruited—"how they are located, and how they're funneled to high schools and colleges in the United States." He continues:

> For me, the key quote in the stories was uttered by a lawyer in Nigeria, who's been active in sending players here. He said:
> "I invest a lot in the kids, and I don't get anything. This is a problem, I don't even have a shoe contract. I am aware that somewhere down the line, some people are making money, and I'm beginning to get ticked off. Because I don't get anything."
> *I don't even have a shoe contract.*
> A lawyer in Nigeria wants a shoe contract.
> It's a small world after all.
> And you know what makes the small world go round?
> Money, money, money, money.[7]

You'll note the critical writing cited above strikes even at sports once treated very gently—high school basketball and college football, as well as professional sports. On sports with more sordid auras—particularly professional boxing—modern sports columnists take, shall we say, a gloves-off approach.

When Mike Tyson chewed off part of Evander Holyfield's ear in their heavyweight championship fight, sports columnists were uniformly critical of Tyson and, further, the world of boxing:

- Dave Kindred, in *The Sporting News* writes, "Now we have seen our time's most uncivilized fighter end a fight the way Neanderthals should end their fights. How wonderfully satisfying to those of us who believe boxing is beneath contempt to have our belief reconfirmed."[8]
- Jack Newfield, *The New York Post*, writes of Tyson's and boxing's "thug nation night world of violence, gangs, criminality and self-destruction."[9]
- Mike Lupica, one of the greats in sports analysis today, writes in *The New York Daily News* that Tyson "behaved like the crazy hoodlum kid he once was ... behaved like the heavyweight champion of the gutter."[10]

Modern sports commentary doesn't stop at critically assessing athletes. It extends to *fans*, too. Here's Sam Smith of *The Chicago Tribune*, in his syndicated column on basketball player Dennis Rodman:

> There was only one incident last week worse than Dennis Rodman assaulting a courtside cameraman in Minneapolis.
>
> It was the standing ovation Rodman got from the Chicago crowd for his 10,000th rebound.
>
> The NBA can't stop Rodman from embarrassing and making a mockery of himself and basketball. Neither can the Bulls.
>
> Their punishments merely provoke Rodman to more outrages, like an angry adolescent.
>
> This is a man who learned from Madonna. Once you shock, you have to shock even more the next time to get attention.
>
> The only way to control Rodman and return some dignity to the Bulls is to boo Rodman. ...

Smith lays into Rodman—and, by implication, the myth of professional athletes as role models:

> Here's a man who does everything you counsel your children not to: He kicks people, for heaven's sake. He curses in public and on television. He attacks officials of the game. His fellow players regard him as the dirtiest in the game. He pushes from behind and after a play is over. He's cursed out by his coach after coming out of a game. He misses practices when he feels like it. He feels a responsibility to no one but himself.
>
> This is a man being celebrated. And for what?

Then, columnist Smith calls into action the parents among his readers:

> How, as a parent, can you expect any discipline or respect from your children when you cheer someone who behaves as Rodman does?
>
> Boycott his products and show.
>
> Boo the guy.[11]

So, young writer, lesson: If you're headed into sports commentary because of a lifelong passion for games and those who play them, be advised that's not enough for a ticket into Big League journalism. You will need a heavy overlay of dispassionate, even critical analysis in your reporting and gloves-off hard hitting in your writing.

Here's another lesson: Bring to sports commentary some *business sense.* Even a cursory study of sports pages reveals much news in sports—and commentary on it—revolves around contract negotiations, labor strikes, owner and league squabbles and other off-field business aspects of sports.

Understand also how to report the law and legal process. Occasionally, you'll need to comment knowledgeably on such things as the arrest and imprisonment of sports heroes!

Is that too cynical? Are today's noted sports columnists too adversarial, too focused on business squabbles and the legal difficulties in sports? Are sports columnists burdened by an attack-dog mentality that seems to guide many journalists these days?

Not really. Read sports columnists and you'll see that generally the emphasis still is on the fun—the magic—of sports. And you'll see that leading sports columnists make serious attempts to build insider knowledge that yields added-value reporting for today's increasingly knowledgeable reader-fans.

You Must Know the Game

Do you know the meaning of the following paragraph?

> So here are the Mets, worrying about their infield and nervous about the starting rotation, knowing that its overachieving nature needs care and feeding, if not an influx of fresh arms.[12]

And, what is the significance of the following?

> The Seminoles lost Warrick Dunn a three-time 1,000-yard rusher. Peter Boulware and Reinard Wilson, who totaled 42 tackles for loss and 22.5 sacks last season, kicker Scott Bentley, who made 52 of 53 pats and 16 of 18 field goals, and improving lineman Walter Jones have also departed.

If you don't know the meaning of the first example or significance of the second you may not know enough about, respectively, major league baseball and college football to qualify as a Big League columnist.

In the first example, Claire Smith, in a regular column, "On Baseball," is writing for knowledgeable *New York Times* readers about the New York Mets. The subject is the defensive strength of the team's infielders and management of the team's pitchers.

In the second example, Neil S. Cohen, senior editor of *Football Action,* is commenting on polls ranking Florida State's football team as likely national champions in the forthcoming season. He continues:

So why are the Seminoles still the choice? Because when one superstar leaves, all coach Bobby Bowden does is slide another blue-chipper in his place. Quarterback Thad Busby is in his second year as a starter and will be that much better. E.G. Green will be another deep threat.

On defense, Daryl Bush is a possible All-American linebacker and Andre Wadsworth is the new sackmeister. The rich get richer ... freshman running back Travis Minor was *USA Today's* Offensive Player of the Year, while frosh defensive end David Warren won the honor as the paper's Defensive Player of the Year. The Seminoles have their usual gauntlet of a schedule, facing USC, Miami (Fla.) and Florida for their non-league battles.[13]

Note in the examples above three points:

1. Columnist Smith assumes *Times* readers have a high level of baseball expertise. "The starting rotation," for example, is reference to the sequence in which pitchers will be used. Understanding that is second nature to true reader-fans. Sports columnists routinely communicate with readers through such "sports shorthand." In almost no other form of journalism do we use so much shorthand. Even *Wall Street Journal* columnists writing for readers expert in business and finance are expected to avoid such shorthand and spell out what they mean. *Journal* writers even explain terms in everyday business use. (Note, for example, how they always explain the meaning of "prime rate" and similar terms.)
2. In the second example, note how columnist Cohen writes in great detail, citing individual players by name, even freshmen. *And that's for his magazine's national audience.* Fan interests are national—global, even, in some sports—and successful columnists write to that universality of interest. Simply put, football fans in Oregon want to know—by name—about freshmen running backs in Florida.
3. Good sports commentary often is built on relaxed, even slangy writing. Note Cohen's reference to a "blue-chipper" player and a "new sackmeister." David Broder's readers—or editors—wouldn't buy equivalent loose writing very often in his *Washington Post* column on politics. William Safire of *The New York Times* wouldn't get far with calling national leaders "warmeisters" or "blue-chipper" politicians.

Reader-fan interest—and expertise—extends beyond the Big Three sports (football, baseball, basketball) and into sports that just a few years ago were limited in fan appeal. Note in the following the assumption by Dave Anderson that he's writing his column, "Sports of The Times," for real experts in golf:

Troon, Sco   d—Before he teed off yesterday in the British Open's third
round, Tig   Woods told friends, "I need a 29 on the front nine."

His r.   matical projection was understandable. With a seven-under-
par 29 on   d Troon's mostly downwind front nine, he would shoot 64 for
a 210 tota   ee under par going into today's final round.

As it   d out, he would get his seven-under-par 64 with 32-32, tying
the British   n record at Troon that Greg Norman shot in the final round
in 1989 be   osing to Mark Calcavecchia in a playoff.

But if   Woods were to have a chance to win this 126th British Open
on Scotland   ny western coast today, he might need another 64, if not a
62.

"If the weather stays like this," said Sweden's Jesper Parnevik, the leader
at 11 under par, "Tiger has to get close to breaking 60 to have a chance."[14]

Now, do you think you'd have a chance to get Dave Anderson's coveted
job at *The Times* if you didn't know golf and were forced to write something
like the following?

Troon, Scotland—Tiger Wood faces a stiff challenge today in his effort to win
the 126th British Open. ...

Nope. Write such pedestrian, shallow leads and you'll not be a sports
columnist for *The Times* or any other newspaper or magazine of consequence.

Knowing the game permits you to lay your analysis and opinions
over important elements in any game or contest that reader-fans want discussed:

- *Strategy*, be that a coach's game plan or Tiger Woods' mathematical projection.
- *Key plays or turning points*. Just as a political columnist surveys an entire
  presidential campaign to find the precise point between winning and losing, so must the sports columnist finger that moment in a game when fortunes shifted.
- *Individual or team performances* that make a big difference. Particularly
  important is the performance of stars, whose lives on field and off literally
  are the stuff of daily conversation between fans.
- *The statistical context* for performances by individuals and teams. Sports
  fans are insatiable in devouring statistics. Sports commentary without statistics is financial writing without dollars and cents, humor writing without punch lines.
- *The look-ahead angle*. All of sports is preparation for more sports. The significance of today's game is found, in major part, in its meaning for next
  week's game. Look again at Dave Anderson's column on Tiger Woods. The
  entire thrust is forward, taking readers toward expert discussion of Tiger's
  chances later *today*, not merely looking backward at what Tiger accomplished *yesterday*.

Note my emphasis above on columnist Anderson's *expert discussion* of Tiger's chances. Writing sports isn't nuclear science. But sports readers are just as quick to find errors in your writing as nuclear scientists would be if you were reporting science.

Know your game!

Get Beyond Winners and Losers

To be effective, sports commentary must probe far more deeply than merely who won, who lost. You must write with two competitors in mind:

- Your own newspaper will carry *news stories* on the outcome, and on major events will publish *sidebars*—related but separate stories that treat different angles, such as post-game interviews with coaches and players or trainer reports on injuries. You'll fail in sports commentary if you merely dance across all that spot-news reporting. If you're writing for a magazine, you must remember true reader-fans will have seen daily newspaper coverage of the game or event.
- Whatever your print medium, you must never touch a keyboard without considering electronic competitors. Television and radio cover all major sports events and sometimes even prep games. So, your reader-fans frequently know the basics—who won, who lost—well before your plastic-wrapped column plunks in their driveway.

In angling your commentary it's particularly important to understand there have been fundamental changes in how sports news stories are written: Today, news stories are strongly framed in analytical dimensions by *reporters* who know they, too, compete with see-it-now television.

For example, on the day that columnist Felser went inside the brawling football camp of the Buffalo Bills, his own *Buffalo News* sports section printed these "news" leads:

> Fredonia—It didn't take running back Antowain Smith long to realize he was no longer at the University of Houston. All it took was one look across the line of scrimmage.
>
> "I saw all those big guys over there, people like Ted Washington, Bryce Paup, Chris Spielman and Phil Hansen," Smith said. "I didn't see anything like that in college."
>
> Welcome to the National Football League.
>
> Smith, the Buffalo Bills' top draft pick, completed his first full week of training camp Saturday. Like most rookies, his head has been on a swivel most of the time as he tries to absorb a new offense.[15]

> Cleveland—Are the Boston Red Sox for real, or are they just teasing their fans again?

John Valentin hit two solo homers and Wilfredo Cordero had a three-run double Saturday as the Red Sox won their fourth straight game, 6-3 over the Cleveland Indians.[16]

Atlanta—Pedro Astacio figured he would beat the Atlanta Braves eventually. He just didn't think it would take six years.

Astacio allowed three hits in 7⅓ innings to beat Atlanta for the first time Saturday, leading the Los Angeles Dodgers to a 4-1 win over the Braves.[17]

The first example above is by *News* Sports Reporter Allen Wilson. It *led* the *News'* sports section. The baseball leads are from The Associated Press, renown for its "straight" news reporting but obviously also probing these days beyond the winners and losers in sports.

Note those three "news" stories all have "soft," featurish intros. Their writing tone is analytical, and they explore angles that in days bygone were left to columnists. And, of course, all three leads are designed to take readers beyond what they saw on television.

Your media competitors create such pervasive coverage that only rarely can you peg sports commentary to truly exclusive information. Too many spot-news reporters are pursuing all the angles to leave you the luxury of relying principally on pulling in readers with exclusive scoops. (*However*, you'd better be exclusive once in a while with important stories or you'll not be a columnist for long!)

Neither can your sports commentary be tied to featurish writing that merely "moves furniture"—writing that addresses, in a different way, in different language, the same facts and angles covered in spot news stories.

Obviously, your commentary must be structured around your expert insights, your informed opinions and your unique writing style.

Or, you can go where the sports-writing pack doesn't go, which is what David Ramsey did for *The Syracuse* (N.Y.) *Herald American*. Columnist Ramsey led his paper's Sunday sports section with this:

Barry Powless ripped a shot into the goal at the Onondaga Nation's box lacrosse field, and he started a wiggly, joyous dance. As he moved Friday under a bright moon, car horns blared in the night and his friends and neighbors shouted their support.

Powless plays and coaches the Onondaga Nation team in the Iroquois Lacrosse Association, started in 1993 to offer the chance for summer competition and fellowship.

The dusty box lacrosse field at the Onondaga Nation presents the game in its simplest, purest form. Other teams in the league play indoors in cozy arenas. Other teams have roofs over their heads. Other teams, Powless said, pay players.

The Onondagas play under the stars. They play, for free, on a field where it is impossible to complete a game without getting a face full of dust. The field is lined with plywood and chainlink fence. Spectators sit in bleachers or stand to look over the fence or sit in their cars. After Onondaga goals, horns blast for a minute.

Now, columnist Ramsey turns to "added value" reporting—the extra dimension of information—that must separate commentary from spot news reporting:

> Lacrosse is closely entwined with Native American culture. "We believe lacrosse to be the creator's game," said Kent Lyons, who plays for the Onondagas. "The game was given to us by the creator for him to enjoy."
> Playing outside, Lyons said, strips the game down to its most basic, and best, form.
> "You can see the spiritual connection," he said. "That's the biggest thing we've got here. We've still got that spiritual connection. It's one of the last places where you'll still see that strong spiritual connection. That's what drives a lot of these boys."

Reflect on what you've read in David Ramsey's column about lacrosse played under a bright moon on a dusty field in upstate New York. Anything missing? How about who the Onondagas played and who won? *That,* Ramsey holds to the 13th paragraph, hundreds of words deep in his column, and only on the "jump" from the sports section's front page to page 9 does he tell you this:

> Lyons, Powless and their teammates lost, 11-10, Friday to the Akwesasne Thunder in a emotional, crisp, tense game. The game featured plenty of checking and scuffling and imaginative stickwork. ... [18]

J. Michael Kelly, who writes an outdoor column for the *Syracuse Herald American,* goes off the beaten track in pursuit of fish-and-game commentary. He features a combination of hard-news reporting and how-to-do-it guidance.

For example, Kelly reports 39 million Americans 16 or older went fishing or hunting last year, and:

> They spent more than $72 billion on tackle, transportation, lodging, licenses and other expenditures related to their outdoors pursuits.
> That's an average of $1,828 apiece.

Later in his column, Kelly gives readers the advice many are looking for:

> King salmon have been hitting in Lake Ontario between Fair Haven and Nine Mile Point, Oswego charter captains say.
> Most days the fish are about 80 feet down in 200 to 500 feet of water. They've responded well to cut bait or spoons trolled behind downrigger balls.[19]

Lesson: *Participatory sports* are gaining widespread attention in America, and winning columns are written on jogging, camping, tennis-for-oldsters, tennis-for-youngsters—you name it. When casting about for an idea for *your* column, don't overlook writing about what you and many of your neighbors do on weekends.

Try Roundup Columns

Mostly, however, successful columnists stick to major sports because that's where most reader-fans are. (The National Football League is the most popular sport with readers.) And, successful columnists get beyond merely reporting winners and losers through imaginative reporting and writing.

For example, *The Philadelphia Inquirer*'s Jayson Stark, in his column, "On Baseball," noted related bits and pieces of news breaking throughout the country and did a *roundup column* with this intro:

It may be too late now for baseball to ever be our true national pastime again. Ah, but there's always Plan B:

It can still be our international pastime.

And it was a stunning week in the globalization of baseball. Let's take them one by one:

Now, columnist Stark discusses the New York Yankee's new pitcher from Japan, Hideki Irabu:

Irabu-gate: In the latest twist in the Hideki Irabu soap opera, the Yankees last week handed San Diego possibly their two best prospects (outfielder Ruben "The Next Mantle" Rivera and pitcher Rafael Medina), plus 3 million spare George Steinbrenner dollars. What did they get back? The right to give Irabu $15 million or so, plus three marginal prospects.

The clear winners: The Padres, who got all that for a player they never had and had no hope of signing. ...

Next, Stark turns to Tampa Bay:

Cuba? Si: Meanwhile, the Tampa Bay Devil Rays upped the ante on Cuban defectors by signing former Cuban ace Rolando Arrojo for a $7 million signing bonus. It then took about 30 seconds for the Devil Rays to start fielding flak. ...

Around the leagues goes columnist Stark, pulling together the week's bits and pieces on foreign players and enormous salaries paid them. Each news development draws comment from Stark, including this on moves for a "World Cup" in baseball:

... what a wonderful world this could be—unless everybody goes broke first.[20]

Note the characteristics of a roundup column:

- It is distanced from the daily "who won, who lost" and thus lets the writer sit back and take a wider perspective.
- It is a perfect vehicle for pulling together separate news developments and *revealing patterns* that might not emerge in scattered daily reporting.
- It lets the columnist *comment* on the bits and pieces, to take the long view in analyzing likely outcomes and directions. *Any* competent sports writer can pull together bits and pieces for a roundup; *your* roundup can qualify as distinctive commentary only with the addition of insightful analysis.

Nothing Succeeds Like "Scoops"

If you want to push your column beyond the superficial daily coverage, if you really want to win big, *nothing* succeeds like an old-fashioned, unrivaled, look-at-me-first scoop. Like this one columnist Peter May dropped on his *Boston Globe* readers:

> M.L. Carr says he's going to take some time at the beach this week and ponder his future with the Boston Celtics. To coach or not to coach? To oversee or not to oversee?
>
> The decision already had been made.
>
> Sources have told the *Globe* that Carr will surrender both his head coaching job and his job as director of basketball operations. He will, however, remain an active part of the Celtics, possibly getting involved in some way in ownership, which always has been his main goal.
>
> It also was learned that the Celtics have settled on the person to replace Carr in the front office. The identity of that individual could not be determined, but don't be surprised if, after all the fuming, fussing and non-sightings, that Larry Bird's name emerges. ...

As any principled journalist would, columnist May now gives coach Carr opportunity to comment. ("That's premature," is his response. "That's all I'm going to say. You're being premature.") May then moves swiftly ahead:

> Carr told a throng of hungry reporters after yesterday's fitting finale—a 125-94 loss to Toronto that he would take some vacation time this week and that no decision will be announced while he's sittin' on the dock of the bay. He deflected repeated queries about his future, but did note that "as far as coaching goes, it's management who picks the coach, not the other way around." That seemed to be a shot at those who have dared to express interest in the job or who set conditions on whether they would accept it.[21]

Note in the example above the combination of superb reporting ("Sources have told the *Globe*" ... "It also was learned" ...) and May's judgmental commentary ("That seemed to be a shot" ...) Such inside reporting—going beyond who won, who lost—combined with insightful analysis makes columnist May one of the country's best. In this case, it won him front-page display in the *Globe's* sports section.

It's worth repeating: Columnists must be superb *reporters*, as well as insightful analysts and skillful writers.

Game Columns Demand Interpretive Reporting

All those attributes must come into play especially in writing a "game column" —a column built around interpretive reporting of an event also covered by a colleague who is doing the spot-news story.

For example, Nancy Gay of *The San Francisco Chronicle* does this *spot-news lead* on an important game:

> Officially, the Giants have style—a winning one. Their well-schooled brand of white-knuckle play—the bunts, the singles, the RBI-whatevers—makes them the best darn track team in all of Major League Baseball.
>
> Atlanta was looking for a two-game sweep, but the Giants wanted to win again. The shifty winds of Candlestick Point became their ally and reckless abandon became their trademark yesterday in a 4-3 victory over the Braves before 17,050 at 3 Com Park, an outcome that restored the Giants' record (14-4) as the best in baseball.[22]

That story above leads—takes the upper-righthand position—of the front page in the *Chronicle's* sports section. Note that despite its featurish tone, the lead fulfills the basic requirement of a spot-news sports story: It quickly gets to who won and what the score was.

On the same *Chronicle* page, beside the story above, is a column by C.W. Nevius on the same game. His intro goes beyond merely reporting winners and losers:

> Those amazin' Giants did it again yesterday, beating the Braves in what we like to call typical fashion, which is to say a wind-blown, three run, inside-the-park homer and a go-for-broke slide across the plate in the bottom of the ninth.
>
> Heck, if all the games were this wacky and exciting, baseball might catch on around here.
>
> The locals have won four of their last five in their last at-bat, have the best winning percentage since the 1971 team won the NL West and are leading the league in grit. That's "grit" as in pluck or toughness, not the stuff that blows in your eyes, a category in which they've led the league for years.[23]

Examine what distinguishes the *Chronicle's* column from its spot-news story:

- Columnist Nevius doesn't worry about the score, attendance or precise (14-4) record of the Giants. That routine statistical backdrop is left to reporter Gay.
- Nevius is breezy in his writing ("Those amazin' Giants ..."; "Heck, if all the games were this wacky ...") Reporter Gay is much more straightforward, sacrificing winsome writing for workmanlike reporting of precise details.
- Columnist Nevius demonstrates he *knows the game*. Note his fast first-graf summary of key elements in the Giants' win.

Such division of writing responsibility between spot-news reporter and columnist is evident in *Los Angeles Times* coverage of a major basketball game.

First, the spot-news lead by Scott Howard-Cooper:

Updated list of Laker problems: Injuries ... disappearing players ... suspensions ... themselves.

The latest reached the surface Thursday night, with the Houston Rockets waiting. The Lakers compounded the difficulties the two-time defending champions bring anyway by having their offense go AWOL, shooting a season-worst 34.9% to lose Game 1 of the playoffs, 87-83, before 17,505 at the Forum.[24]

Alongside, that fact-filled game story, the *Times* plays columnist Mike Downey. Note his intro isolates one factor—player suspensions—as key in the outcome:

All those suspensions caught with the badboy Lakers, who were rusty, reckless and really out of sync in Game 1 of their playoff series against the Houston Rockets, losing and losing ugly, 87-83.

Back after time off for bad behavior, neither Nick Van Exel nor Magic Johnson remotely resembled his old self Thursday night. Van Exel was a brutal one for 11 shooting, and Johnson spent most of the night trying to make a pass that led to a basket. This keeps up, and the Lake Show is going to be in for a quick cancellation.[25]

In *Chicago Tribune* coverage of a game, staff writer Terry Armour produces this spot-news lead:

Miami—It was supposed to be a statement game. Or a message game.

If the Miami Heat beat the Bulls for a second time this season, as they did with their 102-92 victory Wednesday night at Miami Arena, it was supposed to give them some kind of mental edge if the two teams should happen to face each other in the Eastern Conference finals—as many expect.

But while everybody in the Bulls' post-game locker room conceded the Heat is the "second best" team in the East, they insist there was no true statement made.[26]

The *Tribune's* Sam Smith, in a side-by-side column, analyzes the same game with focus on individual performances:

Miami—He apparently had no interest in Toni Braxton.
But Pat Riley still liked his style.
"I think Jamal Mashburn fits in a small forward probably better than Juwan Howard would have with P.J. Brown and 'Zo' [Alonzo Mourning]," Riley said of the Miami Heat front line he had hoped to have before the NBA rejected his signing of Howard last summer.
"Now, looking at it in retrospect, it may be the best thing for the franchise. We're more balanced. We have prospered with the two great-player mentality and other role players. And it gives us a player who can be dropped right into that position and give us versatility."
Mashburn did just that Wednesday. He scored a team-high 23 points, grabbed 10 rebounds, had five assists and three steals and shared ballhandling duties with Tim Hardaway most of the second half as the Heat held off the Bulls 102-92 for its 60th victory.[27]

Note the *Tribune's* spot-news lead gets quickly, in the second graf, to the score. Columnist Smith, however, backs into the game, not even mentioning it until his fifth graf. And he then isolates for analysis the performance of Jamal Mashburn.

Now, hang on. There's more. On the *same* page, spot-news reporter Armour and columnist Smith do *two more stories* on the same game.

Armour compares this season's Bulls to last year's:

Miami—Comparisons between last year's Bulls and this year's version have been going on all season. Only recently have the comparisons heated up.
Michael Jordan thinks it's hard to make comparisons because the current team has been saddled with injuries all season. The victories haven't been as easy as last year. Wednesday night Chicago lost to the Miami Heat for the second time this season.[28]

In his second piece, columnist Smith looks ahead to the playoffs:

Miami—So what do the Bulls want to do?
Tie the 1985-86 Boston Celtics' record of 40 home wins in a season and win at least 70 games for the second straight season?
Or end up possibly having to face both New York and Miami in the playoffs?
While the Bulls were losing to Miami 102-92 Wednesday night, the Knicks were beating Atlanta, and, by virtue of a tie-breaker, moving ahead of the Hawks into the third spot in the Eastern Conference playoffs.[29]

Additionally, the *Tribune* publishes photos of the Bulls game and a full column of linescore, single-graf descriptions of key plays, player quotes and other statistical esoterica beloved by reader-fans.

Note these characteristics of the *Tribune* coverage:

- Both columnist and spot-news reporter demonstrate incredible grasp of the nuances of basketball. ***And, their writing assumes readers know the game, too.***
- All four stories are written with the assumption that fans already have seen the game or highlights on television or at least know the score. Note none of the four lead paragraphs reproduced above mentions the game score. All go beyond winners and losers.
- Despite their heavy side-by-side coverage, columnist Smith and spot-news reporter Armour avoid redundancy. Each story focuses on a different angle. When you write commentary side-by-side with a spot-news reporter be sure to sort out in advance who will take which writing angles. Expect some tension in this. Smart reporters and columnists will head for the same key writing angle. If fraternal competition becomes disruptive—and journalists are competitive people—sports editors normally move in to delineate writing guidelines.
- Both the spot-news reporter and columnist focus on people, the players and coaches. In sports, people are the news.

Focus on People

Here are two questions for your roommate or a classmate:

1. Do you know the name of the U.S. secretary of the treasury?
2. Do you know who Michael Jordan is?

Two more:

1. Do you want to read a column about alcohol abuse by athletes?
2. Do you want to read about Terry Thomas Allen of the Washington Redskins putting his Ferrari into a tree at 133 miles an hour?

Such questions can help you sort out two important lessons for aspiring sports commentators:

First, and simply put, sports stars are better known than are most Americans. Even readers with only passing interest in sports are aware of—interested in—famous (and infamous) athletes. *Name recognition* in sports is a greater reader draw than name recognition in politics or other endeavors.

Second, you'll draw readers more readily into a column on ***people who represent a larger issue*** than you will into a column on simply the issue itself. A famous player charged with driving under the influence is a much more effective writing peg than a flat, dull discussion of off-field conduct by athletes. That's why columnist Rhoden of *The New York Times* cited Terry

Thomas Allen by name as a lead-in to his column on sports as a business, which opened this chapter.

Note how these pros do it:

Columnist Timothy Dwyer of *The Philadelphia Inquirer* and staff writer Tim Panaccio go to Pittsburgh for a hockey game between the Flyers and Penguins. Panaccio writes the game story. Dwyer focuses his column on the star performer:

> Pittsburgh—There was a moment when time seemed to stand still. Mario Lemieux had the puck on the blade of his stick. The Pens were on a power play, and he was standing about three feet from Garth Snow.
>
> This was early in the game, and the Flyers stood and watched him. Super Mario held on to the puck, dribbling it from one side of his blade to the other.
>
> It seemed as if five minutes went by. The Igloo was silent. Snow's legs opened for a second, and that instant, Super Mario snapped off a shot to the opening.
>
> Snow's knees clamped together, and you could hear the thud of rubber meeting pads up in the rafters.
>
> Everyone began to breathe again.
>
> Snow won the first shoot-out with Super Mario, but he could not stop the rest of the Pens. And it was Lemieux who ended the evening with a goal that breathed new life into his team. ...

Now, I'm no hockey fan, but columnist Dwyer had me hooked with that intro. I read eagerly ahead, following Dwyer on the jump from section front to page nine—hundreds of words on the game. Then this kicker for an exit:

> Near the end, nearly everyone in the place got up and began to chant: "Mario! Mario!"
>
> Super Mario came out for what may have been his last shift at home, and, once again, the puck got behind the Flyers' defense.
>
> Lemieux picked it up. He broke toward Snow. But this wasn't like the first period. Time did not seem to stand still. Lemieux faked. Snow went down. And Super Mario shot.
>
> This time, Snow could not stop him.
>
> The crowd roared. It was a perfect ending for the game in every way.
>
> A breakdown by the Flyers. A score for the man they had come to praise and bury.
>
> But Super Mario and his Penguins are still alive.[30]

In the example above, the *Inquirer's* Dwyer builds his entire column around a single player. It's Mario Lemieux against Garth Snow, shooter against goalie, star against the odds. Readers are enticed forward with the drama of personalized battle.

Below, Rick Gosselin of the *Dallas Morning News,* writing in *The Sport-*

ing News, uses a single player—Reggie White—in a quick reference designed to open discussion of a larger issue, free agency in football. Among football fan-readers, mere mention of "Reggie White" is like a blinking neon sign that says, "You must read this."

> In April 1993, the Packers gave Reggie White $17 million to lure him from Philadelphia to Green Bay. The Packers sought a simple return on their investment—The Super Bowl—and last season, they got it.
>
> But White is one of the few players who had proved worthy of his millions since NFL free agency began four years ago. Free agency has not become the great equalizer many people thought it would.
>
> "How many (free agents) have been with winning teams?" asks Chuck Schmidt, the chief operating officer of the Lions. "How many of them have been to Pro Bowls? It's startling how many have not accomplished what you'd hope they would have accomplished."[31]

Broadly, then, your column can have enormous impact if you focus on people and (1) use a star's performance as the vehicle to carry readers all the way through or (2) simply open with a quick reference to a well-known athlete, then move on to a larger issue (that is, using a single mention of Reggie Smith to pull readers into a wider discussion of free agency).

And never miss a chance to personalize *your* involvement when it's pertinent.

Guess what Bryan Burwell has in mind with the following lead. Burwell, an analyst for Turner Sports and HBO Sports, writes for *The Sporting News:*

> My little girl has a jump shot. She steps up just inside the free-throw line, places her left hand under the ball, her right hand on top, raises the ball up in front of her face, and with a little hop and gentle flick of her 8-year-old wrists, she releases the ball on a curious arch towards the 8-foot-high rim. ...[32]

With that intro, Burwell is pulling readers into a discussion of women's professional basketball, and that like all little girls, his little girl now "has a marketplace" for her skills, just as do boys who aspire to professional basketball.

In *Time,* Jack E. White injects himself into an essay on the 50th anniversary of the racial integration of pro baseball. White's personalized approach offers something special:

> I wish I could really remember the time in 1950 when my dad took me to Ebbetts Field to see Jackie Robinson play for the Brooklyn Dodgers. But I was only three years old, and the day is a blur. No matter, my dad explained to me many years later, he wanted me to be in the presence of history. The hopes and fears of millions of African Americans were inextricably connected with every clutch hit, every stolen base, every acrobatic catch in Robinson's

career. Not just Robinson but an entire race was coming to the plate—and he knew it. He stood up to the pressure with extraordinary grace and performed at a Hall of Fame level. His is surely one of the most remarkable and inspiring accomplishments in sports history, or just plain history.[33]

And, I find columnist Michael Lev drawing an *unforgettable* personalized image in this column for *Pro Football Weekly*:

> This was 1973, and Mac Bledsoe was about to welcome Oakland Raider WR Fred Biletnikoff to the football camp Bledsoe ran at Whitworth College in Spokane, Wash.
>
> Bledsoe never had met Biletnikoff but recognized the man who that day had taken off his shoes to wade into a nearby lake. Bledsoe walked over to Biletnikoff to introduce himself.
>
> "Fred, I'm Mac Bledsoe, and I think we're going to know right off whether we're going to be friends, because I think those are your shoes my son's peeing in."
>
> Even at the ripe old age of 1, Drew Bledsoe could find his receivers. And he's been on target ever since.
>
> Mac Bledsoe's son, who quarterbacked the New England Patriots to last season's Super Bowl at the ripe old age of 24, always has been ahead of his time. A prodigy. A wunderkind. Drew Bledsoe isn't "the Man." He's "the Young Man."[34]

Write to Achieve Intimacy

So, you're talking sports with a friend and you lean in close to confide:

> In all his ebullient cacophony, Don King dubbed tomorrow night's rematch between Mike Tyson and Evander Holyfield "The Sound and the Fury." He knew the phrase came from "Macbeth," but Act V was hardly Shakespeare's preamble to pugilistic noise and ferocity in a large Las Vegas, Nev., hotel.[35]

Or, do you say something like the following?

> You wonder what Tiger Woods thought watching Michael Jordan these last two nights of the NBA Finals. You wonder if Woods understands, even at 21, how flattering comparisons to Jordan are, and will always be.[36]

Or, is the following even closer to your conversational style?

> One thing I learned from last year's Cubs is they can't wait around all summer to make a trade. Again. Because they won't be able to. Again.
>
> When they tried last July, which they said was the plan, they got nothing. No one was really dealing because everybody was like the Cubs: With delusions of contending.
>
> My thinking is, make the deal earlier. Like right after you get shut out by a Colorado Rockies pitcher—a Colorado Rockies pitcher, do you hear me?—

and lose a record 12th straight to start a season the way the Cubs did Wednesday.

You have to make deals sooner. The wild-card races have changed the way teams can do business. That's what I learned. ... [37]

No contest, right?

Shakespeare (*Shakespeare!*) comes off very heavy as the intro to a column on a prizefight, in which, remember, Mr. Tyson bit off a piece of Mr. Holyfield's ear.

Not to suggest you should write like you talk. You shouldn't. Conversational communication is terribly inefficient, full of hems and haws, uhs and gasps; it circles and wanders. Writing that way drives off readers.

Nevertheless, the best sports commentators write to create the intimacy of one-to-one conversation. They write to *include each reader in a chat about a common love, sports.*

"You wonder what Tiger Woods thought" ... comes from the keyboard of Mike Lupica, one of our greatest, in his *New York Daily News* column, "Shooting from the Lip."

"One thing I learned" ... is from Steve Rosenbloom, author of the *Chicago Tribune*'s enormously popular column, "Foulline," in a *conversation* with readers on why doesn't Chicago Cubs General Manager Ed Lynch make trades earlier (and you can almost hear reader-fans saying to themselves, "Yeah! Why doesn't he?").

Shakespeare is the writing peg of Richard Sandomir of *The New York Times,* a newspaper justifiably proud of having sports columnists who know the works of the Bard. But in pegging a prizefight story to Act V of "Macbeth," Sandomir labors to make a point that, frankly, eludes me and, I'll wager, even upscale, well-educated readers, of which the *Times* boasts many.

Dumb Down Your Writing?

Am I condescending? Do I suggest you must "dumb down" your writing to score as a sports columnist? Not at all. Sports readers span all demographic groups—rich, poor; the well-educated and the less well-educated. But whoever—whatever—they are, what do they seek in sports writing?

The Philadelphia Inquirer's Timothy Dwyer writes about hockey as if he thinks his readers want a chat about sports:

This is the way you want it to go, isn't it? In the first round you are chairman of the Super Mario retirement committee. In the next round you want them to face the Rangers and Gretzky. Then Jersey and the ghost of two springs ago. And, quite literally—finally—you want them in the finals against The Team That Lindros Built—the Avalanche.

This is the way you want it to go, isn't it?

A month ago, I did not think the Flyers would make it to the Stanley Cup finals, but now, if the Flyers continue to play with the intensity they showed against the Pens, if their goaltending just stays average, it is very possible. ... [38]

In *The San Francisco Chronicle,* Glenn Dickey opens his column the way a fan might open a conversation:

It seems to me: Cal is in a pickle because of the exodus of basketball players.[39]

Dan Shaughnessy of *The Boston Globe* reaches not for Shakespeare but, rather, slangy street talk to open a column:

It's the worst start in Red Sox history. Worse than during the Dick Stuart/Pinky Higgins era. Worse than liverwurst.

The Sox are so bad they're almost good. They're as camp as "Showgirls." The uglier they get, the more beautiful they become. ... [40]

Frederick C. Klein, author of graceful essays on sports for *The Wall Street Journal,* interrupts a column on the first interleague play in professional baseball to let readers in on a secret:

I was about to write here that it's a mystery why the game's powers-that-be took so long to get around to allowing the clubs from the National and American leagues to play each other in games that count, but it is no mystery. Thickheadedness is the reason. ... [41]

And, it doesn't hurt to poke fun once in a while. After all, these are *games* we're writing about. Here's Jim Murray, one of the truly all-time greats, in his *Los Angeles Times* column:

Tennis, historically, has been played and indulged in by guys with Roman numerals after their names, or Sir in front. In the western world, it's not only considered honorable but a distinction for young men and women who show a talent for the game to go around in white sweaters tied round their necks by the sleeves, play in shorts and accept the accolades of their society because they excel at it.[42]

And do remember, from Chapter Seven, the "goat column." Hold *yourself* up to a bit of ridicule once in a while, as does Bernie Linicome of *The Chicago Tribune* in a column reprinting mail he's been getting lately. This exchange follows a column in which Linicome complains about losing dough in an office pool:

Bernie:

I have nothing but the utmost respect for the *Tribune,* but I think it is time they see the error of their ways and get rid of any columnist who would let a personal vendetta and anger over losing an office pool affect his or her writing. Arizona took your money and made you look stupid to your peers, didn't they? Every time I look at your picture in the *Tribune* I will see a tired, worn out old curmudgeon with egg on his face—Jeff A. (Jones), Des Plaines.

    Jeff:

    That's eggs Benedict, actually.[43]

Summary

- Sports is serious business: 88 percent of adult male newspaper readers and 68 percent of females read sports.
- Of all news magazines launched each year, sports magazines are second-most numerous. (Magazines about sex always are No. 1!)
- Electronic media and the more than 500 online services offered by newspapers emphasize sports coverage.
- Sports readership grows apace with TV viewing; fans read sports columns for explanations of something they saw but don't understand, or simply, for confirmation of their own view of what happened.
- If there is a single point of departure between sports commentary in days bygone and how it's written today, it's this: Sports analysts today are liberated from the unabashed boosterism of the past that often drew one-dimensional (and uniformly favorable) portraits of sports figures.
- Many college sports writers pull their punches on their home-towner college teams because they fear tough commentary will cost them access to coaches and players or simply because they grew up worshipping the teams they're covering.
- Bring to sports commentary a heavy overlay of dispassionate analysis and some business sense, necessary in covering off-field stories such as player strikes or difficulties with the law.
- Knowing the game—all its nuances, all its subtleties—is an absolute must because reader-fans have a high level of expertise in sports.
- Columns must cover the strategy of games, key plays or turning points, outstanding individual or team performances, the statistical context, and always must look ahead to the next contest.
- To be effective, sports commentary must get deeply beyond merely who won, who lost, offering added value reporting or analytical insights not offered by your own newspaper's spot-news stories or TV coverage.
- Many columnists leave the beaten path of major sports and focus, instead, on participatory sports, such as fishing, hunting, jogging, tennis.
- Sports is about people, and, thus, so must your sports writing focus on the people factor.
- Great columnists write to achieve intimacy with each reader, using "you" and "I" and humor and, even, street slang to create a conversational mood.

Recommended Reading

The best teachers of sports writing are the great sports columnists of our day. Read them. In addition to those mentioned in this chapter, follow Frank Deford anywhere. He's formerly of *Sports Illustrated* and the now-defunct *National,* currently writes freelance for magazines, and is a sports commentator on National Public Radio.

See particularly *The Sporting News* and its annual publication of best sports stories.

If you're shaky on the statistical context of sports writing, check the "Sports Guidelines and Style" section of AP's *Stylebook.*

Sports Illustrated carries sports analysis to new heights. Great sports writing is in *The Los Angeles Times, Chicago Tribune, Dallas Morning News, Miami Herald, Atlanta Journal and Constitution, Washington Post,* all New York papers (*Times, Post, Daily News*) and *Boston Globe.*

Notes

1. *Facts About Newspapers 1997,* Newspaper Association of America, quoting SMRB Fall 1996 study of Media and Markets, p. 6.

2. Dr. Sami Husni, University of Mississippi, makes an annual study of new magazines. For details see Conrad C. Fink and Donald E. Fink, *Introduction to Magazine Writing* (New York: Macmillan Publishing Company, 1994), p. 10.

3. *Facts About Newspapers 1997,* op cit, p. 33.

4. William C. Rhoden, "Sports of the Times," *The New York Times,* July 12, 1997, p. 27.

5. Larry Felser, "Glenn Parker's Not the Only Toss-Up in Camp as Bills Sort Themselves Out," *The Buffalo News,* July 20, 1997, p. B-6.

6. Dave Anderson, "Sports of the Times," *The New York Times,* July 9, 1997, p. B-13.

7. Tony Kornheiser, "Even Overseas, It's Show Me the Money," *The Washington Post,* March 27, 1997, p. C-1.

8. Dave Kindred, "Biting Off More Than He Can Chew," *The Sporting News,* July 7, 1997, p. 8.

9. Jack Newfield, "On Tyson," *The New York Post,* July 10, 1997, p. 2.

10. Mike Lupica, "Shooting from the Lip," *The New York Daily News,* June 30, 1997, p. 3.

11. Sam Smith, syndicated column for Jan. 18, 1997, played that day in *The Athens* (Ga.) *Daily News and Banner-Herald* under, "After Latest Boo-Boo, It's Time to Just Boo," p. B-1.

12. Claire Smith, "On Baseball," *The New York Times,* June 15, 1997, p. 7.

13. Neil S. Cohen, "Football Action '97 Top 25," *Football Action '97,* p. 6.

14. Dave Anderson, "Sports of the Times," *The New York Times,* July 20, 1997, Section 8, p. 1.

15. Allen Wilson, "Smooth Sailing So Far for Bills' Top Pick," *Buffalo News,* July 20, 1997, p. B-1.

16. The Associated Press dispatch for July 20, 1997.

17. Ibid.

18. David Ramsey, "Nation Player Sees Culture in Box Lacrosse Games," *The Syracuse Herald American,* July 20, 1997, p. C-1.

19. J. Michael Kelly, "Survey Show Anglers, Hunters Are Dedicated," *The Syracuse Herald American,* July 20, 1997, p. C-10.

20. Jayson Stark, "On Baseball," *The Philadelphia Inquirer,* April 27, 1997, p. C-7.

21. Peter May, "Carr's Route: He'll Surrender Jobs, Remain with Team," *The Boston Globe,* April 21, 1997, p. D-1.

22. Nancy Gay, "Giants Run Up a Win Over Braves," *The San Francisco Chronicle,* April 24, 1997, p. B-1.

23. C.W. Nevius, "Even Mother Nature Likes Gritty Giants," *The San Francisco Chronicle,* April 24, 1997, p. B-1.

24. Scott Howard-Cooper, "L.A., You Have a Problem," *Los Angeles Times,* April 26, 1996, p. C-1.

25. Mike Downey, "Stale Players, Rotten Game," *Los Angeles Times,* April 26, 1996, p. C-1.

26. Terry Armour, "A Whisper, Not a Statement," *The Chicago Tribune,* April 17, 1997, Section 4, p. 5.

27. Sam Smith, "On Pro Basketball," *The Chicago Tribune,* April 17, 1997, Section 4, p. 5.

28. Terry Armour, "Inside the Bulls," *The Chicago Tribune,* April 17, 1997, Section 4, p. 5.

29. Sam Smith, "A 70th Win Could Make Post-Season More Difficult," *The Chicago Tribune,* April 17, 1997, Section 4, p. 5.

30. Timothy Dwyer, "About to Retire, Lemieux Isn't About to Quit," *The Philadelphia Inquirer,* April 24, 1997, p. D-1.

31. Rick Gosselin, "Shuffling the Deck," *The Sporting News,* July 7, 1997, p. 40.

32. Bryan Burwell, "Ladies' Choice," *The Sporting News,* July 7, 1997, p. 9.

33. Jack E. White, "Essay," *Time,* March 31, 1997, p. 90.

34. Michael Lev, "Drew Believers," *Pro Football Weekly,* July 20, 1997, p. 6.

35. Richard Sandomir, "TV Sports," *The New York Times,* June 27, 1997, p. B-15.

36. Mike Lupica, "Shooting from the Lip," *The New York Daily News,* June 15, 1997, p. C-26.

37. Steve Rosenbloom, "Foulline," *The Chicago Tribune,* April 17, 1997, Section 4, p. 2.

38. Timothy Dwyer, "A Good Start on the Way to the Cup," *The Philadelphia Inquirer,* April 27, 1997, p. C-1.

39. Glenn Dickey, "Player Losses May Threaten Harmon Plans," *San Francisco Chronicle,* May 9, 1996, p. B-3.

40. Dan Shaughnessy, "And You Know Nipper Caused Blizzard of '78," *The Boston Globe,* May 2, 1996, p. 35.

41. Frederick C. Klein, "So Far, So Good: Interleague Play Is Resounding Hit,"

The Wall Street Journal, June 20, 1997, p. B-8.

42. Jim Murray, "His Game Was Held Hostage," *Los Angeles Times,* May 2, 1997, p. C-1.

43. Bernie Linicome, "In the Wake of the News," *The Chicago Tribune,* April 18, 1997, Section 4, p. 1.

Exercises

1. Do a story count on the sports section of today's *New York Times* (or another paper your instructor designates) and, in about 300 words, discuss the balance of coverage. What proportion of coverage is devoted to on-field sports and how much is on off-field or business developments in sports? Do you think off-field events, such as the personal lives of athletes, receive too much coverage?

2. Examine two recent columns by your favorite sports columnist and discuss, in 350 words or so, whether the writer demonstrates detailed knowledge of the sports event being discussed.

How do you characterize the writer's level of expertise? Does the writing display true understanding of nuances and subtleties of sports? What level of *reader expertise* is assumed by the writer?

3. Examine side-by-side coverage of a single event by a spot-news reporter and a columnist.

Does the columnist avoid duplicating the spot-news story? Does the columnist focus on different angles? Is there added value reporting that distinguishes the column from the factual and dispassionate news account?

Do this in about 350 words.

4. Study at least four columns by your favorite sports columnist. Does the writing assume readers have seen on television the events being discussed?

How does the columnist advance the commentary beyond what reader-fans will have seen on television?

This should be done on a columnist who covers events normally televised. Write your analysis in about 350 words.

5. Pick a sports event on or near your campus and write a column of about 600 words expressing your personal opinions.

Be sure to focus on people and get beyond merely who won and lost. Show your intimate understanding of the sport you're discussing. Use writing devices discussed in this chapter to create a conversational one-to-one tone with your readers.

PART FOUR

Arts Reviews
and Criticism

I T WAS just a rumor, but word circulated in Chicago that *The Tribune* planned changes in its policy of publishing overnight reviews and full arts coverage.

Quickly, *more than 13,000* arts patrons signed petitions circulated by theater owners protesting any changes.[1]

Yet, Fintan O'Toole, an Irish critic has the general agreement of many when he writes that "critics continue to occupy a place in the esteem of artists somewhere below that occupied by sewer rats." [2]

Welcome to arts criticism, a journalistic form read avidly, it seems, by everybody associated with, or interested in, all forms of art—and simultaneously reviled joyously by the same cast of characters.

All to say that when you turn to arts reviewing and commentary you don't retire from hot-seat journalism to a quiet, sleepy corner of the newsroom. Arts coverage done properly is as fully on the cutting edge as commentary on politics, sports or any other subject you and I are discussing in this book.

For many newspaper and magazine readers—and, thus, editors—arts commentary is of compelling interest. Witness coverage in virtually every newspaper and magazine of music, dance, painting, books, television and other artforms.

Outstanding arts commentary is offered on a global scale by papers as diverse as *The New York Times* and *The Wall Street Journal.* Rare is the community newspaper that doesn't cover—and comment on—local county fair music festivals or amateur theatricals. Alternative newspapers and magazines dedicated solely to the local arts scene flourish in many cities. Specialized publications reporting on a wide range of subjects cover the arts. (For example, *The Economist,* panoramic in its reporting, despite its name, gives readers full coverage of the arts. So does *Scientific American.*)

Why do arts reviewing and commentary stir such interest, such passion? We'll consider that in the single chapter of Part Four. And, we'll explore reporting and writing techniques you can use to get started in this journalistic specialty.

9 | You and Arts Commentary

As you approach arts commentary you must sort out your personal answer to two questions:

First, to whom or what do you owe your principal journalistic loyalty? To the artform you're covering? The artist(s)? Yourself? Your audience?

Second, will you write for *insiders*—those intimately involved in the sometimes tiny and tight world of art? Or, will you write for *outsiders*—write as a translator converting the esoterica of art, its specialized language and its principles into everyday language and concepts a general newspaper or magazine audience can understand?

There often is disagreement on these questions, particularly (as you might guess) between editors and writer-critics, but also among artists.

Who Gets Your First Loyalty?

One day, Dennis Britten, editor of the *Denver Post,* swept through his newsroom and replaced his movie reviewers. He explained:

> We were writing about films, and our readers go to the movies, they don't go to films.[3]

No question where Britten thinks a critic's loyalty lies: with the newspaper's readers. To most editors, arts reviews and commentary are an offering to readers, an *inducement* to build circulation. Just like editorials and commentary on politics, sports, business.

Now comes critic O'Toole, invited by *The Economist* to answer the question, "What are critics for?" O'Toole is clear:

Critics should be honest enough to accept that they represent nobody but themselves—not the artform, not even in any real sense the newspapers that employ them. Their job is not to report on how a work was received by an audience. It is not to sell books or tickets. It is not to reform or mold the practice or theatre or music or poetry. And it is not to maintain, as arbiters of taste and value, the authority of the institutions who print their opinions.

The job of the critic is to try to ignore the magnifying effect of print and hyperbole, to preserve a sense of proportion, and to give a genuinely individual opinion. It is a modest but by no means a contemptible task. And it is one that is inextricable from the artistic process itself.[4]

So, editor and critic differ: Translate for my readers, says the editor; no, the critic says, I write for myself. There is a third view.

For more than 30 years, Walter Kerr was a theater critic for *The New York Herald Tribune* and *The New York Times*. His following was enormous, his influence huge. On his death, actress Carol Channing wrote a letter to *The Times*:

If, rightly, we regard theater as family, then Walter Kerr was a beloved family member. The supposedly adversarial relationship between performer and critic was never apparent where Walter was concerned. His opinions were contributions to our work, his commentary was insightful, and he strengthened the art of the theater with his word.[5]

Note that whereas critic O'Toole sees his role as "inextricable from the artistic process itself," actress Channing goes much further. She sees Kerr as a member of the theater "family" who strengthened the art with his commentary.

Kerr's death stirred comment that assigned yet another role—that of teacher—to the critic. Arthur Gelb, editor of *The Times*' cultural coverage during much of Kerr's era, said:

He was a man of such integrity, wit and far-reaching theater knowledge that he was incapable of writing a review that wasn't lively and brimming with intelligence. In his wry and unassuming way, *Walter was also a great teacher* [emphasis added]. All of us who love the theater were proud to be his students.[6]

So, young writer, which will it be? Will your first loyalty go to translating the arts for readers? Or, do you want merely to express your personal opinion? Will you join the art world's "family" in a supportive role? Or, be a teacher?

Be careful which option you select. Your choice can effect your career.

To get started, in campus journalism or "real world" writing, you probably will need to emphasize your journalistic skills—your *reporting* strengths—more than your analytical and interpretive qualities. To be taken seriously as a *critic* with a meaningful message (as distinct from *reporter* or even *commentator*) requires elaborate career preparation and serious study of the artform, just as political commentators must be serious students of politics, just as business analysts must learn business.

If college newspaper arts commentators suffer a single weakness it is a tendency to be stridently (and predictably) adversarial in their criticism, to attack and slash—and all on a base of limited or, even, faulty understanding of what critic O'Toole calls the "history and the conventions of whatever artform is under scrutiny."[7]

For certain, artists spot immediately any weakness in a critic's technical knowledge. And, you'll not fool music lovers if your writing confuses Bach with Beethoven, Blue Grass with New Orleans jazz. Poet Brendan Behan turned on his attackers, arguing they lacked understanding of his artform:

> Critics are like eunuchs in a harem; they know how it's done, they've seen it done every day, but they're unable to do it themselves."[8]

As for readers, if you're writing for general-circulation newspapers or magazines, they need help.

Box 9-1	A Professional's Viewpoint

The thing that separates Tim Page from the mass of critics is not his immense technical grasp of music from Palestrina to Steve Reich. It is his ability to write about music in a way that opens it up to a huge universe of readers. He has found ways to relate music to Stonehenge, Gertrude Stein, classified ads, Thomas Pynchon, Jack Nicholson, butterfat and the Italian scientist Guglielmo Marconi—without in any way diminishing the sophistication of his essays.

The Washington Post, commenting on the award of a Pulitzer Prize to the paper's Tim Page "for Distinguished Criticism."

Are You Writing for Insiders or Outsiders?

The great Walter Kerr acknowledged he got into criticism largely because it let him go to movies eight times a week.

Kerr was 13, writing a column titled, "Junior Film Fans," for the weekly *Evanston Review* in his hometown, Evanston, Ill. Kerr loved movies, and that started his lifelong obsession with the theater.

A *New York Times* colleague, Frank Rich, a renowned critic himself, writes that Kerr was "drunk on theater." Rich says he was "stage-struck" himself and "in love with the theater."

See the danger for journalists—*journalists who happen to be critics?*

Invariably, it's love of art—be that movies, jazz, Bach, whatever—that attracts young writers to arts reviewing and commentary. Total immersion in the art world follows. Friendships are made with artists or others passionate about art. It's art for breakfast, lunch and dinner—followed by more art.

It's easy to begin writing for your fellow insiders, those who share your passion (and your understanding) of art. It's easy to assume a commonality of expertise with your insider readers, to write in the "shorthand"—jargon, almost—that enables one expert to communicate with another expert and waste no time with backgrounding or explanatory writing.

And it's *very* easy to forget those newspaper and magazine readers *out there*, far removed from your art world, who are immersed not in art but in the challenge of daily living. They worry a lot about jobs, children and crab-grass in the lawn, and they need your help, your *powers of translation* as they dip irregularly and perhaps infrequently and inexpertly into the very specialized and sometimes self-centered and closed world of art.

Those readers—those outsiders—need your help.

If you accept that equation, if you agree your essential duty as a journalist is to communicate information, to enlighten and assist, you must structure your career as a reviewer and critic accordingly. That is, you must select events to review with general-circulation readers in mind; you must report for them, you must write for them. For a performer's view of your responsibilities in all this, see Box 9-2.[9]

| Box 9-2 | A Professional's Viewpoint |

Karen Woods danced professionally throughout the world with the Merce Cunningham Company and now teaches dance at Ohio State University. Here she looks at critics and their role from the perspective of an artist.

A Dance Critic's Role

Dance critics play a valuable function in arts reporting if they draw from a rich background of experience and education to make insightful observations about the described work. Ideally, dance critics have opportunities to see more dance than the average audience goer, so they can draw connections between the work being described and the broader context of dance and the performing arts. Critics should provide the reader with necessary information about who is performing, where and when, etc., but even more importantly, weigh in with some finely honed judgment about the work as a whole. The critics' role is to describe what they have seen and experienced in watching the event and then to offer "the bigger picture."

The Bigger Picture

No two people see the same thing in a dance performance. Ideally, the first step in writing about an event is to detach oneself as much as possible from subjective notions of "good" or "bad" art and see and hear what is there. No two works may be judged with the same criteria: An educated critic knows what kinds of questions to ask about an individual work. That is, one cannot ask the same questions (harbor the same presuppositions or assumptions) of an abstract modern dance work and a Broadway musical. One form does not necessarily represent "bad" art and the other "good": Each is different from the other and requires the critic to look at it within a different context. It is the critics' responsibility to educate themselves in all that they see so as to constructively evaluate each work.

Opinion Matters

Contrary to expectation, the critic's individual opinion about a work does count for something: Readers repeatedly turn to a particular critic because they value what he/she has to say, what he/she feels and thinks about a work. While it is the critic's job to restrain from making judgments during the initial observation of a performance, the real work comes in writing the review when the critic must pursue his/her "gut" reactions. The critic asks: What I saw made me feel this way. Why did it make me feel that way? How did the work as a whole produce that intuitive reaction in me? (Try to separate as best you can, the bad Chinese dinner you may have eaten beforehand. Are your responding to the work or to food poisoning?)

Why It Matters

There are many reasons for the dance critics to take their jobs seriously. Among them, of course, are professionalism and the reputation of the newspaper or periodical. But there are wider implications as well. Dance critics should always remember that they are writing about the lives and expressions of others. Ultimately, the critic is not omnipotent and needs to retain respect for the artists at all times. Also, in an era of increasing competition for limited arts funding sources, the critic's few lines tossed off late at night, have the potential to seriously impact an artist's funding source. Be aware that arts organizations often turn to critics as reliable information sources. The responsibility is on the shoulders of the critic to then write with rigorous attention to his/her privileges and obligations.

Hidden Traps You'll Confront

Every form of journalistic writing has its own special dangers. Arts reviewing and commentary are not exceptions.

Here are some traps to watch for as you begin writing arts criticism:

- The Cheap Shot Syndrome, a tendency among some writers to stretch for the cute—and devastating, if meaningless—phrase, to word-dance for amusement and thus neglect the basic journalistic mission of informing.
- Fairness vs. your personal likes/dislikes, which forces you to consider, for

example, whether your review should focus on your personal dislike for how the soprano struggles toward a high C or whether it should focus on her total performance and how the audience loved her despite the cracked high C.

- Clarity vs. jargon, the trap of writing in the shorthand language of artists, to the total confusion of non-expert readers.
- Manipulation by the arts world, whether simply because you buy into the arts so totally (like home team boosterism in sports writing) that you develop blind spots or because you fall victim to the powerful public relations apparatus controlling access to many events and performers.

Danger #1: The Cheap Shot Syndrome

They linger in journalistic lore, those cheap shot one-liners written more for newsroom colleagues huddled around the water cooler than for readers trying to get some sense of what a play or concert is all about.

Invariably—and repeatedly—they go something like this:

Pianist Alvin Smith played Mozart at Concert Hall last night. Mozart lost.

Or,

Soprano Gwendolyn Smith as Mimi died on schedule last night in the final act of La Boheme. So did the opera.

Or,

The Community Players rolled through Shakespeare at Playhouse Theatre last night. As for the Bard, he must have been rolling over in his grave.

Though perhaps faintly amusing when first written, or even somewhat informative, such cheap shot one-liners normally signal that a critic (1) is unable to write without grabbing for horrible cliches and (2) is determined to disguise the fact that he or she really doesn't know much about the artform being reviewed.

Not to say amusing, wry, agile and *hard-hitting* writing isn't part of professional arts commentary. It is, *if* it's backed by insightful, even profound understanding of the artform and *if* that writing truly communicates that understanding to readers.

For example, Drew Jubera is an experienced television critic whose commentaries in *The Atlanta Journal* and *Constitution* are widely recognized by TV experts as insightful *and* by readers as informative. Secure in his knowledge of television entertainment, Jubera writes engagingly:

Monday night's Academy Awards ceremony will long be remembered for its incomparable lack of memorable moments.

It was a nightlong sleepwalk that occasionally woke only to find itself sleeping, snoring through an endless parade of limousine liberalism, I'm-speechless acceptance speeches and a tribute to women in film that was dull and lifeless when it wasn't patronizing and plain dumb.

But through it all, viewers got what they wanted: Billy Crystal and lots of Oscars.

The big award winners were ... [10]

That mood-setting intro out of the way, critic Jubera settles down to detailed *reporting* of what transpired during the Academy Awards show, liberally inserting, however, the analytical comments that are the duty of a critic. (Al Pacino, for example, delivered "a rambling speech.")

Walter Kerr could hit hard, but there were no cheap shots in his reviews. Rather, he took his readers into the theater and *let them discover* why he disliked (or liked) a performance.

For example, Kerr reviewed a musical, "Portofino," and clearly disliked it—and told readers why. He noted the star, Helen Gallagher, tried hard

... in spite of the fact that the spotlight that was supposed to be following her was flickering out, the men who were supposed to be operating it were engaged in a loud, heated conversation in the booth, and the dress that was supposed to be so dazzling was ripping rapidly up the back.

Kerr concluded his review (published in 1958) with this kicker:

I will not say that "Portofino" was the worst musical *ever* produced, because I've only been seeing musicals since 1919.[11]

Note above that both Jubera and Kerr, though writing under deadline pressure as cruel as any in journalism, tell readers *why* they disliked a performance. That explanatory dimension—letting readers understand—separates cheap shot one-liners from the thoughtful, if sometimes harsh criticism that marks professionalism.

The New Yorker, a magazine that blankets New York City's arts scene, features highly disciplined writers who get the *why* into even one-paragraph snippets or reviews of fewer than 100 words.

For example, *The New Yorker* was there when radio shock jock Howard Stern's movie, "Private Parts," premiered, and the reviewer opened with this:

Howard Stern's bid for the love of millions has plenty of isolated hilarious bits, and Stern, who plays himself, is surprisingly photogenic. But the film asks us to see him as both unusually lovable and bravely moral, and that's just too much.

Quickly, the reviewer explains why "that's just too much": The film "rushes through" Stern's "awkward youth"; the screenplay is "disingenuous" and "leaves out a lot of his radio show's true meanness."[12]

To explain *why* you dislike a performance you sometimes must get into such things as staging, sets and even how musicians and instruments are placed on stage. Here is jazz critic Don Heckman of *The Los Angeles Times* explaining why trumpeter Wallace Roney wasn't up to par one night at LA's Jazz Bakery:

> ... his apparent unfamiliarity with the venue's tricky acoustics resulted in sound that can most charitably be described as jarring. For no obvious reason, Roney chose to place the grand piano facing the audience—that is, with pianist Carlos McKinney looking out toward the seats. Bassist Clarence Seay stood in the crook of the piano but turned toward the side of the room, and drummer Eric Allen was placed in the center.
>
> If the clustered positioning was intended to create a better listening environment for the players, it didn't manifest itself in the music.[13]

Danger #2: Fairness vs. Your Personal Views

Now comes into play your *personal* definition of your role as a critic: Do you consider yourself strictly a *commentator*, obliged only to deliver your opinion? Or, are you a *reporter as well*, required to labor for journalistic balance and fairness to report the wider environment of an event—including audience reaction?

Although critic Fintan O'Toole says a critic's job "is not to report on how a work was received by an audience," many reviewers do add audience reaction to their own views.

Here is *The New Yorker* in a balanced—and, I think, fair—review of Jackie Mason in the play "Love Thy Neighbor":

> His range may be limited but his timing is perfect, and the house rocks with laughter.[14]

The New Yorker didn't like Jonathan Larson's rock opera "Rent," which "stands every assumption of the traditional musical on its head." The review explains why, *then presents balancing comment*:

> ["Rent"] can't support the narrative overload (eight separate stories are told), yet by the end of the evening Larson's talent has taken the audience to places the musical never ventures these days.[15]

Audience reaction is *the writing peg* for Matt Diehl of *Rolling Stone* as he reviews an appearance by Motley Crue. His lead:

> If heavy metal is dead, the sweaty throngs chanting "Crue!" as Motley Crue hit the stage at New York's Roseland hadn't been clued in. ...

After that opener, critic Diehl continues to *report* audience reaction: fans give the band an "enthusiastic greeting" ... the "biggest raspberries" go to drummer Tommy Lee ... "

And when the band kicked into powerful renditions of old hits like "Dr. Feel-good" and "Shout at the Devil," the crowd was transformed into something out of "Triumph of the Will," pumping its fists and screaming along with every lyric.[16]

Fairness must include internal structuring of a review to ensure balance. It doesn't take much.

- Scott L. Powers of *The Boston Globe* reviews four albums of The Byrds, newly released on compact discs. Powers' review is positive, and his writing is an affirmative, enthusiastic recall of the early days of rock. But, "The Byrds were far from perfect, and were often frustrating by keeping what seemed like album filler and indulgences." One piece by David Crosby of The Byrds is "annoying, silly, sophomoric and chaotic."[17]
- Writing for *Rolling Stone*, Parke Puterbaugh describes Ozzy Osbourne on tour as "cheerleading for insanity" but notes that when guitarist Joe Holmes got going "the crowd roared more loudly the more gruesomely atonal it got."[18]
- Skip Ascheim of *The Boston Globe* reviews—and loves—an adaptation of "Charlotte's Web" but terms it "not entirely satisfying"—and outlines his reservations.[19]
- Esther Iverem of *The Washington Post* likes a staging of "A Fool and His Money" but notes that bursts of song come at "pivotal—and sometimes odd—junctures" and that "the show slides between moments of melodrama and too-sweet sweetness."[20]

Sometimes, more elaborate reporting is required to achieve fairness and balance in a review. Here is Anthony Tommasini of *The New York Times* reviewing the Lincoln Center recital debut of soprano Barbara Bonney (emphasis added):

> At 41, Ms. Bonney seems at an artistic peak, as this program, accompanied by the fortepianist Melvyn Tan, made clear. Her exquisite lyric soprano voice is pliant and true, and retains a rosy youthful radiance. She has found her ideal repertory in German Lieder and in the lighter operatic roles of Mozart and Strauss, and has wisely not gone far afield. Her diction in three English canzonettas by Haydn was not always clear, *but there was great beauty and musicality in her work*, especially in high-lying pianissimo passages. Her low range is not strong, *but instead of pushing her voice, she darkens the colors and thickens the vibrato, giving the sound richness and presence.*
>
> As befits her background, her German diction in songs of Mozart and Schubert was crisp and clear. It will be a long time before I forget her wistful way with Mozart's "Abendemfindung an Laura."[21]

In an effort to be fair to the *totality of an artist's work*, some critics go beyond the event they're reviewing and write about broader performing quality.

For example, *Philadelphia Inquirer* theater critic Clifford A. Ridley reviews Nicol Williamson's opening in "Jack: A Night On The Town With John Barrymore." Ridley likes the actor but not the play, noting that "Williamson, when he wants to be, is one of the finest actors of our day" but "the show is an empty, self-indulgent bore." [22]

John Anderson, *Los Angeles Times* movie critic, uses his review of a strong current performance by Julia Ormond to explain away an early—and lousy—performance. Anderson writes that in the current "Captives," Ormond "shows why people are excited about her and why we have to hope (her earlier) 'Sabrina' was an aberration." [23]

Yes, fairness to the artist can be accomplished by lacing a critical review with positives, by finding past career strengths to counterbalance current weaknesses. Struggling artists thus are treated fairly (and, no matter what they say, most suffer what fiction writer Norma Rosen calls her "anticipatory anxiety" over reviews). [24] And, art is served—a consideration these days when a bad review can close a play, drive moviegoers from the box office or kill sales of a book. Yes, fairness to artist and art is important.

But how about *fairness to readers*?

I believe the first responsibility of any journalist—in reporting politics, sports, business or the arts—is to be fair to readers. In arts criticism, readers seek from you knowledgeable reporting, insightful analysis, clear writing and opinions founded in fact and reason. *And being kind to struggling artists by throwing puff balls isn't being fair to readers.* Wide-eyed uncritical adoration of entertainers is no more acceptable in arts criticism than in writing about politicians or football players.

Yet, arts commentary today is full of unquestioning, superficial writing that's demonstrably unfair to readers.

Thus, Peter Johnson writes admiringly in his "Inside TV" column for *USA Today* about Matt Lauer (he of "good looks and jovial personality"), who is co-anchor of NBC's morning show, "Today." Johnson has Lauer "munching on a toasted bagel after the show" (why do stars always "munch"?) before heading off to a charity appearance in Connecticut. Lauer drips good-guy charm, and nary the negative does writer Johnson mention to spoil the unadulterated ooze. [25]

Now turn to an old pro, John J. O'Connor of *The New York Times* and one of journalism's most respected television critics. For his readers, O'Connor takes a look—a hard look—at Jack Paar 25 years after he walked away from his role as host of NBC's "Tonight Show." Here is O'Connor's blemishes-and-all lead:

He whimpered. He whined. Sometimes he actually cried.
In short, Jack Paar was a television natural.

O'Connor writes that Paar's "career chart is a checkerboard" and that he was masterful in television at gathering guests who were "generally charming raconteurs." But O'Connor continues: That same Paar was a "full-blown eccentric," whose tone at the time was described by one critic as being "unacceptably sullen, tired and arrogant," and Paar was "notoriously touchy."

This critic doesn't present a profile of unadulterated oozing charm. He is fair to readers, balancing his admiration for Paar's strengths with hard-hitting commentary on his weaknesses. Witness this paragraph:

> The audience was fascinated, idly wondering if he would actually have a nervous breakdown on camera as he rambled, sometimes incoherently, through everything from sentimental musings about his wife, Miriam, and his daughter, Randy, in Bronxville to a somewhat fawning interview with Fidel Castro.[26]

And, yes, young writer, being fair to readers *can be hurtful to others*, and not only to artists but also to those who in many cities keep art alive through donations of time and money. As in Los Angeles, at the UCLA/Armand Hammer Museum of Art, which staged an exhibit that drew attention from Christopher Knight, *Los Angeles Times* art critic. His review opens this way:

> "Sexual Politics: Judy Chicago's 'Dinner Party' in Feminist Art History" is the worst exhibition I've seen in a Los Angeles museum in many a moon ...

From there, it's all downhill for critic Knight. He writes the exhibition is "a fiasco" and "a blunder" marked by "curatorial trivialization" and, "You want to run screaming from the room." Knight's wrath knows no bounds. He exits with this kicker:

> It's always disappointing to come upon an ambitious but failed work of art, like "The Dinner Party." But to witness a museum actively participate in the trivialization of art is infinitely worse.[27]

| Box 9-3 | A Professional's Viewpoint |

I got the worst reviews I think I'll ever receive. It was a little like losing your virginity to a rapist. There's no way to prepare for that kind of media attention.

Chicago actress Paula Killen on the critics' view early in her (later successful) career, quoted in Sid Smith, "On The Outside, Looking In," *The Chicago Tribune,* April 25, 1996, Section Two, p. 2.

Danger #3: Jargon: The Communication Killer

This is a snap quiz. Be quick!

What is a *Los Angeles Times* critic saying with the following in a review of The New York Music Ensemble?

Pablo Ortiz's "Story Time" was an animated but hazy discussion for four, its participants subject to tangential thoughts. Wayne Peterson's sextet, "Vicissitudes," traversed dreamy voluptuousness and hyperkinetic frenzy. Ross Bauer's "Stone Soup," for quintet, contained furtive and nervous impulses, and edgy sostenuto—rough on the digestion.[28]

Well, you say, that's Big League reviewing of classical music. How about somebody who reviews *my* music and speaks *my* language? OK. What is Armond White of *Spin* telling you with the following in his review of Notorious B.I.G. videos?

Stretched into wide, anamorphic letterbox frames, these scenes hanker for a movie glamour that eludes most rappers but still serves as the primary subtext for most hip-hop videos.[29]

Or, explain what *Rolling Stone* is saying in this review of the British group, the Prodigy:

Liam Howlett labored on "The Fat of the Land" for the better part of two years, and the results speak for themselves. His grasp of rhythm and texture—and of basic song structure—has matured immeasurably from the days when the Prodigy were churning out frenetic rave novelties such as "Charly." Howlett may reject the cerebral world of ambient, but he also has left behind the simplistic, hyperventilated hard-core techno of old. Squelching synths bounce round each other on "Mindfields," creating a mesmerizing funk force field. ...
    Nevertheless, the Prodigy are greeting the dystopian future with a crazed kind of glee—there is no premillennial tension on this album. [30]

The point is clear: much arts commentary isn't.

Slipping into jargon or simply taking poetic flight can push your commentary beyond reach of your readers. *You* may feel creatively fulfilled by your musings but unless you translate, *they* will feel little but confusion and a desire to take a flight of their own—away from your byline.

It's possible, however, in arts commentary—as in any journalism—to stretch in your writing for just those right words, those right phrases that express your emotions and still communicate effectively with non-expert readers.

For example, Michael Manning of *The Boston Globe* reviews a Brahms concert and addresses the performance by pianist Leslie Amper of Brahm's "Study After an Impromptu by Schubert":

Amper played it with almost every note in place but without any of the character of the original piece, which is probably not the lesson Brahms had in mind.

I'm okay so far, then I wonder at this next sentence in Manning's review (emphasis added):

The two "Rhapsodies," Opus 79, *lacked a certain fastidiousness.*

Whoa! What does that mean? Well anticipating that question from a reader (the mark of an excellent critic), Manning explains in the next sentence:

> Brahms suffers without details, and when he writes a four-against-three rhythm, one must at least try to play it.[31]

Ah! Now I understand!

At *The Washington Post,* pop critic Mark Jenkins reviews new albums by Nusrat Fateh Ali Khan, a Pakistani singer suddenly and hugely popular in the United States. Jenkins writes that Khan is influenced by *qawwali,* the sacred music of Sufism, a mystical Islamic sect, and that *qawwali* sounds much like Indian ragas.

If ever a critic has opportunity to take poetic flight, this is it. Jenkins can let his keyboard soar into the mysticism of the Indian subcontinent; he can unleash his imagination and let the jargon tumble forth. But he doesn't.

Like any good reporter, critic Jenkins inserts that paragraph—call it the "nut graf" of the "housekeeping graf"—that lets readers understand what Khan and his artform are all about:

> Khan's albums provide musical evidence of the strong cultural tie between those bitter political enemies, India and Pakistan. Qawwali compositions sound much like Indian ragas, the lengthy improvisational pieces played on the sitar, an instrument that has up to 20 strings. The role that the sitar plays in the raga, however, is taken in qawwali by the voice. A qawwali singer must have more than a pleasant tone and the ability to sing on key; he (the genre has no female vocalists) must possess exceptional range and a talent for improvisation. Endurance is important too: Kahn's concerts last up to four hours, and the four tracks on Khan's "Intoxicated Spirit" (Shanachie) range from 12 to 24 minutes long.[32]

Jargon-filled writing is more than a disservice to your readers; it's a disservice to *you,* because it prevents you from truly expressing your opinion or clearly making your central point. Note how these critics cut through the malarkey and drive directly—clearly, simply—to their central point:

The New Yorker reviews a new theatrical production, "Ancient History":

> The superficial point of conflict is that he is Catholic and she is Jewish, but [playwright David] Ives seems to be asking a much larger, more unsettling question about love: Doesn't anybody here know how to play this game? Unfortunately, the twosome [the lead couple] is tedious, and the play, unlike the relationship, goes on forever.[33]

David Norman in *Scientific American* reviews Michael Crichton's book, *The Lost World,* and drives directly to (or *into*) the heart of the matter: "*The Lost World* is a blatantly commercial enterprise— 'Jurassic Park II' in transparent disguise." [34]

And, Jay Carr of *The Boston Globe* is enormously effective with a jargon-less, clearly stated opinion of the David Hogan movie, "Barb Wire," featuring Pamela Anderson Lee:

> Pamela Anderson Lee's signature line in the title role of "Barb Wire" is "Don't call me babe." But of course this latest attempt to hit the female action-hero jackpot is nothing but a babewatch. As a stiletto-heeled terminator in a Mad Max world in 2017, Lee often seems undecided whether to kick butt or expose some. It's easy to understand her puzzlement. She can't act a lick, but the role of Barb Wire isn't about acting. It's about being not quite contained in clingy black duds.[35]

Danger #4: Manipulation by the Arts World

Because his political affairs column stirs presidents and prime ministers, David Broder of *The Washington Post* is targeted by high-powered PR types and spin artists in the capitals of the world.

Coaches, players and a huge well-financed PR effort seek to manipulate sports columnists such as Dave Anderson of *The New York Times.*

As an arts critic, you will be a target, too—whether you're reviewing the local theater group in small-town journalism or nationally famous rock groups for *Rolling Stone* or the Metropolitan Opera for *The New York Times.*

It's the power of your newspaper or magazine the spin artists seek, of course—power to boost careers or sink them; power to draw crowds to the theater, or drive them away; power to inspire a bookstore sell-out or help sentence even a great book to oblivion simply by ignoring it.

It's heady stuff, this power of the keyboard, and, young writer, when *you* are being wined and dined, it's good to remember the spin artists are courting your newspaper or magazine for its power, not you, for your wisdom or scintillating personality.

Make no mistake: The effort to manipulate critics is widespread, determined and, at times, vicious.

A survey by the University of Southern California School of Journalism of critics, reporters and entertainment editors found, for example, that Hollywood studio "manipulation of the media has never been more rampant."[36]

As in any manipulative effort directed at journalists, the carrot—and stick—used by studios is *access.*

Compliant critics willing to shill a movie and unthinkingly sign off on a rave review get exclusive interviews with stars and front-row seats at prestigious pre-opening screenings. Critics who think independently and write what they think can get frozen out and thus be at serious competitive disadvantage.

Glenn Lovell, entertainment writer for Knight Ridder Newspapers and the *San Jose Mercury News,* in reporting the USC survey, wrote, "We turned up accounts of everything from forcible ejection from pre-opening screenings to blackballing by a studio for 'the tone' of one's coverage." Lovell said he was blacklisted by studios for "not playing by the rules."

Lovell said even "the Thumb Boys"—Roger Ebert and Gene Siskel, two of our time's most famous film critics—were dropped from the pre-opening screening list by one studio because they badmouthed a film. Because they have such enormous clout, Ebert and Siskel were reinstated in less than three weeks.[37]

As a beginner critic, in campus or small-town journalism, you'll not have that clout, of course. But you'll be a target, nevertheless.

For example, with huge sums invested in producing films, Hollywood studios are desperate to create box-office draw wherever they can find it, and that includes courting reviewers at small newspapers. The entertainment editor of *Red & Black,* an independent student-run newspaper serving the University of Georgia, was offered an all-expense-paid junket worth thousands of dollars by a Hollywood studio for pre-opening screening of a film aimed at young viewers. College newspapers throughout America received similar offers.

This PR tactic raises complex *ethical questions*:

- Since *any* review, good or bad, is better for the studio than no review, does the student critic surrender an essential journalistic judgment—*which* film to review—by accepting a junket and thus automatically agreeing to review the studio's film?
- Even though the studio may ask no special consideration in return for a junket, and the student critic sets forth determined to give none, isn't there danger of feeling so good (and well-fed) about the occasion that a positive review results?
- And, of course, isn't winging free to Hollywood on a junket the same as a political affairs columnist taking a free Caribbean vacation on a political party's cuff, or a sports commentator riding free on a football team's charter jet? And, wouldn't we run out of the business any political columnist or sports writer so caught?

On the other hand:

- Foreign correspondents eat with the U.S. military in the field and ride U.S. helicopters into combat without buying a ticket. And don't those correspondents retain their independence and freedom to be critical?
- And, if a studio offers a student critic a unique opportunity to go to the scene of the action, on behalf of his or her readers, isn't it okay to accept? After all, student newspapers can't afford to pay their own way to such events, and why deny student readers the right to read about them in their own newspapers?

In case you're wondering, the University of Georgia student critic, with permission of *Red & Black* editors, took the Hollywood junket. It sparked considerable debate over the ethics of junkets. The consensus was that it's okay for student critics to fly and eat free on Hollywood's credit card—*if readers are advised, in an editor's note or the review itself, of the circumstances.*[38]

You can get ambushed by a more insidious manipulative effort—Hollywood's attempt to divert a critic from examining a movie's artistic accomplishments to reporting how much was spent producing the movie or its box office receipts.

Michael Lewis, writing in *The New York Times Magazine,* notes a film studio advertised "in obscenely giant print" the worldwide take of "Babe," not the film's art, and that "Even 'Braveheart,' which you might think would be sold on the strength of its Oscar triumphs, is feted financially."[39]

And, hundreds of newspapers dutifully publish weekly box office receipts of top movies; television entertainment shows feature them—and *money* becomes the critical standard for measuring films.

Box 9-4	A Professional's Viewpoint

Critics move over. Just about everyone's view of the movies is clear. And it looks like this: $$$.

> —Michael Lewis, "All Grossed Out," *The New York Times Magazine,* in reporting Hollywood's tendency to judge films' success not on art but, rather, on box office receipts.

Of course, it's *their own love of art* that traps many young critics into thinking their journalistic mission is to serve art, not readers.

It's the critic's form of boosterism—backing the local team without reservation, sticking with "our guys," good or bad. It's the art world's version of "good-cause" columnists who can be counted on to lend full and uncritical support to "good causes."

In campus and small-town journalism, the pressure is heavy. You *do* support campus culture, don't you? You *do* want community theater (or music or art shows or dance) here in small-town Illinois (or Idaho or Tennessee or Michigan) don't you?

Well, if writing a local political column, you would expect to report and comment on *all* sides of, say, a controversy over a school bond issue (even though you personally support better schools).

If writing local sports commentary you would report the local team's weaknesses as well as strengths (even though you hope the team wins)!

So, approach your journalistic duty as an arts critic by arriving objectively and dispassionately at your own honest and independent opinion (even though you love all art, good or bad).

Form and Structure (or Lack of)

Arts commentary accepts—nay, *demands*—writing originality and individualism that's seldom seen in other types of journalism.

In language, tempo and pace, reviews and critical arts commentary are expected to reflect the uniqueness of the artforms they describe and the writer's personal opinions. Editors and readers expect arts sections to look different, *to be different.*

Which is to say, you'll find in this book no writing formulas for critics—no required writing forms for reviews, no schematic drawings of "appropriate" structures for commentaries. In arts criticism, if your own unique writing approach works, use it.

Nevertheless, your readers (and, certainly, your editors) will demand that whatever your writing form and structure, your reviews and commentaries weave in certain essential information. Yes, as a critic you have license to soar as a *writer*; no, as a *journalist* you can't neglect your key role of reporting facts.

And, you must do it all—report *and* comment—within cruel newshole restraints. Editors simply don't have enough space in any newspaper or magazine to cover the world, its triumphs and its miseries, *and* let you run to thousands of words in reviewing routine events. Use your best news values and judgments (as your editors will) in deciding whether a performance merits long or short treatment. And do remember the pros *write tight*—100 words or so for reviews in *The New Yorker,* sometimes 250-300 in *The New York Times* even for major events.

For young writers, it's a good idea to approach the *reporting function* in arts criticism by ticking off those old faithfuls, the Five Ws and How. But, I'm talking here about Five Ws and How dramatically modified by your interpretation—your opinion—of what would be basic facts simply stated in a news story. Let's look at how pros do that:

Who

In a *news* story about Primus, stating the group's name is enough. In a *review* of the group's "Brown Album," Tom Moon of *Rolling Stone* characterizes the "who" factor by inserting his opinion of the group's musical quality and thus expanding his readers' understanding of who he thinks the group really is:

> ["Brown Album"] is precisely the type of weirdness that Primus have been peddling for years—progressive-rock instrumentals camouflaged in the tattered rags of punk and the absurdist narratives of a junior Zappa.[40]

For Moon of *Rolling Stone,* then, the real "who" is not just "Primus." Rather, it's Primus, a group that *peddles weirdness.*

A reporter would write that jazz guitarist Bill Firsell appeared at the Knitting Factory in New York City. For jazz critic Ben Ratliff of *The New York Times,* the "who" factor is, "Bill Frisell, *the most significant and widely imitated guitarist to emerge in jazz since the beginning of the 1980s.*" [41]

Terry Lawson of the *Detroit Free Press* describes "who" in a commentary on a film studio: "Harvey and Bob Weinstein, *the streetwise brothers* who run the Miramax film division." [42]

Chicago Tribune rock critic Greg Kot expands reader understanding of the "who" in reviewing "master song-writer Ray Davies": Davies "was, and remains, an entertainer and a loner, a loose-screw and a lovable loser, a brilliant conceptualist and a sometimes sloppy performer." [43]

Often, just a few words carry your critical appreciation of the "who" beyond the factual reporting of a news story. For Olin Chism of *The Dallas Morning News,* reviewing a new classical video, lead singer Grace Bumbry is "a natural."[44] Timothy Mangan of *The Los Angeles Times* reviews the Los Angeles Philharmonic and tells his readers the "who," the conductor, is "a relatively novice batonwielder though a seasoned pianist." [45]

What

In arts reviewing, your definition of "what" is pivotal. Your interpretation of the "what" factor expresses your personal opinion and sets the stage for your critical analysis.

Sarah Vowell of *Spin* defines "what" right away in her review of the Geraldine Fibbers' album, "Butch." Vowell's lead:

Country music boils down to "How come you don't love me?" while punk wonders, "Why do you hate me?" The two questions, like the two genres, are inherently oppositional, alienated, confused. Each depends on who's doing the asking which is why singers make or break both kinds of songs. Though vocalist Carla Bozulich of Los Angeles' Geraldine Fibbers slips in and out of styles, defiance is her best color.[46]

Matt Roush of *USA Today* is up-front, too, in reviewing, "On Seventh Avenue," an NBC television show:

Transplant the milieu of "Models, Inc." to the land of "Central Park West" and you get ... another flop in the making.

NBC wisely saw the light and didn't order a show from this sleek two-hour pilot masquerading as a TV movie. (There's far too much story line and too little focus for this to be anything other than a series tease.)[47]

Film critic Bob Strauss of *The Boston Globe* reviews films produced by studio types "born after 1965, the age cohort that hates to be known as Generation X," and sums up the "what" factor: Generation X is producing "some of the very best romantic-comedy films to come along in years."[48]

Tom Shales of *The Washington Post* reviews a "grim and gripping" CBS miniseries, "A Season in Purgatory," and decides the "what" is a number of "depressing messages" from an author who "specializes in crime among the filthy rich."[49]

Robert Bianco of *The Pittsburgh Post-Gazette* reviews "Tornado!" on the Fox network, and decides the "what" is a made-for-TV movie that "sounds suspiciously similar to this week's big-screen blockbuster, 'Twister.'"[50]

Kinney Littlefield of the Costa Mesa (CA) *Orange County Register* writes the "what" of a new book is that it's a "violent and sexually graphic murder mystery." Critic Littlefield then details the book plot and the author's views, providing a well-rounded description of what the book is all about.[51]

Too often, critics neglect to give readers a complete, well-rounded view of what is happening on stage or screen and, instead, launch into opinionated interpretation that, absent factual reporting, can leave readers only confused.

For example, Anna Kisselgoff, widely considered one of journalism's leading dance critics, reports the New York City Ballet closed its season with a farewell performance by soloist Michael Byars. She reports to her *New York Times* readers that fans showered him with bouquets and a fellow performer kissed him on stage in "a moving tribute." Reader anticipation builds: *What*'s going on? Why is Byars leaving? Where is he going? Those questions are not answered; readers are left dangling.[52]

Be certain your reporting of "what" gives readers good insights into the plot of a movie, the substance of a book, the technical artistry of a singer. Explain what the artist or writer is *trying* to accomplish. Build a factual base of understanding in your readers' minds, then cast your opinion against that.

Of course, your explanation of "what" should not be carried so far that you give away a book's plot or strip a stage performance of all surprise. Let your review entice and suggest, but don't deprive your readers of the joy of discovering for themselves.

Where, When, Why (and Also, How Much)

Two factors should influence your judgment on how to handle this type of operative information.

First, you *are* a journalist and *are* obliged to give readers—oh, call it, "news to live by." Newspapers, historically have offered readers detailed information on where to go, when, why and how much it costs when they get there. Even *Wall Street Journal* editors, who usually have their minds on other things, decided to give readers this type of information by publishing daily television, cable and theater schedules.[53]

Second, you must judge the news importance of "where," "when" and "why." In most reviews this information is given passing reference. But not always.

When Jon Pareles of *The New York Times* reviews a Garth Brooks performance the *where* is crucial because although Brooks might be "the best-selling performer of the 1990s and one of the most commercially successful singers in pop history" this performance is *in New York City, in Central Park*. Imagine! Country music attracts thousands of New Yorkers to an evening in the park.

The "where" is important to Pareles for another reason: Brooks "has remade country music for arena-size audiences" and during the performance he "raced from end to end of a very broad stage in Central Park." [54]

Bob Massey of *The Washington Post* tells readers that rapper Toni Blackman and her hip-hop group, Daughters of the Cipher, are appearing tonight at the 9:30 Club in Washington and "don't dress for cocktails" because there will be bands, body painting, a drum and dance circle, self-defense demonstrators, a deejay and an all-female group of visual artists.

That's the "where" and "when." Now Massey provides the "why":

Tonight's spectacle benefits the Empower Program, which works with pregnant teens, teenage mothers and emotionally disturbed youths. The event is the latest collaboration between (deejay Neville) Blackman and local arts promoter Dave Kasdan, whose organization, Artists' Collective Endeavors, tries to bridge the gaps between seemingly disparate disciplines.

Massey's preview concludes with concise "news you can use":

Tickets are $10 in advance from Protix, 703-218-6500; $12 at the 9:30 Club box office, 202-265-0930. Proceeds benefit Empower Programs, 202-882-2800.[55]

Okay, that's the Five Ws—"who, what, where, when and why." What about "how"?

Well, young writer, figuring out precisely *how* to write a review is something only *you* can do. Study the artform you intend to analyze, approach your reporting task with good conscience, meet the basic information requirements outlined in this chapter, then state a reasonable opinion founded in fact and logic—and good luck in developing your own unique, personalized writing style!

Box 9-5	Book Reviewing

Of all artforms, none is given the critical attention that books receive from newspapers and magazines. All publications review books, an old, enduring and, for many, beloved artform.

For aspiring arts commentators, book reviewing often is a starting point. Review copies pour into newspapers and magazines, and they're doled out to staff writers and free-lancers for review.

Subscribers assign high priority to book news, so newspapers and magazines devote enormous newshole to reviews. *The New York Times, Philadelphia Inquirer* and other newspapers publish daily reviews and full pull-out sections on Sundays.

Like most arts commentary, book reviewing doesn't—shouldn't—fit any preconceived notion of how you must structure your writing. Skim reviews in any major newspaper or magazine and you'll see many forms and structures—and highly individualized writing tones and styles.

Broadly, however, many reviews take one of two directions:

- They discuss the book *as a literary achievement,* analyzing the author's writing skill, the plot, structure, characterizations and descriptive language. This is the thrust of much commentary on fiction, which, as much as any artform, is critiqued for creative imagination and technical skill. Many reviews contrast the work with the author's previous writing or, if the book is a first, assign it some degree of comparative merit: Is the book strong? Weak? Why? How does it rank with other similar works? Thus, *The Los Angeles Times* opens a review of a new novel by Kem Nunn by noting his books "have been compared to the works of a latter-day Flannery O'Connor."[a]
- Or, again broadly, reviewers use a book merely as *a peg for wider discussion,* as a means of passing on information about a subject that will spark reader thinking. Thus, *The New Republic* discusses good and evil in authoritarian regimes for 700 words *before mentioning the book it is reviewing.*[b] Thus *The Wall Street Journal* publishes what purports to be a review of *two* new books on the cosmos but which really is a highly personalized, extended discussion of the reviewer's own thinking on the "Big Bang" theory of creation.[c]

Whichever your approach, your review must contain basic information: title, author, publisher and price, in addition to your plot sketch and your outline of what the author is attempting—and your judgment whether successfully.

Always—explicitly or implicitly—you must answer this question: Is this book worth your readers' time and money?

In addition to weaving such information into the body of reviews, the Portland (OR) *Sunday Oregonian* publishes "boxed" summaries such as this one:

A Chance to See Egypt
Sandra Scofield
HarperCollins, $22
Bottom Line

One of the fiction accomplishments of the year, a story of personal renewal in a Mexican village, "Egypt" snares several contrary communities in a web of love, spirituality and terrific humane wit.[d]

As for writing length, use basic news values and judgments. A good book likely to catch your readers' interest—be that "literature" in the widest sense or tree pruning in the narrowest—should get major newshole. Books of little interest to your readers obviously should get less—just as you trim (or eliminate) coverage of *any* news of secondary interest. Newspapers and magazines devote *columns* of type to a major book or, as *Business Week* does in its regular feature on best-sellers, cut a review to the minimum. Like this:

Warren Buffett Speaks by Janet Lowe (Wiley: $16.95) Quotes, droll and otherwise, from Omaha's wealthiest citizen.[e]

Ebony publishes roundups of reviews likely to interest its black audience. Two major books open this "Book Shelf" feature:

Using vignettes of her experiences and personal reflections on events in her life since the publication of Report From Part One, Gwendolyn Brooks—the first Black awarded the Pulitzer Prize and the State of Illinois' poet laureate—presents the second installment of her autobiography, *Report From Part Two* (Third World Press, $21.95).

Robert Fleming gleans a wealth of inspirational quotations from the speeches and writings of some of Black America's most esteemed men and women in *The Wisdom of the Elders: Inspiring Reflections from the Heart of African American Culture* (One World/Ballantine, $15).

In the same column, *Ebony* merely acknowledges publication of another book:

How to Love a Black Man (Warner Books, $17.95), a relationship guide, by Ronn Elmore.[f]

[a]Connie Koenenn, "Shortcuts," *The Los Angeles Times,* April 18, 1997, p. E-3; [b]Ian Buruma, "Wolf in Wolf's Clothing," *The New Republic,* July 14 & 21, 1997, p. 40; [c]Jim Holt, "Blast From the Past," *The Wall Street Journal,* June 17, 1997, p. A-16;[d]John Domini, "A Mourner's Pilgrimage," The Portland (OR) *Sunday Oregonian,* April 28, 1996, p. E-5;[e] "Books," *Business Week,* May 26, 1997, p. 24;[f] "Ebony Book Shelf," *Ebony,* April 1996, p. 16.

Summary

- Arts criticism is a journalistic form read avidly, it seems, by everybody associated with all forms of art—and simultaneously reviled by the same cast of characters.
- Newspapers and magazines of all types offer arts criticism and book reviews as circulation-building inducements to readers.

- Arts critics must decide early whether they owe principal loyalty to the art-form they're covering, the artist(s), themselves or their audiences.
- Critics also must decide whether they're writing for *insiders* intimately involved in the world of art, or *outsiders*, those readers who need the esoterica of art and its specialized language translated into terms they can understand.
- Young writers getting started in arts criticism should lean more on their reporting strengths than analytical or interpretative qualities.
- To be taken seriously as a critic with a meaningful message requires elaborate career preparation and serious study of the artform, just as political commentators must be serious students of politics.
- If college newspaper arts commentators suffer a single weakness it is being stridently and predictably adversarial in their criticism, with limited understanding of what critic Fintan O'Toole calls the "history and the conventions of whatever art-form is under scrutiny."
- Dancer Karen Woods of Ohio State University says critics play a valuable function in arts reporting if they draw from strong experience and education to make insightful observations.
- Young writers face the danger of the "Cheap Shot Syndrome," a tendency to stretch for cute but meaningless phrases and thus neglect the basic journalistic mission of informing.
- Being fair in reviews requires balancing your personal likes or dislikes by reporting audience reaction.
- Avoid writing in jargon, the shorthand language of experts and other artists, which can confuse non-expert readers.
- Arts commentators can be manipulated if they buy into the arts so totally that they become "home-team boosters" or they can fall prey to the powerful, well-financed public relations apparatus that controls access to artists and performances.
- Arts commentary demands writing originality and individualism, so there are no writing formulas for critics; if your unique writing approach works, use it.
- Whatever your *writing* approach, as a critic you must perform the *reporting* task of any journalist and give readers the operative information behind the Five Ws and How.

Recommended Reading

Aspiring critics must read voraciously to develop strengths on what might be called horizontal and vertical planes. That is, while reading (and writing) generally—or "horizontally"—to develop strong, broad-based skills as a journalist, you also should read in depth—"vertically"—in the artform(s) in which you intend to specialize.

"Vertical" reading for aspiring critics should be in specialized newspapers and magazines—*Rolling Stone* and *Spin,* for example, if your musical interests lie in their direction. *Dance* and *Opera News* are examples of arts "trade" magazines available to serious students of specialized artforms.

Among daily newspapers, *The Los Angeles Times* is strong in coverage of the film industry and reviews of new movies. *The New York Times*' "Arts & Entertainment" section is outstanding reading for any aspiring critic. *The Chicago Tribune* is strong on coverage of Chicago, a major arts center, and the Midwest. *Boston Globe* critics range far and wide—and expertly; they're worth reading.

Notes

1. Mark Fitzgerald, "Mixed Reviews for Chicago Tribune Arts Coverage," *Editor & Publisher,* April 20, 1996, p. 21.

2. Fintan O'Toole, "What Are Critics For?", *The Economist,* Oct. 12, 1996, p. 91.

3. Iver Peterson, "Denver Ain't Big Enough for Both of 'em," *The New York Times,* Dec. 16, 1996, p. D-1.

4. Fintan O'Toole, *The Economist,* op cit.

5. Carol Channing, "A Kerr Farewell," *The New York Times,* national edition, Oct. 15, 1996, p. A-14.

6. John Corry, "Walter Kerr, a Dominant Critic During Broadway's Full Flower, Is Dead at 83," *The New York Times,* national edition, Oct. 10, 1996, p. A-19.

7. Fintan O'Toole, *The Economist,* op cit.

8. Fintan O'Toole, *The Economist,* op cit., quoting Jonathon Green, *Dictionary of Insulting Quotations* (London: Cassell).

9. In the spirit of full disclosure, which I believe is any journalist's duty, I report that Karen Woods is my daughter.

10. Drew Jubera, "A Fistful of Oscars," *The Atlanta Constitution,* March 30, 1993, p. B-1.

11. Frank Rich, "The Drama Critic Who Made the Pulse Race," *The New York Times,* national edition, Oct. 20, 1996, p. H-6.

12. "Goings On About Town," *The New Yorker,* March 31, 1997, p. 30.

13. Don Heckman, "A Major Voice With Minor Problems," *The Los Angeles Times,* May 2, 1996, p. F-7.

14. "Goings On About Town," *The New Yorker,* Aug. 10, 1996, p. 14.

15. Ibid.

16. Matt Diehl, "Motley Crue," *Rolling Stone,* Aug. 7, 1997, p. 39.

17. Scott L. Powers, "Byrds' CDs Something to Sing About," *The Boston Globe,* May 3, 1996, p. 57.

18. Parke Puterbaugh, "Ozzy Osbourne," *Rolling Stone,* July 11, 1996, p. 25.

19. Skip Ascheim, "'Charlotte's Web' Spins Humorous Fantasy," *The Boston Globe,* April 23, 1996, p. 53.

20. Esther Iverem, "Talbert's Familiar 'Fool,'" *The Washington Post,* May 1, 1997, p. C-11.

21. Anthony Tommasini, "After a Steady Climb in Europe, She's at Home With Her Lieder," *The New York Times,* Aug. 9, 1997, p. 11.

22. Clifford A. Ridley, "Review: Theater," *The Philadelphia Inquirer,* April 28, 1996, p. F-9.

23. John Anderson, "'Captives' Gets Locked Into Own Darkness," *The Los Angeles Times,* May 3, 1996, p. F-12.

24. Norma Rosen, "My Son, the Novelist," *The New York Times Magazine,* Aug. 3, 1997, p. 60.

25. Peter Johnson, "Inside TV," *USA Today,* June 30, 1997, p. D-3.

26. John J. O'Connor, "A Master of the Small Chuckle," *The New York Times,* Feb. 2, 1997, p. H-42.

27. Christopher Knight, "More Famine Than Feast," *The Los Angeles Times,* May 2, 1996, p. F-1.

28. Timothy Mangan, "New York Ensemble Takes Complex Path," *The Los Angeles Times,* May 1, 1996, p. F-8.

29. Armond White, "Don't Believe the Hype," *Spin,* August 1997, p. 84.

30. Barney Hoskyns, "The Fat of the Land," *Rolling Stone,* Aug. 7, 1997, p. 59.

31. Michael Manning, "Emmanuel Puts Brahms Series to Bed," *The Boston Globe,* April 23, 1996, p. 56.

32. Mark Jenkins, "From Pakistan, Genius Khan," *The Washington Post,* May 12, 1996, p. G-10.

33. "Goings On About Town," *The New Yorker,* June 10, 1996, p. 12.

34. David Norman, "Views and Commentaries," *Scientific American,* April 1996, p. 108.

35. Jay Carr, "The Barbie of 'Barb Wire,'" *The Boston Globe,* May 3, 1996, p. 48.

36. Glenn Lovell, "Movies and Manipulation," *Columbia Journalism Review,* January/February 1997, p. 9.

37. Ibid.

38. This incident occurred in 1996. For a more detailed look at "freebies" and other ethical challenges in journalism, see, Conrad Fink, *Media Ethics* (Boston: Allyn and Bacon, 1995).

39. Michael Lewis, "All Grossed Out," *The New York Times Magazine,* May 19, 1996, p. 24.

40. Tom Moon, "Brown Album," *Rolling Stone,* Aug. 7, 1997, p. 62.

41. Ben Ratliff, "Jazz Festival Review," *The New York Times,* national edition, June 21, 1997, p. 19.

42. Terry Lawson, *Detroit Free Press* dispatch for Jan. 5, 1997.

43. Greg Kot, "Thinking Man's Kink," *The Chicago Tribune,* April 19, 1996, Section 2, p. 2.

44. Olin Chism, "Performance True to Life and to 'Carmen,'" *The Dallas Morning News,* May 5, 1996, p. C-7.

45. Timothy Mangan, "Percussively Postmodern Philharmonic," *The Los Angeles Times,* April 27, 1996, p. F-6.

46. Sarah Vowell, "Geraldine Fibbers," *Spin,* August 1997, p. 112.

47. Matt Roush, "'Seventh Avenue': Heavy on Padding, Thin on Foundation," *USA Today,* June 10, 1996, p. D-3.

48. Bob Strauss, "Modern Romances," *The Boston Globe,* May 5, 1996, p. 66.

49. Tom Shales, "The Bad and the Bountiful," *The Washington Post*, May 5, 1996, p. G-1.

50. Robert Bianco, "'Tornado!' Star Breezes Along," *The Pittsburgh Post-Gazette* dispatch for May 5, 1996, published that day in *Dallas Morning News*, p. C-11.

51. Kinney Littlefield, *Orange County Register*, dispatch for May 5, 1996, published that day in *Dallas Morning News*, p. C-4.

52. Anna Kisselgoff, "A Farewell, With Panache," *The New York Times*, June 30, 1997, p. C-11.

53. "*Wall Street Journal* to Print TV Listings," *The New York Times*, Aug. 15, 1997, p. D-2.

54. Jon Pareles, "Garth, Nice Guy, Balancing Lust and Love," *The New York Times*, Aug. 9, 1997, p. 19.

55. Bob Massey, "In Eclectic Company," *The Washington Post*, May 1, 1997, p. C-7.

Exercises

1. In 300 words, explain where your loyalty as a critic lies. Do you think your sole responsibility as a reviewer is to express a personal opinion and define a personal approach to a performance or an artform? Or, must you give loyalty to art or artists? What is your loyalty as a journalist-critic to readers?

Craft this personal statement carefully and make it the standard by which you perform as a critic in campus journalism or as a "real world" beginner with newspapers or magazines.

2. Study the "Arts and Entertainment" section of last Sunday's *New York Times* (or another collection of arts reviews and commentaries assigned by your instructor). In about 350 words, discuss whether the critics and reviewers you've studied are writing in the shorthand language of art-world experts and thus are writing for art-world "insiders." Or, are the writers interpreting the esoterica and translating the special language of art for "outsiders"—non-expert readers who dip into the arts only infrequently and, probably, inexpertly?

3. Cover a campus cultural event assigned by your instructor. *Immediately following the performance* (to gain experience in deadline writing), write a review in the 250-300 word range.

Demonstrate in your review that you have backgrounded yourself in the artform you're reviewing. Show understanding of what the artist(s) are attempting to accomplish. Be certain to *report* sufficient details so readers will gain true sense of what the performance was all about. Base your personal opinion and comments in fact and logic, and demonstrate to readers that you have done so.

4. Tonight, watch a television program assigned by your instructor. Do as much prior research on the program, plot and actors as you can.

Tomorrow, submit to your instructor a review in the 300-word range. In your reporting, define the plot, and background your readers on the network, producer, director, and so forth, if that's appropriate.

Did the artists/producers accomplish what they obviously set out to accomplish? Were plot, writing and acting up to par?

You'll have no audience reaction to report in this exercise. So, let 'er rip with your personal views on the performance.

5. Examine a major review in the "Arts and Entertainment" section of *The New York Times* (or another review assigned by your instructor) and, in about 350 words, analyze how the writer handles the four dangers outlined in Chapter Nine:

- The Cheap Shot Syndrome. Does the writer go for the cute and quick (if meaningless) cheap hit?
- Fairness vs. personal opinion. Is the writer fair, extending beyond his/her personal reaction to report, for example, audience reaction?
- Clarity vs. jargon. Can *you* understand *everything* in the review? Would most newspaper readers?
- Manipulation by the arts world. Is the writer clearly free and independent, or does the review show manipulation? (For example, does the review indicate the critic has "bought into" the arts world so completely that independence is sacrificed? Does the review focus on box-office receipts, rather than a film's artistic merit?)

PART FIVE

Extra Dimensions in Commentary and Opinion

O ur discussion in this book has explored major sectors in opinion writing and critical commentary—editorials, personal columns, sports, the arts.

But there's more—much more.

In the two chapters of Part Five we'll explore additional avenues you can follow in writing opinion and commentary. Note carefully the specialized writing we'll study. In pages ahead are even more ideas on how you can launch an exciting career.

In Chapter Ten, "Specialty Columns and Comment," we'll look at commentary tightly focused on narrow interests for newspaper and magazine readers. Highly talented (and well-rewarded) columnists have dedicated followings for their opinions and comments on everything from the stock market to wine to health foods. We'll also look in Chapter Ten at writing for broadcast and that ill-defined but promising electronic sector called "cyberspace."

In Chapter Eleven, "On Campus Today: How It's Done," I'll report on my study of 45 newspapers from colleges and universities across the nation. My purpose is to guide you to your keyboard *now*—to write *now*—for your most wide-open and accepting market, the newspaper on your own campus.

10 Specialty Columns and Comment

NAME YOUR hobby, your special personal interest or, even, your fantasy. (C'mon, do it now!)

Do you know that the editor of some newspaper or magazine somewhere *pays someone* to write commentary on your hobby, special interest or fantasy?

Is your hobby, say, playing video games? The *Syracuse Herald American* pays Jeff Kapalka to do a regular column on video games for its entertainment section.

Does your special interest lie in keeping fit? Jane Brody is a nationally acclaimed personal health columnist for *The New York Times*.

Do you fantasize about, say, roaming the world and visiting exotic lands? *Many* are the travel columnists who do that and get paid for it.

And, don't try to trick me, as one student did by answering that his hobby was simply "wandering about, looking at tall buildings." As the *Boston Globe*'s columnist on architecture, Robert Campbell does that—and he won the Pulitzer Prize for criticism for his "knowledgeable writing" on the subject.

The Specialty Columnist's Special Responsibilities

It's imperative that you keep in mind two factors as you enter specialty commentary:

- You'll need intense personal backgrounding in your subject. The relatively relaxed reporting of "he said, she said" for a general assignment or personal column doesn't work in commentary on technical subjects.

- You'll need sharpened awareness of the impact you can have on readers' lives with specialty commentary. Stretching for a laugh in a humor column or commenting on the football team's weakness at left defensive tackle is one thing; guiding readers toward, say, Wall Street investments or cancer treatment is quite another.

Your First Responsibility

By moving into specialty commentary you jump from *general* reporting into *technical* reporting and writing on complex, esoteric even, subjects.

And waiting for you, when you get there, are *readers often expert or at least highly knowledgeable in your subject.*

So, your first special responsibility in specialty commentary is to ensure your career preparation, academic and on the job, is thorough, and that your reporting is painstaking and, always, that your conclusions and mindset are based on informed opinion and fact drawn from qualified and authoritative sources.

If you don't know what you're writing about, informed readers—the kind who read specialty columns—will spot your weakness in a minute (if your editors haven't already!).

Start now preparing for your eventual move into specialty commentary. If you aim at one day writing a column on business, take business courses; if you want to be the next Jane Brody, take science courses. Somewhere in your college's course catalogue are specialty courses that can help prepare you.

Then, read, read, read—everything you can find on the subject you intend to eventually write about. Read columnists who today cover the subject you'll write about tomorrow.

You'll need general-assignment reporting experience, of course, and that probably will be your first job at a newspaper. *However*, even on general-assignment reporting you often can maneuver into covering stories about your favorite hobby, personal interest or fantasy. Grab those stories; handling them as news stories is great preparation for later column writing.

Your Second (but Equally Important) Responsibility

A great many people *trust* newspapers and magazines. Despite opinion polls showing low public esteem for the "media," the written word is taken very seriously.

Remember that as you venture into, say, business commentary for readers trying to figure out how to invest their life savings, or into personal health commentary for readers with low-back pain who are wondering whether to see a doctor or stick with their Aunt Gracie's home-treatment remedy.

This is serious stuff.

In addition to getting proper career preparation and doing painstaking reporting, when entering this journalistic danger zone of specialty commentary you should do two things:

- Avoid writing as if you possess The Single Truth. No matter how confident you get (*never* get cocky) about your career preparation and reporting or your analytical abilities and interpretive skills, you should *stay tentative* in your commentary. You'll still be a journalist, and nobody should expect journalists to have all the answers. Even the best experts on Wall Street—and that includes brokers we quote—don't know whether stock prices will rise or fall tomorrow. And nobody (including Aunt Gracie) can diagnose low-back pain from afar.
- Analyze, interpret and comment—but also direct your readers to *additional authority*. You can do this within your column by referring to authoritative sources by name and affiliation (The American Cancer Society on significance of some low-back pains). And, you can identify additional sources—reading lists, Internet web sites, health "hot lines"—your readers can consult. Let your specialty commentary be the beginning, not the end, of your readers' search for operative information, their "news to live by."

Let's look at some attractive specialties.

Writing Business Commentary

Despite immediate, automatic disdain many students have for business writing (ugh!), I turn to it for good reasons:

First, business commentary has its own challenges and rewards. Many journalists find it fascinating. Explore carefully this exciting writing option.

Second, almost without exception, campus newspapers ignore business commentary, which leaves the door wide open for *you* to do a column on subjects of student interest.

Third, big league newspapers pay premium salaries for journalists who can handle business news—and who have clips to prove it.

Where can you get ideas for your own business commentary? From your favorite newspaper or magazine. For example:

- Would your student readers go for a column on why couples should "talk about money before marriage"? Commentator Charles A. Jaffe wrote that for his Page-One column, "Personal Finance," in *The Boston Globe*'s business section.
- Margaret A. Dixon devoted one column in *Modern Maturity*—a magazine for oldsters—to how fraudulent telemarketers steal billions from senior citizens. Could your campus newspaper—a news source for young peo-

ple—use a column on how *students* can avoid telephone fraud?

- Walter S. Mossberg of *The Wall Street Journal* described in his column, "Personal Technology," how to use your browser software to explore the World Wide Web without getting hung up on companies' promotional home pages and "other obligatory stops in cyberhell." Do you know anyone more avid than students for such helpful commentary on personal computer technology?
- Jane Bryant Quinn of *Newsweek,* a highly regarded commentator on personal finance, did a column on, "The Internet is safer for business than you think." Her commentary guided readers toward secure personal shopping via the Net at below-premium costs, particularly for books. Of interest to students? You bet!
- James C. Cooper and Kathleen Madigan wrote their *Business Week* column, "Business Outlook," on U.S. employment rates. We'll pass that one, right? Think again. Who is more interested in jobs than college students, particularly graduating seniors?[1]

Well, use your imagination on business commentary you can get into right away—student loan availability, how to find traps in apartment leases, how students can handle personal finances when on their own for the first time. The list is endless.

Endless also are the imaginative, creative ways you can write business commentary. This specialty not only takes you close to your readers' pocketbooks (and, thus, their hearts), it also gives you opportunity to sparkle in your writing.

For example, in his *Boston Globe* column, commentator Jaffe is *open and inviting* in his intro on what could be a dull piece:

> Summer is here and for many people that means an exchange of wedding vows.
>
> Presumably, couples have taken care of the "love, honor, and cherish" part before they ever set a date for the ceremony.
>
> The "for richer, for poorer" part of the equation is a different story altogether.
>
> Even if your love "makes the earth move," it's going to be your money that provides the earthquake insurance.
>
> The tough part is talking about money before marriage.

Columnist Jaffe now quickly weaves in a great quote from an investment advisor with guidance for couples: "You are going to take your clothes off in front of each other, so why not take off your financial clothes? There is nothing to be embarrassed about. This is who you are and it deeply affects your future together."[2]

Business commentary must be dull? No way!

Note columnist Geraldine Fabrikant in her *New York Times* column, "Market Place":

Hercules can lift many things: houses, mountains, tree trunks.

But so far he has been impotent at his most important task: hoisting the Walt Disney Company's stock price.

In its first two weeks of general release, Disney's latest animated feature, "Hercules," has taken in only about $58 million at the box office—a poor showing, compared with other recent Disney summer releases, like 1995's "Pocahontas," which took in $80 million in its first two weeks, and 1994's "The Lion King," which grossed $119 million.[3]

Or, check out John Waggoner in his column, "Mutual Funds," for *USA Today*:

As the strains of "Pomp and Circumstance" waft from your local high-school stadium, your thoughts might be drifting toward your own children. What will they be like at age 18? What will their interests be? How many banks will I have to rob to pay their college tuition?

Put the ski mask away. If you start saving now, you might actually be able to pay for Junior's time at a Big Ten college without doing time in the Big House.[4]

So, if your writer's muse is moving, let it inject your column with sparkle. But *never* at the expense of accuracy, balance or that tentative "maybe" or "perhaps" or "on the other hand" that can save you considerable embarrassment when future reality catches up with your predictions. The real pros always get balance in their columns.

Thus, Jacob M. Schlesinger writes in *The Wall Street Journal's* front-page column, "The Outlook," that there is strong possibility low inflation will continue. But: "Of course, inflationary fears aren't completely cured."[5]

Richard Korman opens his "Investing It" column in *The New York Times* with favorable comment on a company I'll call "Rapid Expansion": "From many angles, [Rapid Expansion] is a tempting investment." However, Korman concludes his column with this tentative note: "But without a merger windfall, [Rapid Expansion] investors may struggle."[6]

And note the balance and authoritative source quickly inserted in one of financial journalism's most prestigious columns, "Heard on the Street," in *The Wall Street Journal* (reported this day jointly by E.S. Browning, Deborah Lohse and Suzanne McGee. I've added special emphasis.):

Time for the Nifty 2000?

It was the market-darling "Nifty 50" blue chips that led the Dow Jones Industrial Average down 247 points Friday.

Some investors now think the small group of powerful multinationals, loosely dubbed the new Nifty 50, finally is set to cede market dominance to a broader group of stocks. *Big fans reply* that the blue chips, which have driven the market for three years, will bounce right back.

What's surprising is that *few people on either side* seem very worried that the Nifty 50's slide could herald the broad market decline that bears have forecast for more than a year.

Richard Unruh, who heads stock-market investing at Delaware Management Co. in Philadelphia, *says* ... [7]

Finally, the pros always point readers to additional authority. Pamela Reeves of Scripps Howard News Services does so in a column on "reverse mortgages" (particularly attractive to older folks because they can live in their homes without making monthly payments). Reeves concludes her column this way:

> About 400 lenders are offering the new reverse mortgage. You can get a list of lenders who live near you, along with an information packet, by calling Fannie Mae toll-free at 800-732-6643 between 9 a.m. and 5 p.m. ET on weekdays.[8]

Writing Lifestyle Commentary

Newspaper and magazine editors pour enormous resources into lifestyle commentary, a huge journalistic tent covering columns and entire sections variously titled, "Lifestyle," "Living," "Style," or, at the *Los Angeles Times,* "Life & Style."

Readers flock to these sections, seeking guidance on how to look better, feel better, dress better, eat and drink better ... how to handle their sex problems, their children's sex problems. In lifestyle sections is where the world of news is reduced for readers to their basic daily problem—just getting along.

For you as a writer, lifestyle commentary is a gold mine of opportunity *if* you develop the knack of spotting—and getting on—the cutting edge of reader thinking and *if* you can report perceptively, analyze fairly and logically, then write helpful commentary that *carries readers beyond recognition of a problem and toward its solution.*

For readers, that problem can be simply where to get a good restaurant meal or how to keep grubs from destroying their lawns. (See Box 10-1 for a view of one lifestyle columnist who spends many of his days—and nights—searching for a good meal. As for grubs, Carol Stocker *led The Boston Globe's* "Living Arts" section one day with the lowdown on them!)[9]

| Box 10-1 | A Professional's Viewpoint |

Frederic Koeppel is restaurant critic, wine columnist and a book reviewer for the *Memphis Commercial Appeal.* He describes his "work" at the dinner table for his Scripps Howard newspaper:

Nine years. Five hundred restaurants reviewed for the *Commercial Appeal's* Friday "Playbook." Ten pounds.

Those statistics apply to my career as restaurant reviewer since the first establishment I critiqued in 1988.

I could add these facts: lots of great meals, lots of average meals, and far too many I would rather not recall at all.

And something else: criticism from restaurant owners and chefs, telephone calls from readers accusing me of being crazy or prejudiced, a death threat we took quite seriously, and those calls from readers tipping me off to obscure little restaurants I otherwise would not have reviewed.

When readers tell me I have the best job in the city, I don't tell them about the deadlines, about the weeks when I have to rush a review into print, about the bad meals, about the times I would love to sit at home and eat a simple dinner instead of hitting the reviewing trail once again. I don't tell them those things because my job *is* the best job in the city.

How do I do it, week after week, year after year?

First rule: Never clean your plate. It makes waiters, managers and chefs unhappy—"Omigod, he didn't finish his entree!"—but it keeps pounds off the waistline.

Second rule: Eat in a variety of restaurants to represent all type of styles of regional cuisine, as well as to keep my tastebuds from getting jaded. Memphis is rich in ethnic fare.

Third rule: Spread the reviewing around. People live and eat in the suburbs, and I try to make certain the weekly reviews alternate among different sections of the city and its suburban areas.

Fourth rule: Create a balance between old and new. Unlike some metropolitan areas, Memphis does not see frenetic restaurant openings and closings. Promise of a (supposedly) great new restaurant here makes news it wouldn't in New York or Chicago. So I often go back to restaurants I have reviewed before, check out new menus or new offerings or find old places where I have never been.

Our policy is to let a restaurant have a month to get things ship-shape before I review it, though sometimes this doesn't work. I have been to restaurants that advertised for several weeks before they opened the doors, meaning that I reviewed them prematurely. Occasionally, a restaurant will actually issue a challenge: "We're ready for Koeppel now; let him do his damnedest."

I try to be fair and objective, open-minded, nonjudgmental. It's not always easy; confronted with a terrible meal, one wants to cast blame, not to mention aspersions. And I have to work at not sounding as if I'm having too much fun dissing a bad place. Metaphor and humor sting, especially when someone's money is at stake.

☙

The column above is reproduced with permission from the July 1997 issue of *Scripps Howard News*, which asked critic Koeppel questions important for aspiring food and restaurant reviewers:

Q: What qualifies you to be a restaurant critic?
A: First, I love food. I also cook a lot at home. I do a great deal of re-

search when I'm writing a review. I compare the restaurant's menu to what classic menus might be. Basically, I have a life history of learning and teaching myself.

Q: Do you pay for the meals you review?

A: The *Commercial Appeal* pays so it's ethical, objective and as fair as possible.

Q: Are your visits a surprise to restaurant managers?

A: We would like them to be. I am not, alas, completely anonymous because I've lived in Memphis for more than 40 years. ... We try to have an unspoken rule that when I know they know me they aren't going to say, "Are you doing a review?"

Or, the readers' problem can be as serious as macular degeneration, an eye ailment discussed by Jane E. Brody in her "Personal Health" column in *The New York Times*. Her lead:

> Do door frames, telephone poles and the edges of buildings appear bent or crooked, as if you were looking at them through heat waves on a highway?
>
> Do objects at a distance seem clear but those up close are blurry, or vice versa?
>
> When you cover one eye, then the other, do you notice a change in the color or size of objects?
>
> Is there a blurry or blank spot in the middle of your visual field, as if a flashbulb had just gone off in your face?

The *problem* and its symptoms thus outlined, Brody points readers toward a *solution*:

> Do not assume that you need new glasses and can wait weeks for a convenient appointment. See your ophthalmologist right away. Accept no delays.
> ...

Brody's column now discusses technical details of macular degeneration but in language readers can understand (explaining, for example, "The macula is a tiny, highly sensitive region in the center of the retina that allows you to see fine details when you look directly at something."). Brody quotes authoritative sources—physicians, the *Journal of the American Medical Association*—on preventive steps readers can take, including vegetables to eat protectively.

In sum, this lifestyle columnist writes in a serious (but never panicky) tone with helpful how-to guidance and always with reference to responsible authority. ("See your ophthalmologist right away.")[10]

At *The Wall Street Journal*, Marilyn Chase takes a *consumer-oriented* approach in her column, "Health Journal." Her lead on one column:

> Consumers who have been willing to pay more for groceries marked "organic" may soon know exactly what they're buying.

Federal regulators will be affixing a USDA organic products label on certain products that look like the labels for USDA Grade A eggs or USDA Prime beef. That's good news for consumers who want more options for healthful dining, and the standards to back them up.[11]

Serious lifestyle subjects are handled entertainingly by columnists such as the syndicated sisters Dear Abby and Ann Landers. So great is their reader appeal that some newspapers publish both—along with others, such as Dr. Joyce Brothers.

Whereas some columnists, such as Brody and Chase, pursue health and consumer issues in great depth—several thousand words for Brody, at times—the dear Abby-type columnist normally goes for quick, pointed and often amusing commentary pegged to brief letters from readers. (Sex comes up a lot!)

Absent sound academic and professional training, young writers should steer clear of giving advice—which readers might follow—in such highly complicated areas as medicine, law, finance (or sex).

Stick to commentary on what you know. You might be forced to, anyway; lifestyle editors increasingly hire columnists or use syndicated commentators with strong professional credentials, such as degrees in medicine or law. Network television news directors hire "consultants" with specialized backgrounds.

| Box 10-2 | Syndicated Success |

If you develop superior analytical ability and writing skill you one day may extend your reach (and financial success) through syndication.

Instead of reaching only the audience of one newspaper or magazine, you—if you're *highly* talented—may reach *hundreds* of publications through syndication and many *millions* of readers.

Ann Landers is distributed by Creators Syndicate, which reports her personal advice column appears in more than 1,200 newspapers worldwide each day, with about 90 million readers.

Los Angeles Times Syndicate claims more than 400 newspapers for its conservative columnist, Cal Thomas. Roger Ebert, the only film critic to win a Pulitzer Prize, appears via Universal Press Syndicate in more than 200 papers.

Some syndicates grew first as "salvage" adjuncts to large newspapers. *The Los Angeles Times, Washington Post, New York Times* and others developed new revenue streams by selling to other papers news stories, columns and features written for their own pages. Concurrently, feature syndicates sold comic strips, features, columns, photos—news and editorial copy of all descriptions.

Today, scores of syndicates distribute all types of opinion writing—editorials, political commentary, personal columns, humor, specialty writing.

Some columns are written specially for syndicates but most are written by newspaper staffers for their own pages, then syndicated.

David Broder, for example, is a *Washington Post* columnist whose commentary is distributed by the Washington Post Writers Group twice weekly. Other WPW columnists include Jane Bryant Quinn (a personal-finance columnist whose home base is *Newsweek*), William Raspberry (strong on racial and inner-city topics), Robert J. Samuelson (economics), George F. Will (politics), Jim Hoagland (two Pulitzers, one for foreign reporting, another for commentary), Ellen Goodman (humor).

Robert D. Novak is a *Chicago Sun-Times* political commentator who appears nationwide, in both print and television, via Creators Syndicate. His syndicate colleagues include Molly Ivins (liberal politics with humor, from her base at the *Fort Worth Star-Telegram*), Stephen Chapman (libertarianism, *The Chicago Tribune*), Mark Shields (witty political punditry, in both print and television), Tony Kornheiser (*The Washington Post* humorist), Patrick J. Buchanan (right-wing political commentator and sometime Republican Party presidential hopeful).

Opinion, analysis and commentary also are distributed worldwide by **supplemental news services** (so-called to distinguish them from **basic** news services, such as the all-encompassing The Associated Press and Reuters). Widely used supplementals are operated by *The New York Times,* jointly by *The Los Angeles Times* and *The Washington Post,* by Scripps Howard Newspapers, Copley Newspapers Group (whose flagship is the *San Diego Union*) and Knight Ridder Newspapers, among others.

For "hot copy," which is topical and timely, syndicates use high-speed transmission circuits, delivering copy directly into newspapers' computers, ready for electronic editing, headline writing and computerized layout ("pagination"). "Timeless copy"—crossword puzzles, astrology columns and so forth—are prepared weeks in advance, and sometimes are mailed.

For complete listings of syndicates, writers and the soup-to-nuts columns and features they offer, see *Editor & Publisher*'s annual *Syndicate Directory.*

Stick to What You Know

But, you may ask, "Do I know enough about *anything* to qualify as a campus critic or commentator?"

Many student writers, unfortunately, automatically say no. Wrong.

As a student, you're "plugged in" to the thinking of thousands of your fellow students, and you have strong insights into their hopes, dreams, aspirations and problems. With sound reporting and authoritative sources behind you, you *can* move into commentary. For example:

The Club and Party Scene

If your campus is typical, it's surrounded by clubs, bars and eateries clamoring for student business. And critiquing them is an idea clamoring for your attention.

Many newspapers pay close attention to the "scene" revolving around clubs, bars and the social set.

Mary Lou Loper writes, "RSVP: The Social City," for *The Los Angeles Times,* and covers benefits, gala dinners and other "social circuit" events.[12]

The New York Times regularly publishes commentary on where to go and what to do in cities around the world—and travel writers are *judgmental* (with Sarah Lyall commenting, for example, that visitors to Scotland will find "vigor and indeed loveliness in Glasgow").[13]

At *The New York Post,* Lucinda Rosenfeld is, well, *earthy,* in her club-scene column, "Night Owl." One of her leads:

> "Everyone calls it the Genie Bar—they think they made it up themselves," sniffs Richard Barbour with regard to the cheddar round of a drinks room over which he presides just off the front lobby of the Royalton Hotel.
>
> "This is where you come to close the deal with a little strawberries and champagne before retiring to your room upstairs to do the Horizontal Mambo," he says of Vodka Bar (its correct name).
>
> This guy means business, as does the patron base, most of which is West Coast wheeler-dealer types sipping $11-a-pop flavored vodkas with one eye on their "smart phones."[14]

Key to successful commentary on the club scene is weaving in not only your *opinion* on where readers can go for fun, but also *facts* to guide them. Note that Rosenfeld's "Night Owl" look at the Vodka Bar includes prices and descriptions of clientele (answering readers' question, "Will I fit in?"). And, Rosenfeld included this boxed information:

> Vodka Bar at the Royalton Hotel,
> 44 W. 44th St., (212) 944-8844

In your writing about the club and party scene, be informal, chatty. Examples:

- *New York Times* reviewer Ruth Reichl takes readers along as "guests" and opens her critique of a restaurant this way: "For 15 minutes we have been waving our hands in a futile attempt to get the attention of a waiter. Any waiter." Now, the hammer: "An off night at [the restaurant]? Unfortunately, no. The food is usually excellent, but the restaurant is so badly run that each time I am seated in the upstairs dining room I almost walk out."[15]
- Julie Hatfield, in "Party Lines" for *The Boston Globe:*

Nantucket—Wow. Winona Ryder didn't show up, as she was supposed to, but 400 other beautiful young women did. Billy Joel didn't sit down at the piano as he had planned, but a deejay provided a mixture of hip-hop, house, and techno music for club dancing—and dance all night they did. Arnold Schwarzenegger didn't belly up to the bar with Maria Kennedy Shriver, but no one wanted them there anyway.

The Nantucket Film Festival, known as the screenwriters' film festival, is showtime for the "other" Hollywood, the emerging producers, screenwriters, actors, and filmmakers of the small, intelligent, sometimes brilliant, sometimes money-losing independent films. The festival held its second annual celebration this past weekend all over the island. While you might not recognize the faces at the lively parties they throw, you could be talking to the movies' hope for tomorrow.[16]

It's not only on Nantucket, romper room of the rich, where you can write social-circuit commentary. *The New York Daily News* publishes a column called, "Street Eats," with critic Whitney Walker commenting on "ethnic snacks you can eat on the street." In one column, Walker visits Chinese food vendors at their push-carts at Canal Street and makes the judgment: " ... the prices can't be beat. Everything at Ji-chuen Chen's cart costs $1." [17]

Home (or Dorm) Entertainment and Hobbies

Ham radio, computers, stamp collecting, motorcycles and cars, photography—each a hobby and each the subject for regular columns in most newspapers.

If Americans do it—or even *think* about doing it—newspapers and magazines publish commentary about it. Hobby columns have fanatical followers (just ask editors, who get storms of reader protests when a favorite column is dropped). Writing commentary on a hobby—yours—is a perfect way to match personal interest with writing opportunity.

Writing for student readers, you should stick to youth-oriented hobbies, of course. For example, rock climbing and riding mountain bikes are the rage on some campuses, and these new fads, like old fads, create openings for thoughtful commentary. Strong favorites with students are home videos and games—subjects covered very seriously by major newspapers. And, the pros go beyond feature-story description of hobbies; they also comment, judge, criticize, applaud. For example:

- Susan King, in her column, "Home Entertainment," for *The Los Angeles Times,* critiques videos. ("Avoid the colorized version of 'The Absent-Minded Professor,'" she says; "One of the best basketball flicks ever made," she says of "Hoop Dreams.")
- Christopher Cornell, who reviews videos for Knight Ridder News Service,

says "Shine" rates 3½ out of 4 stars and is "compelling" and features "seam-lessness" in its acting.

- Jeff Kapalka, in his "Games" column for the *Syracuse Herald American,* says "the 3-D graphics are great" in "Starfox 64" and rates the video game four stars out of a possible four. (Kapalka also reviews *comics* for the newspaper.)[18]

And, of course, there are turnips and astrology.

Turnips? Yes, turnips were the subject of gardening columnist Georgeanne Brennan in *The New York Times.* (She moaned, "Turnips and their near kindred, rutabagas, have an unfortunate history of being associated with poverty, institutional cafeterias and English cooking at its worst.")[19] Gardening—turnips and all—is a favorite hobby column in most newspapers.

Astrology? Yes, many newspapers publish star-gazer commentary—with suitable disclaimers, such as this warning tagged on Sydney Omarr's "Astrological Forecast" column in *The Los Angeles Times:* "The astrological forecast should be read for entertainment."[20]

Fashion Commentary

Fashion is a multi-*billion* dollar industry, a subject of enthusiastic interest for millions of American men and women, and a major topic of news commentary for magazines and newspapers.

Critics cover traditional topics. For example, writing in *The San Francisco Chronicle*'s column, "Style Counsel," Reena Jana comments on wearing "a short-sleeved turtleneck to make you feel like Sharon Stone." The *Chronicle*'s fashion editor, Trish Donnally, critiques David Letterman's wardrobe for his TV shows. (His "on-air suits have high armholes and smooth fabrics.")[21]

But nontradible commentary is, well, fashionable as well with critics these days. They roam far afield from merely critiquing the clothing worn in the traditional march of models down the runway at a new showing. In her column, "Off the Cuff" for *The Chicago Tribune,* commentator Teresa Wiltz, a black, attacks "the 'blond collections,' where skinny, pale-haired models ruled the New York runways ... the glaring lack of ethnic and/or dark-haired models."[22]

Stuff for Big League newspapering only? Or *Vogue* and *Women's Wear Daily?* Not really. Think of clothing and *behavior* fads that sweep campuses. Think of student interest in them. For example, every campus newspaper probably has done a feature story (or two or three) on body piercing. Why don't you take a different approach? Do a *column* on the fad. Consult a psychologist or two on *why* students do that to themselves, then deliver your opinion whether they *should.*

Critiquing the Media

Here's a column idea begging for your attention: If the media are watchdogs who bark in the night, who barks at the watchdog?

For *journalists*, there is plenty of barking by critics in our professional journals—*American Journalism Review, Columbia Journalism Review, Editor & Publisher, presstime, American Editor, The Quill, Nieman Reports, Broadcasting & Cable*.

But for our *audiences*—our readers, viewers, listeners—there is little regular, painstaking, hard-hitting examination of the media, either as a multibillion dollar industry or as an enormous influence on American thinking and public policy.

Indeed, the media probably are the *only* major industry so free of external, organized public critiquing.

Of the more than 1,500 U.S. daily newspapers, about 50 have a staff "ombudsman" or "reader representative" whose duty is to critique the newspaper and judge staff performance through readers' eyes, then publish the findings for all to see. Most editors say it is *their* job to critique their papers and represent the public interest and, anyway, if the paper isn't doing its job, people won't buy it. Unquestionably that falls short of guaranteeing any disciplined external monitoring of newspapers on behalf of the public, particularly since editors' critiques are mostly internal and effectively hidden from the public (although most newspapers do openly acknowledge and correct even minor errors).

One newspaper that *does* regularly publish notable criticism from its own ombudsman is *The Washington Post.* (In one editorial-page column, ombudsman Geneva Overholser, an experienced newspaper editor, termed "absurd" her own newspaper's grant of anonymity to a government official in the news, and considered—then dismissed—reader letters charging the paper's "Style" section with being "unfair and tasteless.")[23]

Richard De Uriarte, "reader advocate" of *The Arizona Republic,* was given major display for a piece explaining to readers why the paper fired 60 staffers and closed its afternoon paper, *The Gazette.* (A weak and changing economy caused it, he wrote, hastening to add that the comic strip "Doonesbury" would not be cut in the economy move, as some readers feared.)[24]

The Wall Street Journal, New York Times and *Los Angeles Times* publish regular media *news* coverage, particularly of advertising and other business aspects. But few papers have regular commentary on journalistic or ethical performance.

As for magazines, next time you're at your favorite supermarket's magazine rack dip into 10 or 15 of the 11,000 or so titles currently published in America. You'll find no sustained media criticism published *for readers.* Although, many newspapers do publish regular columns titled, "Off the Rack" (*The New York Times*) or "Magazines" (*Chicago Tribune*) that report subjects of articles and content published in magazines (but don't critique performance).

Television and radio offer almost no regular, effective critiques of their own performance—or the media's in general—and have no policy for daily correction of errors (although major goofs are corrected, of course).

To steal (and adapt and probably ruin) a line from Mark Twain, media criticism is like the weather: Everybody talks about it but nobody does anything about it. When you reach the appropriate experience level in your career, why don't *you* do something about it?

Commentary for Broadcast and Cyberspace

Thinking of a career in editorial writing and commentary for the electronic media? If so, consider—carefully—two factors:

- In traditional television and radio, once-promising trends toward significant editorial efforts are disappearing. Many stations once actively airing editorials are dropping regular opinion broadcasting and commentary. Most stations today have no consistent editorial programming.
- In the new electronic media—online newspapers and electronic news services—the future is unpredictable, particularly whether editorials and issue-oriented commentary by professional journalists will have any significant role.

Let's look at both sectors:

Writing for Television and Radio

Into the 1970s, editorials and commentary on the day's compellingly important issues had a role in broadcasting. Leading TV and radio stations aired meaningful commentary—including station endorsement of political candidates and social policies. Then, things changed:

First, the Federal Communications Commission eliminated enforcement of certain regulations governing television and radio, including the so-called "Fairness Doctrine," which required giving equal time to opposing candidates and arguments. In sum, the FCC relaxed pressure on broadcasters to air public service programming to protect their broadcasting license. Editorials (or news) no longer were necessary to keep FCC regulators happy.[25]

Second, broadcast stations, mostly owned by profit-oriented groups, came under extraordinary pressure to deliver ever-greater profits—and they did, particularly in television, where profit ratios often far exceed those of most newspapers. Broadcasters cut costs by eliminating editorials (and, in some cases, news). And, editorials (and, again, news) gave way to entertainment programming, which is more attractive to viewers and, thus, more salable to advertisers and, as a result, more profitable.

Third, driven by its entertainment (and profit) mission, broadcasting redefined news and how it is reported. In commercial radio, air time not given to music generally goes to talk shows (public radio is a notable exception). And in talk radio, opinions expressed by host and listener—often loudly and stridently—push aside the reasoned commentary and editorials we've discussed in this book. In commercial television (again, with public TV an exception), news readers and reporters frequently express opinions, even on what purport to be news shows. This and the trend toward personality or scandal-oriented "magazine" shows blur television's distinction between news, commentary and editorializing.

Fourth—and frankly—many station owners lost the *courage* to air pointed, forthright editorials. *Consensus programming*, not controversy, builds the huge audiences that keep television's golden goose laying enormous profits. Also, FCC regulation (Rule 73.1930) *does* require stations *endorsing* candidates to give free time to other candidates seeking the same office. And, "That can get kind of messy," notes Neil Heinen, editorial director of WISC-TV in Madison, Wis. He points to endorsement by WCVB-TV in Boston of five candidates in a 10-person race in a school board election, which required giving up substantial free air time.[26]

Geri Denterlein, editorial director of WBZ-TV and Radio in Boston, notes television editorializing fell off so rapidly that the National Broadcast Editorial Association merged in 1991 with its newspaper counterpart, the National Conference of Editorial Writers.

Says Denterlein: "The culprit is the bottom line."[27]

Heinen of Madison's WISC-TV spreads the blame more widely:

> I'll argue it's laziness and complacency. It's educators unwilling to add opinion writing to broadcast journalism courses. It's station managers unwilling to rock the boat. It's journalists unwilling to pursue the challenges and rewards of opinion writing. ...
>
> ... Good, serious, compelling, engaging broadcast editorials are an investment. Forward-thinking journalists and managers must make that investment." [28]

Despite discouraging industrywide trends, commentators who have found niches in broadcast editorializing say it is rewarding, particularly because they reach people—nonreaders—who cannot be reached through newspapers and magazines.

Robert S. McCord, a former newspaper publisher and executive editor, turned to editorial writing for KTHV-TV in Little Rock, and recalls an immediate increase in public comment.

"The comments are not only numerous, but multicultural also," he says. "Unlike my days at the newspaper, they come not just from the decision-makers in the community—politicians, activists, business leaders—but from people who are affected by them as well: young people, minorities, working women, blue-collar workers. People I seldom reached on newspaper opinion pages."[29]

A Few Broadcast Style Hints

Teaching broadcast writing demands its own book, of course, and is far beyond the scope of this book. But let's look at a few writing hints in case you want—as I hope—to try broadcast editorials and commentary (with a campus radio station, perhaps?).

The basics:[30]

- You're writing for ears, not eyes, of course, so your tone and pace must match listeners' ability to hear and absorb information *and* your ability to deliver it smoothly, understandably. Read your copy aloud—several times—before going on air. If you must stop, stutter and gasp for breath to get through your editorial, rewrite it.
- Your time constraints are cruel: You have perhaps one minute or, at most, a couple to bring listeners up to speed on an issue, explain the facts, then make—and defend—your position. You must do this in 150-200 words, not the 500 or 800 of newspaper editorials. *Write tight!*
- Informal language patterns communicate best in broadcasting. Use short, snappy sentences with lots of transition words that are understood easily. Write in the active voice.
- Limit your central thrust to a single major idea. If you're endorsing John Smith for mayor, stick with Smith and his qualifications and the lesser qualifications of his opponents. Don't launch off concurrently into city government, clean water and air, the city council and stray dogs. That's too much to jam into two minutes—and too much for a listener to catch.

Sentence Structure

Don't use lengthy modifying phrases or clauses to open a sentence. Most effective are subject-verb-object sentences. For example:

No:

Sixty-year-old, nineteen-year veteran politician John Smith is our choice for mayor.

Yes:

Here's our choice for mayor—John Smith. ... Smith has nineteen years experience in local politics ... experience we need as a leader. ... John Smith is our pick for mayor.

Subordinate Clauses

Eliminate them. Here's why:

No:

Mayor Smith, a graduate of local schools and a lifelong resident of our city, has nineteen years experience in local politics, and that's why he's our choice for reelection.

Yes:

Mayor Smith is our choice for reelection. Smith has nineteen years experience in local politics. He is a lifelong resident of our city and a graduate of local schools ... that's why we support Mayor Smith for reelection.

Write to Signal Emphasis

You can't use exclamation points or question marks in broadcast writing (listeners can't see them!). You've got to use your voice to signal emphasis.

For example, use a dash—like this—to remind yourself that you want to pause or lend emphasis. Or, ellipses ... like that. ... Thus reminded, you can change your tone of voice, pause or speak louder or more softly—devices all useful in delivering clear, emphatic editorials.

Structure Your Editorial Simply

If your mission is to endorse Smith, do so—and go directly to that central theme. You'll have a "lead-in" from an announcer ("The following is a WXYZ editorial ..." or, "The following is a special commentary by WXYZ editorial director Adam Adams ..."). Then you can open this way:

Our City faces many financial
and social challenges over
the next three years ...
and WXYZ-TV recommends you
reelect Mayor John Smith
as the man to lead us in
meeting those challenges.

Now (noting you already have used 31 words!), parcel out your additional thoughts simply and directly:

(*Briefly*, the issues and
challenges.)
(Smith's qualifications.)
(Why his opponents won't
do.)

Finally, you can close out with repetition—broadcast's way of saying to listeners, "Did you hear me?" Something like this:

So, we hope that when you
go to the polls tomorrow
you'll cast your vote
for Mayor John Smith ...
we here at WXYZ think
he's the man to lead us over
the next three years.

Personal Pronouns

Your huge advantage in broadcast commentary is that you can *chat* with viewers and listeners, speak to each of them informally and warmly. On television, you can look 'em right in the eye. Don't waste that advantage.

In print, it's bad form to inject yourself into an institutional editorial. By journalistic convention, the personal pronoun is avoided. Not in television. Thus:

No:

Smith has been frank in
telling reporters that
tough times are ahead. ...

Yes:

I've asked Smith if
tough times are ahead ...
and he's told me
frankly that ...

Homophones

Watch 'em, avoid 'em. Don't describe Mayor Smith as "heir" to problems left by previous administrations. Your listeners might hear "air," "error" or "err."

Homophones (words that sound alike but carry different meanings) include: to/too/two, wear/where, capital/capitol, council/counsel, sex/sect.

Writing for Online Services

This is clear: Computerized, interactive online technology, offering stunning access to mountains of data, will be part of your career as a journalist. You'll collect and transmit information electronically *or* compete with someone who does.

Unclear—doubtful even—is whether interactive communication will detract substantially from the *editorial and commentary* role of print newspapers and magazines. Indeed, online services may not have much use for editorials and commentary written specially for them by professional journalists.

Realities:

First, hundreds of newspapers and magazines offer online news; few are profitable, at least profitable enough to attract the massive capital investment needed for expansive leaps forward.[31] Many media analysts view their future profitability as uncertain. And, active online newspapers and magazines mostly recycle (or "repackage") news and, in some cases, commentary from host newspapers and magazines. They generally limit newly originated copy to *add-on information*. For example, a news story on drunk driving arrests lifted from the host newspaper can be accompanied by a computer address where users will find historical data on DUIs. Or, online editors inform readers how to access the host newspaper's editorial on drunk driving. Relatively little news coverage and almost no significant special commentary is being originated by professional journalists for online newspapers. Star Tribune Online of Minneapolis, a leading service, originates just one feature even close to being commentary—a staff-written column on technical developments on the Internet.[32]

Second, if online services develop as their most devoted supporters hope, they might in fact move even further from offering professional editorial writers and commentators. That's because a central strength of online services is *bypass capability*—giving users direct access to databases and each other, bypassing the traditional approach to newspapers and magazines for editorials and commentary. Online newspapers provide "chat rooms," interactive space where users don't simply read institutional editorials but, rather, chat with each other. That is, users aren't always reading editorials written by professional journalists, then scrutinized by experienced editors for fairness, accuracy, balance, responsibility. Chat room conversationalists often don't know the credentials or professionalism of those who weigh in with opinions online.

All this worries professional journalists now in online journalism. One is Jackie Crosby, news editor of Star Tribune Online in Minneapolis, one of the country's leading online newspapers. Crosby earlier won a Pulitzer Prize for reporting at the *Macon* (Ga.) *Telegraph,* wrote for the *Orlando* (Fla.) *Sentinel* and was a top producer for KSTP-TV in Minneapolis. Crosby says:

> The online medium breaks down traditional communication barriers between the institution and the reader and allows readers to more easily discuss and argue the ideas put forth in institutional editorials. But the result often is chaos. We have thoughtful and authoritative contributors of opinion; we also have wackos.[33] (See Box 10-3 for additional views from Crosby.)

| Box 10-3 | A Professional's View |

Jackie Crosby is news editor of one of the nation's leading online newspapers, Star Tribune Online. She earlier won a Pulitzer Prize for newspaper reporting and was a news show producer for KSTP-TV in Minneapolis. Here she discusses commentary online.

Like many online newspapers, our service contains a section that closely reflects the work published in what we affectionately call, "the crushed-tree version" (*The Minneapolis Star Tribune*).

Our Opinion section offers editorials, syndicated columnists, essays by people in the community, opinions written by the newspapers' editorial board, the readers' representative (ombudsman), letters to the editor and editorial cartoons.

Online editors, however, can enhance the basic editorial in a number of ways—by offering background and context, by providing a simple and immediate vehicle for feedback and by providing a forum to discuss ideas.

Let's say, for example, *The Star Tribune* takes a stand against a controversial school-funding issue endorsed by the governor. Online editors could gather past news coverage and opinion pieces already published on the issue and offer them as background with the editorial.

The online editorial could include links to the text of the bill being discussed in the Legislature and any other related sites on the Internet. Online editors could offer a forum to discuss the school-funding issue—either by starting a discussion and inviting readers to participate or by providing a link to an existing discussion group.

Online editors might also invite the newspapers' editorial writer, the governor and/or an opposing legislator to host an online discussion group, giving users opportunity to interact directly with people involved in the issue. Readers could respond directly to the editorial writer, to the newspaper or to the online news editors via e-mail.

What makes the online environment so fundamentally different from the newspaper is the ease with which readers can react to the editorial, whether that means privately via e-mail to the author, publicly in an online "conversation" or by sending a letter to the editor electronically.

For readers online, many barriers to communication have been removed. Here is an example:

Star Tribune sports commentator Dan Barreiro wrote a column before the Minnesota Vikings played the Green Bay Packers, making fun of Packers fans and dreading Green Bay's probable trip to the Super Bowl (where Green Bay eventually won).

We used Barreiro's column on Star Tribune Online, and his words whipped up a tremendous fury. He received hundreds of e-mail messages from all over the world (as well as phone calls and letters).

Online editors responded to the deluge by creating an interactive game called "Kick Barreiro," in which users could boot a football-shaped photo of the columnist through goal posts. A successful kick would release cheers from the crowd; a miss would evoke a sympathetic, "Awwwww."

The game and original column were packaged with a discussion in which hundreds of people railed against Barreiro (and a few defended him). Barreiro eventually followed up with a column about how his opinion writing took on a life of its own in an environment where people can share information and feedback quickly.

One caveat: Communication via computer is impersonal. People's responses may be more swift, but they also can be more hateful, and sometimes obscene, sexist and racist.

(Want to "chat" with Jackie Crosby? You can reach her at crosby@star-tribune.com)

The New York Times worried (in an institutional editorial) that Internet content must catch up with its technology: "Between abuses of e-mail, some nasty pranks and a careless on-line gossip columnist, the well-established information anarchy of cyberspace has turned more chaotic and even brutish ... users should realize that just because information flashes across their computer screens does not necessarily mean it is all true."[34]

On the plus side, journalists schooled in traditional commentary and editorial writing see online services having two major strengths:

- Editorials online reach users who can't be reached through the printed page. John V. Pavlik, executive director of The Center for New Media at Columbia University, says, "For many of us in this field, the point is to engage the unengaged."[35]
- Online services involve readers personally, bringing them into a conversation and creating a "feedback loop" for their input. *Forbes* editors report that for every regular mailed letter they receive from readers they get five e-mails.[36]

Here's how you can use new technology to interact with professional editorial writers and commentators for traditional newspapers and broadcast stations: Check in with the National Conference of Editorial Writers at their World Wide Web site, http://www.infi.net/ncew

Summary

- There is far more to opinion writing than editorials and commentary on politics, humor, sports, the arts. Specialty columns on business, lifestyle, fashion and hobbies are popular.
- Editorial writing for broadcasting is waning rapidly, and new online electronic services originate very little opinion and commentary written specially for them by trained professional journalists.
- When you move into specialty columns you need expert personal background in your subject; the relatively relaxed reporting of general assignment or personal columns doesn't work in commentary on specialty subjects.
- Writing specialty commentary demands sharp awareness of the impact you can have on readers' lives; commenting on the football team is one thing, guiding readers in Wall Street investments or cancer treatment is quite another.
- Informed readers—the kind who read specialty columns—will spot quickly any writing that's poorly reported.
- Never write as if you possess The Single Truth; nobody should expect a journalist to have all the answers, so stay tentative in your writing.
- Analyze, interpret and comment, then direct your readers to additional authority, either with internal citation of authoritative sources or other sources such as reading lists, Internet web sites or health "hot lines."
- Business commentary is an exciting career option, and aspiring writers can start with columns on subjects of student interest.
- "Lifestyle" is a huge journalistic tent covering columns and entire sections variously titled, "Living," "Style" and so forth.
- A key to effective lifestyle commentary is not only spotting reader interests and describing problems but also leading readers toward solutions.
- Popular lifestyle subjects are restaurant and bar reviewing, health and fitness, consumerism.
- Aspiring writers should stick to commentary on subjects they understand thoroughly, and that can include virtually any subject of interest to fellow students.
- Fashion is a multi-billion dollar industry of great interest to millions of Americans, and, thus, fertile ground for critical reviewing and commentary.

- Experienced writers can critique the media, an industry subjected to very little thorough, professional external monitoring on behalf of the public.
- FCC relaxation of regulation and the broadcast industry's relentless drive for profit are diminishing efforts in radio and television editorials and commentary.
- It's clear that electronic gathering and distribution of information will be part of every journalist's career; unclear is how profitable online newspapers will be and, thus, what their future shape will be.

Recommended Readings

The National Conference of Editorial Writers has included broadcast editorialists as well as print writers since 1991. You can monitor this professional group's activities via its publication, *The Masthead,* or via the Internet, http://www.infi.net/ncew

Broadcasting and Cable is an excellent source of news about radio and television. Watch print industry trade magazines for developments in online services. Regular coverage is in *Editor & Publisher, presstime, Columbia Journalism Review, American Editor* and others.

Leading daily newspapers strong in institutional writing and personal columns also publish specialty columns that provide aspiring writers with valuable examples. They include *The New York Times, The Wall Street Journal, The Los Angeles Times, Chicago Tribune, Boston Globe, Dallas Morning News.*

Notes

1. These examples are drawn, respectively from Charles A. Jaffe, "Personal Finance," *The Boston Globe,* June 23, 1997, p. B-5; Margaret A. Dixon, "Don't Fall for a Telephone Line," *Modern Maturity,* May/June 1997, p. 83; Walter S. Mossberg, "Personal Technology," *The Wall Street Journal,* Aug. 21, 1997, p. B-1; Jane Bryant Quinn, "Capital Gains," *Newsweek,* Oct. 14, 1996, p. 71; James C. Cooper and Kathleen Madigan, *Business Week,* May 19, 1997, p. 21.

2. Charles A. Jaffe, *The Boston Globe,* op cit.

3. Geraldine Fabrikant, "Market Place," *The New York Times,* July 10, 1997, p. D-1.

4. John Waggoner, "Mutual Funds," *USA Today,* June 20, 1997, p. B-3.

5. Jacob M. Schlesinger, "The Outlook," *The Wall Street Journal,* Aug. 18, 1997, p. 1.

6. Richard Korman, "Faith and Doubt for a Maker of Modems," *The New York Times,* Aug. 17, 1997, p. F-7.

7. E.S. Browning, Deborah Lohse, Suzanne McGee, "Heard on the Street," *The Wall Street Journal,* Aug. 18, 1997, p. C-1.

8. Pamela Reeves, Scripps Howard dispatch for July 20, 1997, published that day in the *Syracuse Herald American,* p. B-1.

9. Carol Stocker, "Grubs," *The Boston Globe,* May 4, 1996, p. 25.

10. Jane E. Brody, "Personal Health," *The New York Times,* July 2, 1997, p. C-9.

11. Marilyn Chase, "Health Journal," *The Wall Street Journal,* Aug. 18, 1997, p. B-1.

12. Mary Lou Loper, "RSVP: The Social City," *The Los Angeles Times,* April 21, 1996, p. E-2.

13. Sara Lyall, "What's Doing in Glasgow," *The New York Times,* Aug. 17, 1997, travel section, p. 10.

14. Lucinda Rosenfeld, "Night Owl," *The New York Post,* Aug. 14, 1997, p. 43.

15. Ruth Reichl, "Restaurants," *The New York Times,* June, 27, 1997, p. C-26.

16. Julie Hatfield, "Party Lines," *The Boston Globe,* June 23, 1997, p. C-6.

17. Whitney Walker, "Street Eats," *The New York Daily News,* July 4, 1996, p. C-11.

18. These examples are drawn, respectively, from Susan King, "Home Entertainment," *The Los Angeles Times,* May 3, 1996, p. F-25; Christopher Cornell, Knight-Ridder News Service dispatch for July 20, 1997, published that day in "Stars" section, p. 13, of *Syracuse Herald American;* Jeff Kapalka, "Games," published in "Stars" section, p. 13, of *Syracuse Herald American,* July 20, 1997.

19. Georgeanne Brennan, "Cuttings," *The New York Times,* Aug. 17, 1997, p. 51.

20. Sydney Omarr, "Astrological Forecast," *The Los Angeles Times,* April 18, 1997, E-9.

21. Reena Jana, "Style Counsel," *The San Francisco Chronicle,* May 9, 1996, p. E-7.

22. Teresa Wiltz, "Off the Cuff," *The Chicago Tribune,* April 25, 1996, Section 2, p. 5.

23. Geneva Overholser, "Questionable Etiquette," *The Washington Post,* May 4, 1997, p. C-6.

24. Richard De Uriarte, "Newsroom Layoffs Very Painful to Endure," *The Arizona Republic,* Jan. 19, 1997, p. B-1.

25. Peter Kohler, "Wanted: Editorial Entrepreneurs," *The Masthead,* Fall 1996, p. 24.

26. Neil Heinen, "FCC Handicaps Broadcast Endorsements," *The Masthead,* Spring 1997, p. 11.

27. Geri Denterlein, "Broadcast Editorializing Back in the Picture," *The Masthead,* Winter 1992, p. 18.

28. Neil Heinen, "Bold, Relevant Opinion Holds the Key," *The Masthead,* Fall 1996, p. 33.

29. Robert S. McCord, "Move from Print to Broadcast Brings Surprises," *The Masthead,* Winter 1994, p. 5.

30. I discuss broadcast writing in more detail in Conrad C. Fink, *Introduction to Professional Newswriting,* 2nd ed (New York: Addison Wesley Longman, 1998).

31. Steve Outing, "Interactive Communications," *Editor & Publisher,* Jan. 18, 1997, p. 26.

32. Material on Star Tribune Online is drawn from an interview with Jackie Crosby on Aug. 22, 1997, and from her letter to author, May 27, 1997.

33. Jackie Crosby, interview, ibid.

34. "www.internet,anarchy," editorial in *The New York Times,* Aug. 15, 1997, p. A-30.

35. John V. Pavlik, "The Future of Online Journalism," *Columbia Journalism Review*, July/August 1997, p. 30.

36. Guy Kawasaki, "Technology," *Forbes*, July 28, 1997, p. 86.

Exercises

1. In 300-350 words, describe your hobby, special personal interest or fantasy that you think might be an appropriate subject for a column of commentary *directed at fellow students*.

Is there broad interest on your campus in the subject? What reporting approach would you take? What would be your writing tone? What would be the most valuable news, information and opinion in your column.

2. Reflect on this chapter's discussion of the "specialty columnist's special responsibilities." In about 300 words *aimed at publication* in a campus newspaper or magazine, explain to a general reading audience your personal views of a columnist's responsibilities to be fair, balanced, accurate and to offer opinion and comment founded in logic and fact.

View this assignment as one of explaining ethical, principled commentary to an audience skeptical about journalists and journalism.

3. Critique five successive issues of your campus newspaper (or a newspaper designated by your instructor) and, in an essay of about 350 words, answer these questions:

- Is the newspaper offering specialty columns and commentary that meet the needs of its audience?
- In which types of specialty columns is the newspaper strong? In which is it weak?
- What would you tell the editor of that newspaper he or she must do to bolster content and meet reader needs for specialty commentary? What type column could *you* write for that newspaper?

4. Reflecting on the discussion of lifestyle commentary, describe in about 350 words the lifestyle column you would like to write for your campus newspaper (or another newspaper designated by your instructor).

Which lifestyle sectors already are covered? Which aren't?

What special reporting or writing experience do you have that qualifies you to write such a lifestyle column?

What would be its form and structure?

5. Read five successive issues of your campus newspaper (or a newspaper designated by your instructor) and write a column about its professionalism and journalistic performance.

In this exercise, you are that newspaper's reader representative or ombudsman, so write as an "insider" for those on the outside, the readers.

In about 450 words, address what you believe to be issues of compelling importance to readers. Have there been shortcomings in reporting? Has writing been sloppy? Have there been ethical lapses?

11 | On Campus Today: How It's Done

FOR MANY STUDENTS, it comes as a hard reality, a disappointing surprise:

"Where," says the job interviewer, "are your clips?"

There you are: Smiling, dressed to kill, edge-of-seat alert, strong grade point average in hand, and you're desperately seeking entry-level work in newspapers or magazines.

And *all* the interviewer wants is to see your clips, the published proof of your commitment to journalism, the track record—in ink, on newsprint—of your progress from faltering beginner to accomplished campus journalist.

No clips? Forget it. In fact, most leading newspapers and magazines won't even waste their interviewers' time with you unless you have a clip file and résumé that demonstrate in advance you are serious about journalism.[1]

Your best chance to build a clip file—and, more importantly, a personal foundation of priceless experience—is at campus newspapers. Most need you. They are understaffed and desperate for the innovative writing we've discussed in this book. In return, your campus newspaper can give you, at minimum, two things you need: ink and newsprint.

Campus newspapers generally are a wide-open and accepting market for even the least-experienced writer. Seize the opportunity, even if you've never written a line for publication. Campus journalism may be your last easy access to newshole, a precious and limited commodity doled out carefully at most professional newspapers to only the very best writers.

To help you, I've studied 45 newspapers from colleges and universities across the nation, examining how they handle opinion and commentary, how they perhaps can improve—and always looking for hints on how *you* can get a piece of the action.[2]

Strengths and Weaknesses in Campus Journalism

It's an old one but (I think) a good one:

Question: What is the difference between beginner journalists, doctors and lawyers?

Answer: Beginner doctors bury their mistakes, lawyers wave goodby as theirs go off to prison, and journalists put their mistakes on front pages for everybody to see.

All to say that an examination of campus journalism, which, after all, is produced by beginners, inevitably will reveal many errors, many weaknesses. But strong opinion writing—some excellent, some courageous—is being produced out there on campuses. Based on my more than 40 years in journalism and teaching it, here's what I see:

Lessons in Courage and Commitment

Courage has many faces in journalism. It can be a foreign correspondent bracing under mortar fire or a White House reporter daring to take on the President of the United States and Leader of the Free World.

Or, it can be a form of courage that profoundly stirs my admiration: Newspaper people (largely unsung) laboring long, hard hours to cover the news and do their best to analyze and interpret it for readers, many of whom are apathetic toward the day's important issues and most of whom, it sometimes seems, are suspicious of the "media" and all who labor for them.

College editors are displaying this courage. With too few staffers to help, and too little money to pay them, editors of campus daily and weekly newspapers are producing some fine journalism—clearly at severe cost to themselves.

Here's Matt Snyder, editor of *The Daily Iowan,* at the University of Iowa, in Iowa City, in a column designed to tell readers how his newspaper covers the news (an *excellent* means of building credibility and reader rapport):

> I spend most of my day in the newsroom, only leaving to catch a bite to eat. I work for ten to twelve hours a day, sitting in meetings, working with fellow editors and staff members and answering phone calls.[3]

Lesson No. 1

Call it courage, call it commitment—long hours and hard work are what Big League journalism demands, and every newspaper recruiter who visits your campus is looking for evidence you can hack it. That recruiter likely was a campus journalist, too, and knows the commitment it takes to become editor or to publish a soundly-reported, well-written editorial or column.

Your name on the masthead's list of editors or your byline on an outstanding column is just what that recruiter is looking for.

Courage also is willingness to take on hot issues and powerful personalities. There's lots of this courage in campus journalism.

The Plainsman of Auburn University went hunting for big game, in an editorial charging Gov. Fob James with circumventing Alabama's constitution in his dealings with Auburn's trustees. *The Plainsman* fired both barrels:

> The governor is guilty of trying to play king with laws of the state. He obeys the ones that suit him and disregards the ones that crimped his plans.[4]

William Lutz of *The Daily* at the University of Washington in Seattle hunted closer to home (which can take more courage than shooting at distant politicians). Lutz filed a public records request for university documents and wrote that university officials were "finding a clever new way to trumpet the UW's accomplishments to the Legislature."[5]

At Iowa State University in Ames, under the headline, "More Outrage in the Classroom: Pretentious Professors," columnist Robert Zeis of *The Daily* examined one teacher's syllabus, his attitude toward students and grading system. Zeis concluded his lengthy column this way:

> There is a lesson to be learned here. Though you may think what your teacher says is gospel, it isn't. If you think an instructor in any class is placing undue pressures on you as a student, you have outlets to air your grievances. Use them. We have a right to demand the most for our education dollar, and those who are not cost effective (for the students) should be let go. It appears we need to shop around for another teacher.[6]

At the University of Southern Maine in Portland, *The Free Press* reported on Page One a university policy that allows (but doesn't encourage) students to use university computers to access pornography on the Internet. That same day, *The Free Press* took a strong position in its lead editorial:

> The computer labs on the Portland campus and in the law library have very enlightened policies on the subject of viewing pornography. ... This is a university, not a high school. Internet access should not be censored.[7]

Lesson No. 2

Campus editorials and commentary can require courage in the face of authority. Do sound, ethical reporting, base your opinions in fact and logic, then suck it up and write what you believe. If you can't envisage yourself criticizing the governor or writing tough about a professor you know or taking on your university's administration—if that's too hot for you, re-examine your career plan.

For student commentators and editorial writers, there are even hotter topics, of course: criticizing *fellow students* for their drinking habits or sexual mores, speaking out on campus racism or homophobia, abortion, religion ... hot buttons, all.

The Arkansas Traveler, at the University of Arkansas in Fayetteville, commented editorially on heavy drinking in fraternities and sororities, and, predictably, a storm ensued. One letter writer accused the paper of ignoring higher GPAs earned by Greeks and their community service and charitable efforts.[8]

Columnist Paul Turner of *The Daily Barometer,* at Oregon State University in Corvallis, described his friendship with a lesbian and concluded that, "Friends are not in the details. ... Friends are in the people. People should always be more important than the details."[9]

Racism, real or imagined, is an explosive topic on some campuses. But that doesn't force college editors to back off.

Editor in Chief Scott Lamar of *The Current,* at the University of Missouri-St. Louis, wrote a column counseling his fellow students to, in sum, cool it and not attribute every black vs. white parking lot scuffle to racism. He wrote:

> I am aware that many white on black (or vice versa) crimes are race related. However, I don't believe we should treat every incident as if it were. The fact is, in most cases, stupidity is to blame. Since stupidity will exist until life on Earth ends, we realize one thing: People are ignorant, but that doesn't necessary mean they're a racist.[10]

In the same issue, *The Current* published a reader's letter complaining a recent cartoon threatened to ignite a "racial powder keg." In an editor's note, the paper said the cartoon was an expression of opinion, that editors wouldn't censor opinion, that the cartoon was "clearly identifiable" as entertainment—but that the paper regretted any "negative racial undertones" readers may have detected.[11]

Columnist Chris Robertson of *The Tartan,* at Radford University in Radford, Va., took a strong stand on Ebonics (black English). She wrote:

> Where will we stop? Will there be Chinabonics, Hisabonics and Koreanbonics? If it ever comes to this count me out. I'll just be different and speak English.[12]

Lesson No. 3

Courage is part of the job, taking the cold stares (or worse) as you walk to your dorm, or getting the late-night harassing telephone call or the hate mail. And, it's good training for getting the same treatment, as you will, on occasion, in Big League journalism.

Examples of Excellence

A high degree of professionalism is achieved by some campus opinion writers in selection of issues for comment, reporting for editorials and in bright writing.

For example, *The Rice Thresher* at Rice University in Houston jumped on a U.S. Supreme Court finding that Brown University was violating Title IX, which requires equal funding and facilities for women's athletics. That ruling was on a Monday. The following Friday, the *Thresher* published a detailed editorial that—importantly—*localized the issue*.

The *Thresher* said the ruling was a "wake-up call to the nation's colleges and universities. Rice included." Note the *reporting* in the editorial:

> Looking at data from 1995-96, women made up 45 percent of Rice undergraduates but just 31 percent of varsity athletes. That's pretty far from the "substantially proportionate" that Title IX requires.
>
> Women also receive only 31 percent of athletically related student aid. Recruiting expenses for men's sports more than triple those for women's sports, $364,627 as compared to $104,523.
>
> More troublesome are the average salaries for head coaches of men's and women's sports; they are $83,424 and $43,122, respectively. The average salaries for assistant coaches, which aren't skewed by a single high-profile salary like that of Football Head Coach Ken Hatfield, are $38,473 and $22,526. That's a long way from "equal treatment" in terms of coaching quality.

Now, in a fine display of balance, of *fairness*, the *Thresher* editorial continues:

> Rice is far from the top of the heap in terms of gender equity, but common sense says that we aren't doing a horrible job, either. Football and baseball aside, Rice's men and women athletes share what are basically the same facilities.

The *Thresher,* having detailed the problem in a fair manner, now *points toward solutions*:

> Of course, the most important thing about the Brown decision is that schools like Rice may have to change whether they want to or not.
>
> Compliance with Title IX can be accomplished in several ways. Some

schools have simply decided to eliminate entire men's sports teams. Brown's solution is to cap roster sizes on men's teams and set minimum roster sizes for women's teams.

A far better idea, and certainly a lot more worthy of Rice, would be to increase the athletic opportunities available to women.

Not only would that be a good thing for the university community, it would also begin to establish the "continued history of expansion" that would immediately put Rice in a good light.

Monday's decision means that sometime in the not-so-distant future we may not have a choice, anyway. But we shouldn't wait until then. Now is the time for Rice to make a bold move in the right direction.[13]

Examine the elements that make the *Thresher* editorial worthy of any Big League newspaper:

- *Thresher*'s editorial board is **news-aware**, watching distant news horizons for developments that must be **localized**. A court ruling in Washington about a university in Providence, R.I., is examined for its new merits at Rice University in Houston. **Watch your news horizons.**
- *Thresher*'s editorial is in print quickly, just four days after the court ruling and while front-page news coverage of the ruling is fresh in readers' minds. **Stay close to the news.**
- **Strong reporting** localizes the editorial; hard figures—dollars and cents—put muscle in the commentary. "Added-value" reporting is much more effective than empty ranting and raving.
- *Thresher* is fair ("we aren't doing a horrible job..."). Readers quickly spot—and reject—patently unbalanced diatribes. Take strong one-sided positions in editorials, if you desire, but let readers see all arguments, all sides before you lead them, through fact and logic, to your position.
- *Thresher* doesn't only define the problem or simply point an accusing finger. The editorial **suggests solutions**. If your editorials don't suggest solutions you become part of the problem.

Many campus editorial writers strive to localize distant issues and provide strong reporting. At Southern Illinois University in Carbondale, *The Daily Egyptian* does both in an editorial on discussions in Congress over extending student health insurance after graduation. The editorial reports about 17,500 SIU students (and "almost 3 million nationwide") are covered by university health insurance and 6,100 eligible to graduate from SIU "could be covered as early as August, if the bill is passed."[14]

The Call to Action

If you believe (as I do) that newspapers have a responsibility *to lead*, the editorial page is where the trumpet sounds the call to battle.

Report the facts in your editorials, yes; explain the alternatives, point to solutions—but, in some cases, also stridently call on readers *to act.*

At the University of Tennessee in Knoxville, *The Daily Beacon* does that in an editorial on students having problems with landlords. Some apartment owners are demanding students not only pay rent and utilities, but also chip in for structural repairs. That, says the *Beacon,* is wrong, and the Graduate Student Association is sponsoring an informational program on student rights.

The editorial concludes:

> ... tips will be provided for how to handle lease dealings and problems with your residence. There will be a panel of experts to discuss the Landlord/Tenant Act.
>
> Tenants, you do not want to miss this great opportunity to find out your rights. If you currently are living in a residence hall and plan to move off-campus, you should attend the program so you will move into your new place knowing your rights.[15]

The Daily Texan, at the University of Texas in Austin, approaches a presidential election facing, as do all newspapers, this question: Do we endorse a candidate? *The Daily Texan's* answer:

> First, it publishes on its editorial page a lengthy piece by Bill Clinton (bylined, somewhat coyly, "Guest Columnist"). It's one of those canned pieces churned out by any candidate's speech writers during a campaign, but, nevertheless, it makes Clinton's case.
>
> Second, on the same page, *The Daily Texan* runs a column by one of its commentators, Hunter Stanco, recommending students not vote for Clinton on character grounds (youthful marijuana, womanizing).
>
> Third, *The Daily Texan's* institutional editorial endorses neither candidate but still calls for student action—*vote,* says the paper, despite the usual student preoccupations:

> Understandably, students couldn't care less right now about most things.
>
> You've kissed your 4.0 semester goodbye. You're stuck in an 8 a.m. microbiology class, your creditors are jumping down your neck and your roommate has become a manifestation of Satan.
>
> None of these factors is a viable excuse for not voting Tuesday.[16]

On its op-ed page, *The Daily Texan* lists addresses of polling booths on and near the campus.

Specialized Commentary Is Strong

Campus commentators and critics focus on student interests in specialty columns that often feature clever planning and writing.

For example, *The Shorthorn,* at the University of Texas in Arlington, joins a national debate over *fashion*—whether children should wear school uniforms.

In hilarious side-by-side columns, two *Shorthorn* commentators take opposite views. With wonderful provocative, tongue-in-cheek language, Dareen Barber opens his argument *for* instituting school uniforms.

> Children are morons. There's just no getting around that. Stick a kid in the bush with a survival knife, a can of Spam and a blanket and he'll be dead in seconds.
>
> And that's all right.
>
> But at least the little ones should *look* civilized while they writhe in agony over algebra.
>
> Let's get them uniformed. ...

In making the *no* case, Dave Wilson recalls his chubby childhood and his efforts to carefully select personalized clothing "to disguise my lack of muscle mass." He concludes:

> As the poster boy for the crusade against school uniforms, I'm telling you it's a bad idea. The plan is designed to squash individuality. It's designed to level the playing field.
>
> Instead, it would make things worse. Weaklings would be exposed, as would those who are "filling out."
>
> And it would be harder to find the weird girls.[17]

Now, that writing tone won't work at *The New York Times* or *Washington Post.* But Barber and Wilson aren't writing for New Yorkers or Washingtonians; they're writing *for students.* Pegging your style and tone to *your* audience, not somebody else's, is essential to writing success. And, you simply won't be read if at times your writing doesn't swing and sway a bit.

(Incidentally, *The Shorthorn's* editorial page wasn't all spoof that day. The page showed *balance between the serious and the comic.* An institutional editorial demanded the Legislature spend more on education, and a staff columnist, Andy McMillen, attacked President Clinton for selling political favors.)[18]

Some student newspapers are strong in restaurant and bar reviews.

For example, *The Ring-tum Phi,* at Washington & Lee University in Lexington, Va., features critics "Doug and Robin" who dine out incognito and report back on their findings.

One restaurant they visited "is the best option for fine Italian dining in Lexington," and "Doug and Robin's" gives it (on a scale of 1-5) a 4 for food quality and a 4 for food presentation. The restaurant's address is published, along with a small photo of its facade and its price range ($7-$17).

"Doug and Robin's" displays the essentials of professional restaurant reviewing: candid personal opinions plus operative information (location, prices) for readers.[19]

Strong reporting is featured in arts reviews in *The Lantern,* at Ohio State University in Columbus.

Arts writer Richelle Taylor views a multi-media event and *reports* what the sponsoring association's spokeswoman says is the artistic intent. Critic Taylor's piece is fully detailed on where, how and when readers can see the event—and how much tickets cost.[20] Melissa Littleton of *The Lantern* reports similarly on local opera singers offering to sing "vocal valentines," and lists their telephone number—and reports students can use credit cards to order valentines sung.[21]

Arts reviewing and restaurant critiquing are not merely your opportunity to sound off; you also have a *reporting* responsibility to your readers.

Heartening efforts are made by some campus newspapers to critique their own journalistic performance and other media.

Staff columnist Jay Dismukes of *The Daily Mississippian,* at the University of Mississippi ("Ole Miss"), in University, Miss., attacks a Birmingham TV station for refusing to air the comedy "Ellen" episode in which the main character (played by Ellen DeGeneres) "comes out" as a lesbian. Dismukes cites "Deep South" hangups behind the station's decision, which "conjures up visions of McCarthyism." Writes Dismukes:

> Every now and then, as if at the whimsical mercy of some twisted higher power, Birmingham, the state of Alabama, and the Deep South for that matter, feel the overwhelming urge to make asses of themselves. [22]

In an ombudsman-like institutional editorial, *The Paladin,* at Furman University in Greenville, S.C., comments on holes in its own news coverage of turmoil in the Greek system:

> If you are an astute reader, you are asking yourself why none of this appears in the news section of the newspaper. An excellent question. The fact is that, while almost everyone queried was willing to describe to us in detail the circumstances of this travesty, not a single person directly involved was willing to go on record with their knowledge. And so we are left in the immensely frustrating situation of knowing the truth (though we cannot print it as such), but not being able to do anything about it. We cannot simply run a story without willing and substantiated sources, and yet we don't feel that it is something we can simply walk away from. [23]

Defense of the First Amendment and openness in government is strong in many campus newspapers.

Red & Black, at the University of Georgia in Athens, frequently files Open Records demands and lawsuits to obtain university documents that, by law, must be available to the public.

The College Heights Herald, at Western Kentucky University in Bowling Green, defends the *people*'s right to know by using its editorial page power (and no matter how small your paper's circulation, editorials *are* powerful). The *Herald* opens an institutional editorial:

> You may not know it, but you had a door slammed in your face last month.
> On two separate occasions in February, the Board of Regents shut the public out of its meetings regarding the search for Western's new president. ...

Now, the *Herald* editorial reports the paper tried to gain information for its readers. But the Regents refused (illegally, the *Herald* says) to open its meetings and, consequently, "The public still doesn't know what they were talking about."

The *Herald* concludes:

> It's simple: Public business needs to be conducted in public. Just because the Board of Regents can try to sidestep the severity and legality of closing meetings while keeping the community uninformed doesn't mean it's right.
> To do any less would be slamming the door in Western's face.[24]

Hard-nosed defense of the *public*'s right to know is an obligation of all who enjoy freedom of the press.

That's some of what is strong in campus journalism today. Now, the other side.

Today's Problems, Tomorrow's Challenges

Napoleon, by all accounts, was a profound thinker, a great strategist and, except for a battle or two lost here and there, a strong general. But before he got to any of that, Napoleon had to learn how to load a musket, the basic tool of his trade.

So must you student journalists learn your basic tool—the language—before you can write effective opinion and commentary.

Grammar: Learn It!

My survey of campus newspapers shows clearly that a fundamental problem for many (dare I say, "most"?) aspiring journalists today is not knowing simple rules of grammar and sentence structure. Learn them or forget the challenge of becoming tomorrow's journalistic stars.

Face it: No matter how profound your thinking or sweeping your view, if you cannot write clearly and accurately you'll not communicate your vision and, further, you'll be discredited automatically by the very people all of us journalists want to reach, *thinkers*.

How can readers trust the logic and wisdom of your editorial if you confuse subject and verb agreement, foul up sequences of tenses or misplace modifiers? *All signal amateur at work* (and all litter campus newspapers).

Write Short!

Many editorials and columns are written so long that not even the writers' moms would read all the way through.

Don't confuse yardage with impact. To the contrary, the longer your editorial, often the more confused your message.

If William Safire can discuss the Free World in 400 words or so, you can comment on campus crime in about the same wordage. And you humor columnists note: Buchwald does it in 350 or so!

Focus Your Central Point

Remember our discussion earlier in the book about how the pros do it: They limit their central argument to one or two compellingly important points, and express those points clearly.

Too few campus newspaper editorials have the "housekeeping" or "nut" paragraph which precisely states the writer's central point. Tell us—*precisely*—what are you advocating?

You're asking *busy* readers too much if you demand they labor over your editorial, as over a crossword puzzle. Make them work to figure out *what* you're saying, and they won't stick around long enough to conclude whether they agree or disagree with you.

Avoid Sweeping Generalizations

As a news reporter, you wouldn't escalate a single parking lot mugging to "Crime Wave Sweeps Campus."

Neither should you, as an editorial writer, fall prey to the Sin of Sweeping Generalizations.

Which is what happened to an editorial writer for *The Second Sun*, at Francis Marion University in Florence, S.C. The writer reported efforts were made by the university administration to determine who voted for a non-confidence motion against the president, and, "Faculty members are now afraid to say anything that is not already written down in a textbook." [25]

Whoa! Whatever the seriousness of the situation and however commendable the writer's attempt to deal with it, the effort failed the moment readers stumbled on that sweeping and obviously overstated generalization.

Defeat Afghanistanism

"Afghanistanism" is that tendency among journalists to discuss news from afar and avoid what's happening on Main Street.

After all, knocking out a quick editorial on Afghanistan is easy. (We're against war, for peace; lock up the bad guys; elect the good guys.) Digging through claim and counterclaim of a complex—and controversial—local issue, like whether to cut down all the maple trees along Main Street, is something else.

For all their efforts to focus comment on local campus issues, student journalists still tend to gaze frequently on distant (and for campus readers, nearly irrelevant) news horizons.

Thus, a columnist for *The Eastern Echo,* at Eastern Michigan University in Ypsilanti, stumbles on for hundreds of words about the White House and presidential politics. Two thoughts: David Broder of *The Washington Post, who is in Washington,* does it better. And, on the day of the editorial, *The Eastern Echo*'s Front Page reported three *campus* stories that merited comment: The university and its staff union reached agreement on a new labor contract, campus police announced new anti-stalker measures, and the National Association for the Advancement of Colored People was reactivated after three years' absence.[26]

Sports writers, among the most active (and, often, most stylish) writers in campus journalism, frequently commit Afghanistanism. Many (I'd say *all,* except for a hatred of sweeping generalizations) want to report major league sports for major league newspapers—and, thus, a sports columnist for *The Northern Star,* at Northern Illinois University, analyzes, from his base in Dekalb, Ill., the play of Tiger Woods in the Masters golf tournament in Augusta, Ga.[27] In the *adjacent column* is fertile local ground for analysis by our wandering sports columnist: Two Northern Illinois grads who played in NCAA tournament *and* professional tennis are coming back to campus to be honored.

If you want—need—to get a piece of distant action, do it the way Brian Ayres did in his column for *The Post,* at Ohio University in Athens. Ayers wrote about the Major League Baseball Free Agent Amateur Draft but *not* from the distant scene of the draft; rather, Ayres obtained and commented on *reactions* by three *Ohio* players picked in the draft.[28]

Watch Those Anonymous Sources

Question: Why would news sources, official or otherwise, give you hot dope for an editorial on a controversial subject and then demand anonymity?

Answer: Because they want to leak information to the public and avoid responsibility for it, that's why. Which means *you* take responsibility.

See the catch? Yet, campus opinion writers and commentators repeatedly peg their arguments—the very core of their positions—to anonymous sources. In some newspapers, readers even are permitted to publish vitriolic—and unsigned—letters, including attacks on other individuals by name.

We all know important stories (including Watergate) that broke on information from anonymous sources. And sometimes you must go with unidentified sources to get important stories before the public.

But keep anonymous sources to a strict minimum. They are sucker bait, and they *shred* your credibility. And make it a rule: Readers who don't sign their letters don't get their letters published.

Take Time to Cheer

Journalists report much bad news. War, famine, murder, rape, arson—all are our daily news fare, and all are on our editorial as well as front pages.

But don't forget to take time to cheer when good things happen to good people, as did *The Collegian,* at Kansas State University in Manhattan, with a lengthy editorial complimenting the women's basketball team for an unexpectedly strong season. *The Collegian* called for campuswide applause under this headline:

Women's Basketball
at K-State Needs
Kudos for This Season's
Big 12 Performance[29]

And, Do Consider Good Taste

Okay, you're away from home (free at last!) and can say anything you want to say. And, you've got the First Amendment and freedom of the press behind you.

But, does that mean freedom (or need) to use the "F" word 18 (*eighteen*) times in a single column, as did a commentator for *The Maneater,* at the University of Missouri in Columbia? (His essay was on various usages of the word, which undoubtedly neither enlightened nor shocked many readers; rather, it simply was a terrible waste of his chance to reach the public with his thoughts on any of the truly important issues that surface on campus.)[30]

And, did a commentator for *The Battalion,* at Texas A&M University, in College Station, waste his tremendous opportunity, *as a journalist,* by devoting his column to explaining how members of the ROTC Cadet Corps and the Aggies Band, in "friendly rivalry," call each other—well, pieces of fecal material?[31]

Good rule on questions of bad taste: Ask yourself, Is there *higher journalistic purpose* in using language or material that would offend reasonable readers? Is such material *essential to communication* of your thoughts? Is such material *in direct quotes* and, again, essential to communication?

If the answer is no to those questions, why not eliminate the material and get on with that higher journalistic purpose?

Summary

- Campus newspapers are wide-open markets for aspiring writers who want to build the clip files demanded by job interviewers.
- Campus journalism is produced by beginners and, inevitably, has weaknesses, but much high-quality opinion writing is published in university newspapers.
- Journalistic courage is exemplified by campus journalists who, largely unsung, labor to cover and analyze news for student audiences.
- Campus papers often take on hot issues and powerful personalities, and if you can't envisage yourself criticizing the governor in an editorial or writing a probing commentary about your university's administration, rethink your career plan.
- Criticizing fellow students in a column and commenting on racism, homophobia, religion and other hot button topics are part of courageous journalism.
- Campus editorial pages often display Big League characteristics—strong reporting, clever planning and writing.
- Many campus editorial writers and commentators need to improve grammar and sentence structure to ensure their ideas are communicated effectively to readers.
- In campus journalism, editorials and columns generally are too long, lack a focused central point, contain sweeping generalizations and tend toward "Afghanistanism," a preoccupation with distant events, to the exclusion of local issues.
- Even considering that they write for student audiences, some campus journalists write in bad taste. Ask this question: Is this obscene or otherwise offensive material necessary to serve a higher journalistic purpose?

Recommended Reading

Many of the writing problems discussed in this chapter are examined in Conrad Fink, *Introduction to Professional Newswriting,* 2d ed (New York: Addison Wesley Longman, 1998). Magazine-style commentary is discussed in my *Introduction to Magazine Writing* (New York: Macmillan, 1994). Excellent for a brush-up on grammar and writing basics: Brian S. Brooks and James L. Pinson, *Working with Words: A Concise Handbook for Media Writers and Editors* (New York: St. Martin's Press, 1989), William Strunk Jr., and E.B. White, *The Elements of Style,* 3d ed. (New York: Macmillan, 1979), James J. Kilpatrick, *The Writer's Art* (Kansas City, MO: Andrews, McMeel & Parker, 1984). *Be certain* to read Rene J. Cappon, *The Word,* 2d ed (New York, The Associated Press, 1991).

Notes

1. I discuss job-hunting strategy and résumé writing in *Introduction to Professional Newswriting*, 2d ed (New York: Addison Wesley Longman, 1998).

2. The 45 newspapers were represented at the second annual conference on management strategies and leadership for college newspaper editors, sponsored by the James M. Cox Institute for Newspaper Management Studies, at the University of Georgia, August 6-9, 1997.

3. Matt Snyder, "Remembering to Look at the Faces Inside the News," *The Daily Iowan*, June 24, 1997, p. 4.

4. "Plainsman Delivers Three Guilty Verdicts," *The Plainsman*, May 15, 1997, p. A-6.

5. William Lutz, "Passing the Buck," *The Daily*, April 10, 1997, p. 4.

6. "In Our Opinion ... ", *The Iowa State Daily*, Feb. 6, 1997, p. 4.

7. "Porno Policy," *The Free Press*, Feb. 3, 1997, p. 4.

8. "Voice," *The Arkansas Traveler*, April 14, 1997, p. 2.

9. Paul Turner, "Ellen DeGeneres Comes Out of Closet, Causes Commercial Coup," *The Daily Barometer*, May 7, 1997, p. 9

10. Scott Lamar, "Everything Isn't as Easy as Black and White," *The Current*, Nov. 8, 1996, p. 2.

11. "Cartoon Could Ignite 'Racial Powder Keg,'" *The Current*, Nov. 8, 1996, p. 2.

12. Chris Robertson, "Schools Attempt to Bridge Language Gap," *The Tartan*, Jan. 17, 1997, p. 26.

13. "Title IX," *The Rice Thresher*, April 25, 1996, p. 2.

14. "Full Coverage," *The Daily Egyptian*, April 25, 1997, p. 4.

15. "Tenant, Landlord Forum Discusses Responsibilities," *The Daily Beacon*, April 1, 1997, p. 4.

16. "One Vote," *The Daily Texan*, Nov. 5, 1996, p. 4.

17. "More Money," *The Shorthorn*, March 4, 1997, p. 7.

18. Andy McMillen, "Supporters Shouldn't Trust Clinton as Far as They Can Throw Him," *The Shorthorn*, March 4, 1997, p. 7.

19. "Il Palazzo, Still the In-Town Reliable Favorite," *Ring-tum Phi*, May 12, 1997, p. 3.

20. Richelle Taylor, "Joan of Arc Film Hits Columbus," *The Ohio State Lantern*, Feb. 11, 1997, p. 13.

21. Melissa Littleton, "Serenade Delivers Valentine Romance," *The Ohio State Lantern*, Feb. 11, 1997, p. 13.

22. Jay Dismukes, "Boycott of 'Ellen' Episode Ridiculous," *The Daily Mississippian*, April 22, 1997, p. 2.

23. "Reign of Error," *The Paladin*, Jan. 17, 1997, p. 6.

24. "Regents: Learn the Law," *The College Heights Herald*, March 4,1997, p. 4.

25. Rebecca Marriott, "Actions Speak Louder Than Words," *The Second Sun*, April 15, 1997, p. 3.

26. Jesse Esquierdo Jr., "Dole Did Not Fail to Dream," *The Eastern Echo*, Nov. 8, 1996, p. 4.

27. Kevin Wendt, "Get Used to the Name of Tiger Woods," *The Northern Star,* April 15, 1997, p. 16.

28. Brian Ayres, "Waiting Game Pays Off as Gick Goes in Draft," *The Post,* June 6, 1997, p. 11.

29. "Our View," *The Kansas State Collegian,* March 5, 1997, p. 4.

30. Peter Bellone, "Maneater, or Wordeater?," *The Maneater,* May 6, 1997, p. 11.

31. David Boldt, "Mean-Spirited Rivalries Block Understanding," *The Battalion,* Oct. 30, 1996, p. 11.

Exercises

1. Recalling the discussion of courage, write about 350 words on the single most impressive example of courage in journalism of which you are aware. This can be courage by an individual journalist, a staff or a newspaper.

Write this as a *commentary for publication.* Treat it as an ombudsman's report, an explanation by a journalism *insider* of courage under fire for an audience of *outsiders,* your student body.

2. Examine your campus newspaper (or another newspaper designated by your instructor) and comment, in 350-400 words, on whether its editorial page is covering—and commenting on—"hot button" topics discussed in this chapter.

Do you find editorials and columns on racism, homophobia, student drinking and conduct, religion? Is the newspaper displaying *editorial courage?*

3. Apply to your campus newspaper (or another newspaper designated by your instructor) the standards of excellence outlined in this chapter. Write your findings in about 300 words.

Do editorials and columns display *strong reporting?* Do they *localize issues?* Are they *balanced and fair?* Do they *point toward solutions?*

4. Examine specialized commentary in your campus newspaper (or another newspaper designated by your instructor). Is the newspaper "covering the waterfront?" Is it addressing issues in fashion and fads, health and fitness, restaurant and bar reviewing, the arts?

Write about 350 words as a critical examination of content for submission to the newspaper's editor in chief as your suggestions for improvement.

5. In about 300 words, comment on bad taste, as discussed in this chapter and as it is treated in your campus newspaper (or another newspaper designated by your instructor).

Is the newspaper guilty of writing in base taste, in your opinion? Would some content be regarded as objectionable by reasonable student readers? Is there difference in how journalists should write for students and for the general public?

PART SIX

You and the Law: Write Defensively!

W
E TURN now to a crucial balancing act you must perform as a writer of opinion.

On one hand, your journalistic responsibility is to probe and inquire on behalf of your readers, to reveal and at times *hit hard* in pointed commentary on people and issues.

Counterbalancing that *always* is a dangerous legal climate that can expose your media employer and you to potentially damaging—ruinous, even—financial risk, especially in libel lawsuits.

Media managers and editors (and authors of journalism textbooks) must achieve a balance of their own—stoking your reportorial ardor to produce great journalism and public service, yet, risk dampening your enthusiasm by suggesting you write defensively.

I hope your commitment to strong, courageous journalism has been buttressed by this book. Be assured my purpose is not to weaken it now. Rather, the single chapter of Part Six is designed to provide hints on how to meet your journalistic purpose *and* write defensively to fend off lawsuits.

Note: I am not a lawyer and Chapter Twelve is not designed as a comprehensive discussion of media law. Use the pages ahead only as a beginning point for your own deeper exploration of media law.

12 Avoiding Legal Traps for Opinion Writers

THIS IS your basic problem:

Widespread disdain among Americans for the media emboldens many to rush to law courts over wrongs—real or imagined, major or minor—inflicted on them by newspapers, magazines, broadcast companies and, now, cyberspace writing.

Public opinion polls reveal many Americans consider the media cold, distant, arrogant, out only for a story and thoroughly insensitive to the people they write about.

Reflecting such negative societal attitudes, juries follow their emotions and return judgments against the media *and writers* in a high percentage of libel cases, passing out awards in the hundreds of thousands or even many millions of dollars.

For example, $2.8 million was the *average* award in 1996 in libel and privacy cases won against the media. Hugely profitable newspaper, magazine and broadcast companies are regarded as "deep-pocket" targets by offended individuals and, importantly, by their attorneys.[1]

Upon appeal to higher courts, where judges presumably rule on law, not emotion, many judgments against the media are overturned and many monetary awards are reduced. In the period 1994-1996, for example, 60 percent of all libel verdicts were overturned, reduced or sent back to trial courts.[2]

That is, you have strong First Amendment defense—but *not* total immunity—for expressing your opinion on matters of public interest and for entering robust debate in the "open marketplace of ideas" with factually accurate journalistic purpose.

However, awards of many millions of dollars against media companies have been upheld by appeals courts in recent years, and, anyway, just defending against lawsuits can cost millions. A.H. Belo Corp., owner of television stations, the *Dallas Morning News* and other newspapers, opted for a costly out-of-court settlement when a $58 million judgment against a company TV station was upheld.[3]

Reporters, writers and editors are personally included even in those libel suits directed at a company's deep pockets. A Houston jury ordered a *Wall Street Journal* writer to pay $20,000 (and the *Journal, $222.7 million!*) in a suit brought by a brokerage firm. (The newspaper's penalty was reduced to $22.7 million by an appeals court.)[4]

The negative societal environment for the media and writers is reflected in jury awards for *punitive damages*, which, of course, are designed to punish. *Actual damages* are awarded to compensate for damage to reputation. Of the $222.7 million in that initial verdict against *The Wall Street Journal,* the jury awarded $200 million in punitive damages.

In sum, the legal climate for journalists is so adversarial that across the media landscape has settled a "chilling effect." That's the tendency—ever so subtle sometimes but nevertheless real—to pull punches, to avoid writing about controversial people or subjects or, in what *is* written, to be inoffensive and indirect in hopes that journalistic indecisiveness will prevent legal difficulty.

Can we do the job as journalists, as discussed in this book, and still protect ourselves in such troubling times? Yes.

First, The Basics

In the beginning, it was majestic in concept, if simple in language:

> Congress shall make no law respecting an
> establishment of religion, or
> prohibiting the free exercise thereof;
> *or abridging the freedom of speech, or*
> *of the press;* or the right of the people
> peaceably to assemble, and to petition
> the Government for a redress of
> grievances.
>
> First Amendment, U.S. Constitution

The First Amendment and nine others—the Bill of Rights—became effective in 1791. In the many court rulings since then, what might appear simply to be a blanket of total press freedom laid down in the First Amendment has assumed considerable complexity.

For writers of opinion and commentary, sorting through the complexities of *defamation law* is most important. Defamation is injury to reputation. What reputation is and whether or how it is injured is decided by judge and jury. But generally it's accepted that you run risk if you hold a person to public shame, disgrace, ridicule, hatred.

Slander is defamation—injury to reputation—through the spoken word. *Libel* is injury through the written word, pictures, drawings.

You can be held to have libeled a person with a single word ("murderer," "criminal"), a sentence, a paragraph, a two-paragraph story—as well as in an investigative "take-out" or lengthy institutional editorial or column.

If you're sued for libel, the plaintiff (the person or company filing the lawsuit) must prove the following:

- That defamation occurred, and that the plaintiff was identified and was the target of the defamation.
- That defamation was published (and, as we'll discuss later, that doesn't mean *only* in a newspaper or magazine).
- That you were at fault in publishing the defamation, through negligence or recklessness or, of course, that you *intended* to defame.
- That defamation harmed the plaintiff, as through financial loss, harm to reputation, emotional distress.

There is a single (yes, just one) *unconditional defense* in a libel suit: That the facts as you have stated them are provably true. Note *provably*. That means *you*—not the cop you talked to, not the high-ranking official who slipped you a document—you must be prepared to convince a jury that *everything* in your editorial or column, including what's in quotes, is provably true.

A second line of defense is *qualified privilege*. This flows from reporting fairly, accurately and without malice official proceedings, such as court hearings and legislative meetings, and from most official public records. Qualified privilege can cover reporting even false or damaging information.

For example, a U.S. senator has *absolute* privilege when stating on the floor of the U.S. Senate that his esteemed colleague is a "crook, adulterer and wife beater." You have *qualified* privilege in reporting fairly, accurately and without malice what he said.

Note: In claiming qualified privilege, you must be certain your reporting is from a privileged proceeding or source. State laws vary somewhat on this.

For example, you're generally on firm ground if you write an editorial pegged to a statement made on a street corner by the police chief, *acting in his official capacity*, that he arrested Fred Smith on a narcotics charge. But, again, state laws vary on who and what are official sources and, thus, under what circumstances qualified privilege applies.

Strong protection exists for *fair comment and criticism*—even commentary that's *unfair*—if it's on people or issues of public interest and importance. But, *facts in your opinion writing must stand the test of provable truth*. It's a point on which we should linger: Courts have held there is no such thing as an inaccurate opinion. Your belief is your belief. However, there obviously can be inaccuracies in the facts in your opinion writing *and in the facts on which you base your opinion*—and that can cost you heavily in a libel suit. Ensure your facts are accurate.

For example, a restaurant critic probably is safe with this *opinion*: "I think the service and food are terrible, and just thinking about Joe's Eatery makes me ill."

But, this is a dangerous *statement of fact*: "It will make you ill to eat at Joe's." Laboratory experts, health officials, physicians, patrons and Joe himself—all could testify that eating at that restaurant does *not* make you ill.

Figurative writing, so often used in critical writing to emphasize a point, can be torn to pieces under the test of provable truth in a court of law.

It's not enough to simply declare, "That's my opinion," and wrap yourself in the defense of fair comment. Judge and jury might require you to prove that your opinion derived from provably accurate facts.

That is, there is legal as well as journalistic and ethical purpose in letting your readers see the facts on which you structured your opinion—to see the honest journalistic motivation and reasoning behind your opinion.

Differentiating fact from opinion can be difficult, particularly in political commentary and the interpretive writing featured on many op-ed pages. In such cases, courts often consider the larger context of the writing and how ordinary readers would interpret it. For example, courts have decided that syndicated columnists whose Washington-datelined columns appear regularly on op-ed pages would be considered by most "ordinary" readers to be writers of opinion. *The Associated Press Stylebook and Libel Manual*—one of a working journalist's best friends—states:

> The right of fair comment has been summarized as follows:
> "Everyone has a right to comment on matters of public interest and concern, provided they do so fairly and with an honest purpose. Such comments or criticism are not libelous, however severe in their terms, unless they are written maliciously. Thus it has been held that books, prints, pictures and statuary publicly exhibited, and the architecture of public buildings, and actors and exhibitors are all the legitimate subjects of newspapers' criticism, and

such criticism fairly and honestly made is not libelous, however strong the
terms of censure may be."
                (*Hoeppner vs. Dunkirk Pr. Co., 254 N.Y. 95*)

Note above the reference to "comment on matters of public interest and
concern." The defense of "fair comment" is particularly strong when opinion is based on provably accurate facts and *directed at public acts, appear-
ances and performances*. This is a sturdy umbrella for comment on public
officials and public figures and for critiques of music, art, dance, drama (and,
alas, textbooks).

Many libel cases have common characteristics, and writing defensively
against them should become second nature to you. If you're careful, you can
head off lawsuits and still do the job, journalistically. And even if despite
your best efforts you are sued, defensive writing can give your attorney the
foundations of a strong defense.

Box 12-1	Professional Viewpoints

Some editors hold that in libel law, the best defense is offense.

Their newspapers let it be known they won't settle baseless libel suits
out of court—that they'll not be "easy pickings" and will force plaintiffs
into lengthy and costly courtroom fights.

Some editors say they will counter-sue attorneys who file spurious lawsuits on patently weak legal grounds. These editors say that even if plaintiffs don't know better, the attorneys should, because they know the law.

James W. Michaels, editor of *Forbes,* issues a warning in a column reporting a "public relations person" sent the magazine an article on a lawsuit
against *The Wall Street Journal.* Michaels writes:

**In sending it, the image merchant was implying: Take it easy on my client or
Forbes may find itself in the same position as the *Journal*'s. (This flack has been
retained by a company that thinks we may be preparing an unfriendly article.)**

Michaels continues:

**I've got news for the gent: We hate spending time and money defending against
libel suits, and so we don't go to press until we are sure of our facts and pretty
darned confident of our opinions.**

Michaels then describes how *Forbes* successfully fought a libel suit and the
judge "took the exceptional step of awarding *Forbes* financial sanctions against
(the plaintiff) and its attorneys."

Michaels concludes:

> I tell the story not to boast, but to remind people who would threaten us that we regard defending against libel suits as part of our cost of doing business. Only by accepting the burden can we help put notorious swindlers like [John Doe] out of business. We take seriously our slogan: No guts, no story.
>
> —James W. Michael, "No Guts, No Story," *Forbes*, August 11, 1997, p. 12.

Defensive Strategy #1: Be Journalistically Sound

Be fair, accurate and balanced in your writing. That is, be *journalistically sound.*

Repeatedly, writing that fails the libel test in court should have failed the good-journalism test by writer and editors before it got into print. Ethical, professional reporting and writing draw much less legal fire than do opinion and commentary that are patently unfair or unbalanced. Although even *unfair* opinion has strong constitutional protection, what we're talking about here is heading off the *career challenge* you'll face if your newspaper has to spend hundreds of thousands of dollars defending one-sided, inaccurate reporting and shoddy writing that you've produced in an editorial or column.

Defensive Strategy #2: Beware Accusations

Be doubly cautious if your writing accuses—*or could be perceived to accuse*—a person or company of illegal or immoral conduct.

Libel cases arise frequently over news stories, editorials or commentary about alleged criminal activity, misconduct in office, dereliction of duty.

Libel is *damage to reputation*, remember, and judges and juries have been dealing harshly with writers who accuse a person or company of improper behavior. That initial $222.7 million judgment against *The Wall Street Journal* stemmed from writing that the brokerage firm alleged was false and drove away clients. Be particularly careful if your opinion writing or commentary might cause a person or company *financial loss.*

Defensive Strategy #3: Double-Check Facts

Check, then double-check facts and quotes in your opinion writing *and* facts on which you base your opinion.

Journalistic lore is incorrect: Quoting a source on facts does *not* relieve you of responsibility for proving the truth of what the source told you. *You* take ultimate legal (and ethical) responsibility for everything in your writing.

And here is a courtroom reality: Any error—even one you might consider journalistically insignificant—can give plaintiff's attorneys an opening to convince a jury that your entire piece is discredited.

The context of a fact—or error—can be significant in a lawsuit. In lawsuits, there are no "little" errors, and surrounding the larger central truth of your editorial or commentary in a context of even insignificant errors can damage your defense.

| Box 12-2 | Seeking Professional Help |

Acting as your own lawyer—like diagnosing your own illnesses—can be dangerous. Seek expert advice when you *even suspect* you have a legal problem.

Aside from your own editor and your publication's attorney, here are sources for preliminary advice:

- *The Associated Press Stylebook and Libel Manual,* available on most newsdesks and from all bookstores. This contains an excellent summary of libel law in language non-lawyer journalists can understand.
- Your state press association. It has legal counsel on call for member newspapers and publications.
- The Libel Defense Resource Center, a media-financed organization in New York City, telephone (212) 889-2306.
- Media law experts in your nearest university law or journalism school.

Defensive Strategy #4: Investigate "Privilege"

Don't assume reporting from "public records" is "privileged" and thus safe.

First, you must determine whether under your state's laws the records truly are classified as public and official records and thus are privileged. Obtaining a piece of paper from a police officer or lawyer doesn't mean it's public, official or privileged.

Second, if you do obtain a genuinely public and official record the material you draw from it is privileged *only* if your reporting is fair, accurate, balanced.

Defensive Strategy #5: Question "Neutral Reportage"

Don't lean too heavily—or, at least, unthinkingly—on "neutral reportage" as a defense in libel.

Some courts accept the principle that a writer has privilege in reporting, for example, damaging statements or charges made by responsible sources if the circumstances are newsworthy and concern public officials or public figures *and* if the reporting is impartial, balanced and provides opposing views. An example is coverage of charge and counter-charge by shareholders critical of how a chief executive officer is running a company.

However, other courts reject "neutral reportage" on grounds it merely licenses journalists to report damaging charges they know may be false.

Again—as with all legal nuances—check your state's legal precedent.

Defensive Strategy #6: Don't Lean on "Cute" Writing

Don't assume indirect or cute language strips libelous material from your writing. For example, you need not name a person to identify him or her. "Pipe-smoking, bushy-eyebrowed professor ..." is enough if your entire university community knows instantly that is dear old Professor Frank Franklin. And, you've made a dangerous leap if you mistakenly write that the "pipe-smoking, bushy-eyebrowed professor ... was reported swept up on a police visit last Saturday night to a certain Broad Street club"—and everybody in town knows that was a raid by narcs who arrested heroin addicts.

Courts hold that identification is complete if the identity of a person can be inferred from an editorial or column. And, it's not only literal language in a published statement that can make it defamatory. Innuendo or the *context* of what you write and the *overall impression* it creates also can defame.

And—always—watch those "informed sources." It's journalistically unsound to litter your writing with them. In a legal (or ethical) sense, (1)*you* are responsible for proving everything the source said, and (2) you may be required in court to reveal your source's identity or accept the alternative, which can be a citation for contempt of court, a fine and a jail sentence.

Incidentally, inserting "alleged"—as in "pipe-smoking, bushy-eyebrowed professor is an *alleged* heroin addict"—is *absolutely no protection*. "Alleged" or no, *you* are making that charge, unless there is formal arrest.

Defensive Strategy #7: Take Care With Groups

Don't think there is automatic safety in numbers—safety if you avoid naming an individual and, instead, label as "child molesters" a group of 25 unnamed dissident members of a local church.

You may draw a lawsuit from all 25, and because that's a small group whose members could be identified by friends and family, the law generally would be on their side.

Conversely, the law probably is on your side if you want to write about large groups of 100 or more—"all those sex-crazed nuts who live in California."

Defensive Strategy #8: Beware Humor

Remember that humor and parody can wound *and defame*, and wounded, defamed people sometimes sue, rather than suffer in silence.

So, read again—twice—your clever play on words, your brilliant parody, your marvelous column of humor. Though hilarious to you, your writing may be unfunny in the eyes of your target and libelous in a law court.

A leading textbook, *The Law of Public Communication,* sums up a problem: "A major difficulty for writers is that even the courts disagree on where to draw the line between nondefamatory humor and defamatory ridicule."[5]

Defensive Strategy #9: No One Is "Fair Game"

Forget the newsroom tradition that public officials are "fair game."

In the eyes of the law and public (and, thus, juries), public officials have the right to defend their reputations. And, they're increasingly doing so in lawsuits.

Public officials are held to a high standard of proof. They must prove "actual malice," which means they must show that you knowingly wrote a falsehood *or* wrote with "reckless disregard" for the truth. But even forced to meet that high standard leaves public officials far from being fair game.

You also need to be careful writing about "public figures"—non-official individuals once thought also to be fair game if they thrust themselves, or are thrust, into the public limelight. Some courts have left undefined precisely who is a "public figure." Even a well-known lawyer and a prominent socialite have been deemed "private."

In the new world of libel law it's best to stick with an old rule of journalism: Be accurate, balanced and fair in all your writing, *about everyone*.

Defensive Strategy #10: Handle All Writing Carefully

Treat *every* editorial, *every* column as important and as potential lawsuit bait.

In libel law, there is no defense in claiming you wrote only a "minor" story, an "insignificant" editorial, a "secondary" column. Indeed, many lawsuits arise out of commentaries that journalists would consider minor, and from off-the-cuff columns written quickly on deadline, without second thought.

Major institutional editorials or investigative "take-outs" often are libel-proofed before publication. They usually deal with important people, companies, issues—and everybody in the newsroom knows they can be dangerous legally. Writers double-check, editors double-check writers, and, often, the newspaper's lawyers double-check all of them. And off in the corner, out of that day's action, is a bored columnist idly knocking off a quick, dirty and dangerous piece about a school principal accused of child molestation ... or a securities broker who is ripping off clients.

Defensive Strategy #11: Avoid Outside Comment

Be careful of what you write and say *outside* your editorial page or your column.

A libel must be published to be defamatory—but "publication" can be in a letter to your mom, an e-mail memo to your editor, a cute note on the newsroom bulletin board.

Journalists often trade information with sources. It's part of networking to dig out news. And it can be very dangerous. Don't trade to a source anything you wouldn't put in your editorial or column—or anything you can't stand behind in court.

A businessman won a $9.2 million jury award in a suit filed over a memo two *Alton* (Ill.) *Telegraph* reporters sent a federal agency while researching a story. 'Nuff said?

Defensive Strategy #12: Involve Your Editors

Get your editors involved in potentially dangerous situations.

You may think editors are paid only to harass you, to chop to bits your beautiful prose. But believe it: Editors also are paid to keep you (and thus themselves and your newspaper or magazine) out of trouble.

Look at it this way: Somebody decided your editor has more experience than you, better judgment, more journalistic moxie, or you would be editor, right? With that decision goes better pay for your editor, more benefits and a great deal more responsibility for what appears in print. *Lean on the editor.* Make your problem the editor's problem; make it a corporate problem.

If in writing an editorial or column you receive a threat ("I'll sue if you print that!") be certain to tell your editor. If you are unsure of your facts or see other possible legal problems, alert your editor.

Don't count on potential problems being discovered in the normal editing process. If you've seen newsrooms on deadline you know why: Editors often are overwhelmed and simply shovel copy through to production. Hoist a warning flag if you have a problem. Your editor probably won't be a lawyer, but many editors have considerable experience in libel law and, importantly, may know when to call a lawyer for advice.

Defensive Strategy #13: Handle Complaints Gently

Be courteous when you get a complaint.

Many libel suits are filed by people offended by what is published and who would like to talk it out with somebody at the newspaper or magazine—but nobody will listen.

Tough journalists who have seen "Front Page" too many times like to bark at complainers, "Get lost"—or worse, much worse. Who *will* listen? A libel lawyer, that's who. And, with many lawyers underemployed, it's easy to find one who will sue a publication for no fee up-front—just a healthy percentage of any jury award or out-of-court settlement.

That is, libel law no longer is only the "rich man's revenge," as it once was termed. Many lawsuits are launched by people far from rich and who are unsophisticated in media affairs—but very aggressive in defense of what they consider to be their "good name."

So, when someone calls you with a complaint—and during your career someone will—listen courteously. Say very little; just take notes. Do not acknowledge error, do not apologize, do not confess: "Golly, you may be right ... that *doesn't* look as good today as it did when I wrote it yesterday." Don't rush out a correction, and don't do the very human thing: Don't try to handle the complaint on the hush, hush, promising to write another editorial or column for tomorrow and, "Let's see if I can make you happy." What you say and do following a complaint can repeat a libel or admit to one, and can be as dangerous legally as anything you've written.

Make it a rule: Only lawyers talk to lawyers. If a *lawyer* telephones you, hang up. A lawyer may be seeking your acknowledgment of error, your confirmation of libel.

Thank any complainer for calling, and immediately inform your editor—again avoiding the human instinct to disguise from your superiors that you may have goofed. Only if you are completely forthcoming can your editor and lawyer handle the matter properly.

Defensive Strategy #14: Watch Other Dangers

Don't think libel law is your only danger.

A jury found ABC News, two network employees and the network's then owner, Capital Cities, liable for *fraud, trespassing and breach of company loyalty.* ABC employees used undercover reporting techniques in a story on the Food Lion supermarket chain, gaining employment in a store and reporting "from behind the scenes."[6]

We all know important stories that surfaced through such undercover reporting techniques, and some journalists feel strongly they should be used to break news important to the public. (Out of concerns more ethical than legal in nature, my advice is to avoid using those techniques.)[7]

Invasion of privacy can arise if you write about a private individual who desires to be left alone—a *right* in the United States—and there is *no current newsworthiness* in that person. The heretofore anonymous lumberjack's wife who craves privacy but who was victimized yesterday in a spectacular bank robbery, is of public interest, even against her will, and probably has current newsworthiness. But you are at risk if you drive 10 miles back in the woods and, figuratively, drag her kicking and screaming into the limelight and reveal some intimacy, some private matter if there is no bank robbery, no current newsworthiness.

False light is depicting someone untruthfully in a manner that would offend a person of ordinary sensibility. False-light portrayal ***need not be defamatory***. As in defamation suits your defense is truth. If what you write is true, it cannot hold the person in "false light."

Copyright, Fair Use and Plagiarism

Much journalism is built on previous journalism, and therein lies danger.

Item: A news story breaks in Washington on, say, Japan's auto exports to the United States. All over America, editorial writers and commentators move quickly to analyze and interpret local impact.

Item: Toxic waste dumps are found more (or less) dangerous than thought, and newspaper editorial boards structure their institutional stance on permitting (or denying) local dumps.

Item: A local school bond issue becomes controversial, and opinion writers search out precedents in school districts across the land.

In all three scenarios, writers are strikingly unanimous in their first reporting moves: They get on the Internet and check what other newspapers have written; they consult books published on auto imports (toxic dumps and education financing); they pull out their personal clip files of stories they saw in *The Economist* or *Business Week;* all check The Associated Press, which, in turn, is reporting what other news organizations reported!

See the problem? It's easy to draw on other journalist's work, to pull on their facts and pick up their interpretations and analyses. In sum, it's easy to lose sight of your original thinking and theirs, your originally reported facts and theirs.

How you draw on the work of others can have important legal ramifications. (In an ethical sense, drawing on them without attribution is a mortal journalistic sin.) Here's the legal background:

From our very beginning as a nation we've recognized the right of creative persons to profit from their work. The Founding Fathers wove Constitutional protection around that right, giving Congress (Article 1, section 8) power "To promote the progress of science and useful arts, by securing for limited times to authors and inventors the exclusive right to their respective writing and discoveries." The intent obviously was to encourage creative work that would benefit society.

The resulting Copyright Act protects original work such as news stories, columns, opinion pieces, books, works of art and so forth. Note a distinction: The artist's or author's account or expression is protected; there is no protection for the event or facts of the news break that inspires the author's account or a newsphoto or artist's painting.

That is, the news of Japan's auto exports isn't copyrighted, but *The Economist*'s story about them can be; the danger of toxic dumps isn't copyrighted, but *Forbes'* account of that danger can be.

Under "fair use" doctrine, you have the right to draw from even copyrighted material under certain conditions. The Copyright Act gives special latitude to reporters, authors, poets, composers, academics who draw from copyrighted material for comment, criticism, teaching, research, scholarship. That is, if you're writing arts commentary or book reviews the Copyright Act presumes you will borrow, lift, quote from the work you are critiquing.

Remember that *copyright is a form of property*. The original author or creator owns the copyright and has the right to profit from it, sell it, give it to heirs. Anything you do to *diminish the commercial value of that property* can put you in legal jeopardy.

So, if you are accused of *infringing* on copyright, judge and jury likely will consider whether you diminished the copyright's property value. For example, if you write about, say, a new book and lift thousands of words in direct quotes—the "heart" of the book—the author might argue you exceeded "fair use" and diminished the book's marketplace value. Even using a sentence or two from poems or songs could be questioned, if those sentences were deemed central to the commercial value of the copyright.

In assessing your use of copyrighted material, judge and jury would consider the *purpose and character* of your use (whether for commercial or non-profit, educational purposes); the *nature of the copyrighted work*; the *amount and "substantiality" of your use* in relation to the work as a whole (whether, for example, you extracted in lengthy excerpts the significant "guts" of an article or book); the effect of your use *on the work's market value*.

Note: The law grants copyright to the creator of an original work the moment it is created, whether on paper, film or another medium. The creator gains stronger ability to recover damages for infringement by placing "Copyright" on the work (or (C) or "Cop.") and registering the work with the Copyright Office in the Library of Congress. Some publications automatically include copyright notification covering the entire issue.

Writers of the opinion and commentary discussed in this book normally don't have difficulty under copyright law except in cases involving lengthy excerpts deemed to destroy the market value of a book or other form of writing.

Plagiarism is quite something else because it involves copying someone's work and ideas and using them as your own.

Inevitably in journalism, you'll sometimes begin your writing from a base of ideas developed by other journalists—you'll write an editorial after reading a news story about Japanese auto exports or after studying editorials and commentaries from a number of publications. The law recognizes that is the nature of journalism.

However, note this distinction: It's *plagiarism* to merely rewrite the words and ideas of another and not cite attribution. In the law, that can be *misappropriation*, and it can draw a lawsuit. It's *accepted journalistic practice* to read another writer's words and ideas *and* do additional research and new reporting to advance the debate, to carry the story ahead into new dimensions. To avoid the legal (and ethical) complications inherent in plagiarism take two steps: (1) Give credit to any original author from whom you draw unique ideas, and (2) present "added value" reporting that pushes your discussion beyond that of the original author.

| Box 12-3 | A Professional's Viewpoint |

If you see something somebody else has said or written that is so good you have to use it, the way to do it is simple: Put it in quotation marks, and attribute it. Sometimes ideas should be attributed, too. If, in pondering the workings of the universe, you independently arrive at the conclusion that E=MC2, it's worth noting that Einstein got there first.

—Ed Williams, editor of *The Charlotte Observer*'s editorial pages, in "A True Horror Story," *The Masthead*, Fall 1995, p. 45.

Who Owns Your Work?

Broadly, you *lose* ownership of your work—your automatic copyright— when you write "for hire."

First, if you are employed by a newspaper, magazine or other medium and you write as part of your job, your employer becomes "legal author" and, thus, owner of your work.

Second, if you are commissioned to freelance under a write-for-hire agreement, your writing is owned by the medium that pays you.

In freelancing, the key is to retain whatever rights you can negotiate. As a beginner you don't have much leverage, but remember that secondary usage of your writing—in reprints, sale to other publications, films—can be profitable.

Try to limit your freelance sale to "first North American serial rights." That means the newspaper or magazine has one-time right for publication in North America, and that you can sell your piece outside North America and share in proceeds from secondary use.

If you're considering a serious career in freelancing you can get valuable guidance in contract negotiations from the American Society of Journalists and Authors, Inc., 1501 Broadway, Suite 302, New York, NY 10036, telephone (212) 997-0947.[8]

And, How About Cyberspace Law?

Like cyberspace technology and operations, cyberspace law is evolving and still undefined. However, factors are emerging as important for writers of opinion and commentary:

First, libel law applies to defamation on the Internet and electronic services, just as it does to defamation in ink on paper. If cyberspace transmission communicates defamation to a third party—a party other than originator and target—libel law can kick in. Note that "publication" need not be in an online newspaper or in journalistically structured writing. It can be achieved with communication posted to electronic bulletin boards, a discussion group or "chat room."[9]

Second, persons who feel defamed in cyberspace likely will take the same deadly serious view they take when offended by something published in traditional print media. A White House official filed a *$30 million* suit against an Internet writer who commented on the official's spousal past. (Still unclear is whether on-line services that carry defamatory material will be liable along with writers or whether, like telephone companies, on-line services won't be liable for information that travels on their circuits but is originated by others.)[10]

Third, for writers, Internet transmission can widen dramatically the geographic area of publication and thus possibly expose them to unforeseen circumstances. For example, your editorial or commentary published in, say, a Phoenix or Philadelphia newspaper could appear via Internet in London and thus expose you to Britain's *much* tougher libel law. Under such circumstances, you'd need to understand much more than only Arizona's libel laws or Pennsylvania's![11]

Fourth, tension is developing between writers—staff and freelance—and their newspapers and magazines over whether writers should be paid extra if material sold for ink-and-paper publication is also distributed electronically. Newspapers and magazines, of course, claim total ownership of staff production and maintain that freelancers shouldn't get extra payment for use electronically. In one ruling that's certain to be only the first of many, a U.S. District court judge ruled in favor of publishers, stating that electronic databases and CD-ROMs of print publications are not new services for which writers should be paid extra but, rather, *revisions of print publications*. (Publishers claim they merely "repurpose" for electronic delivery material already bought for use in print products.)[12]

Summary

- Opinion writers must balance their journalistic responsibility to produce pointed and sometimes hard-hitting commentary against the reality that they write in a dangerous legal climate.
- Widespread disdain among Americans for the media emboldens many to use libel law to punish journalists.
- Juries, reflecting negative societal attitudes, find against the media in a high percentage of libel cases, passing out awards in the millions of dollars.
- In appeals courts, where judges presumably rule on law, not emotion, many judgments against the media are overturned and many monetary awards are reduced.
- Nevertheless, the legal climate is so adversarial that a "chilling effect" leads some journalists to avoid writing about controversial subjects or people.
- Defamation is injury to reputation; libel is defamation through written word, pictures, drawings; slander is spoken defamation.
- Plaintiffs who sue for libel must prove defamation was published, that it identified and harmed the plaintiff and was published through fault, negligence or recklessness.
- A single unconditional defense exists in a libel suit: provable truth.
- Qualified privilege flows from fairly and accurately reporting certain official sources, but state laws differ on what is "official."
- Opinion has strong constitutional protection but facts in opinion writing must be provably true.
- The best defensive strategy in writing opinion is to be journalistically sound—fair, accurate, balanced.
- Beware when your writing accuses someone of illegal or immoral conduct, a principal cause of most libel suits.
- Neutral reportage—reporting impartially and with balance—is a defense in some but not all courts.
- Vague, indirect language doesn't always strip libelous material from your writing; humor or parody can defame and, thus, should be double-checked before publication.
- Contrary to journalistic lore, public officials are not "fair game" and should receive the same accurate, balanced and fair treatment accorded any person in the news.
- Involve your editors anytime you have doubts about legal dangers in an editorial or column, particularly if you get a legal threat.
- Listening courteously to someone offended by your writing sometimes can head off a lawsuit.
- Copyright law gives the creator of a work right to profit from it but under "fair use" doctrine; writers may quote from copyrighted material for journalistic purpose.
- Cyberspace law still is undefined but, clearly, libel law covers defamation

on the Internet and electronic services just as it does defamation in ink on paper.

Recommended Reading

The Associated Press Stylebook and Libel Manual is a thorough source for libel basics explained in lay language. Check also whether your newspaper or magazine has its own libel handbook.

State press associations are excellent sources for information on libel laws and procedures in your state.

Full treatment of media law is in Kent R. Middleton, Bill F. Chamberlin, Matthew D. Bunker, *The Law of Public Communication,* 4th ed (New York: Longman, 1997).

Anyone planning freelance writing should read *The ASJA Handbook: A Writer's Guide to Ethical and Economic Issues,* an excellent summary of contract and writer's rights, published in 1992 by the American Society of Journalists and Authors, Inc., 1501 Broadway, Suite 302, New York, NY 10036.

Notes

1. Figures from Libel Defense Resource Center, quoted in "Study Says Libel Awards Rise in '96," *Editor & Publisher,* March 8, 1997, p. 50.

2. Libel Defense Resource Center Statistics, quoted in Iver Peterson, "Firm Awarded $222.7 Million in a Libel Suit Vs. Dow Jones," *The New York Times,* March 21, 1997, p. C-1.

3. Ibid.

4. "Most of Record Libel Award Thrown Out," *The Atlanta Journal* and *Constitution,* May 24, 1997, p. E-3.

5. Kent R. Middleton, Bill F. Chamberlin, Matthew D. Bunker, *The Law of Public Communication,* 4th ed (New York: Addison Wesley Longman, 1997, p. 88.)

6. Good summaries of this case are in Barry Meier, "ABC Found Guilty of Fraud in Investigating Store Chain," *The New York Times,* Dec. 21, 1996, p. 6; Barry Meier, "Jury Says ABC Owes Damages of $5.5 Million," *The New York Times,* national edition, Jan. 23, 1997, p. 1, and Lawrie Mifflin, "Judge Slashes $5.5 Million Award to Grocery Chain for ABC Report," *The New York Times,* Aug. 30, 1997, p. 1.

7. I discuss ethical ramifications of undercover reporting in Conrad Fink, *Media Ethics* (Boston: Allyn & Bacon, 1995).

8. Also see the society's *The ASJA Handbook: A Writer's Guide to Ethical and Economic Issues,* published in 1992.

9. An excellent discussion of these issues is in Jared Sandberg, "Will Threat of Libel Suits Chill Cyberspace Chatter?" *The Wall Street Journal,* Aug. 29, 1997, p. B-1.

10. Ibid.

11. Jessica R. Friedman, an attorney, is strong in discussing this in, "Libel in Cyberspace," *Folio,* Sept. 1, 1995, p. 57.

12. David Noack, "Publishers 1, Freelancers 0," *Editor & Publisher,* Aug. 23, 1997, p. 7.

Exercises

1. In 350-400 words, write a personal commentary on the "chilling effect." Write for a *student* audience of newspaper readers.

Explain for your readers what the "chilling effect" is, its impact on robust journalistic debate *and your personal views* on whether writers of opinion and commentary are dangerously "chilled" by libel suits or whether lawsuits are rightly checking insensitive, uncaring journalists.

2. You are writing an institutional editorial for a student-oriented campus newspaper. Your subject is the balance writers must achieve between their journalistic responsibility and, as discussed in this chapter, the reality that they write in a dangerous legal climate.

Interview professors of law and journalism, local editors and journalists, and political leaders on campus and off. In 400-450 words, state your newspaper's position on whether libel law as it's exercised today in the United States is shutting down public dialogue and creating timid journalism, or whether that fear is something conjured up primarily by overly concerned journalists.

3. Study five days of institutional editorials in your campus newspaper (or another newspaper designated by your instructor) and, in about 450 words, discuss whether you sense the writers are showing impact from the "chilling effect."

Is the writing robust, pointed at times hard-hitting? Or, are the writers obviously pulling their punches, taking indirect and indecisive approaches to the day's issues in hopes of avoiding legal challenges? In sum, are editorials the type of public-service journalism discussed in this book or are they weak and meaningless?

4. Study five days of columns by your favorite political commentator (or another opinion writer designated by your instructor) and, in about 400 words, describe whether the writer is following the 14 defensive strategies outlined in this chapter.

Is the writer obviously sensitive to legal dangers and writing in a careful, defensive manner? Or, do you detect careless (and, thus, dangerous) writing? As that writer's editor, would you challenge anything in what was written as being dangerous legally?

5. In this chapter, you read about legal dangers confronting writers of opinion and commentary. You saw that writers, as well as "deep-pocket" newspapers and magazines, are included in libel suits and can be ordered to pay substantial damages.

In about 400 words, discuss whether *you personally* feel chilled by this knowledge. Is your personal attitude toward courageous journalism changed? Has your attitude changed toward a journalism career?

Write this exercise as a personal column *for publication* in your campus newspaper or magazine. *Be candid.*

Name Index

Subject Index